professional writing for the human services

professional

writing

HV
41
P759
1993

for the

human

services

Edited by Linda Beebe

National Association of Social Workers, Washington DC

Barbara W. White, Ph D, ACSW, President
Sheldon R. Goldstein, ACSW, LISW, Executive Director

1993 ≡ NASW PRESS

Library of Congress Cataloging-in-Publication Data

Professional writing for the human services / Linda Beebe, editor.
     p.   cm.
   Includes bibliographical references and index.
   ISBN 0-87101-199-9
   1. Human services—Authorship.   2. Social service—Authorship.
 I. Beebe, Linda.
 HV41.P759 1992
 808'.066361—dc20   92-39534
                                                 CIP

Printed in the United States of America

Cover and interior design by Hubert Leckie

contents

PART III NASW QUICK GUIDE TO MECHANICS

Editorial Staff Contributors: Lisa A. Braxton, Christina A. Davis, K. Hyde Loomis, Stephen D. Pazdan, Nancy A. Winchester

PART IV APPENDIXES

preface

Writing is an essential skill for all professionals. For the academic, the connection of writing skills to career success is clear: To be considered productive, one must be published in peer-reviewed journals and books. The practitioner, even if he or she chooses not to seek publication, also needs strong writing skills. Case records; reports; testimony—for local boards and committees, state legislatures, or Congress; letters; and other forms of written communication are a part of the daily work of the practitioner. However, most holders of advanced degrees still need help with writing skills.

The National Association of Social Workers (NASW) has a tradition of helping authors. Beatrice Saunders, who directed the publishing program from its start in 1955 to 1980, delivered hundreds of writing workshops during her tenure and advised countless authors on how they might improve their skills. While Bea was director, NASW's program grew from one journal, a handful of books, and a yearbook to a major program with five journals and an encyclopedia. Twelve years after her retirement, she continues her work, serving as editor-in-residence at Fordham University Graduate School of Social Service and traveling to give workshops and individual consultations.

Jacqueline Atkins, who directed the program from 1981 to 1987, continued the tradition of writing workshops and devoted considerable energy and skill to building the book program. After establishing royalty payments for books, Jacquie set out to attract authors who would build a reputation for NASW books.

I have attempted to follow my predecessors in providing services to authors. When NASW formally established the NASW Press in 1990, one of our major purposes was to offer more prestigious opportunities to prospective authors than we could with a publishing department. Publishing with the NASW Press, we believed, would enhance an author's reputation, whether they published in NASW's well-regarded journals or the book program.

All three directors have carried out their work in support of the NASW members to whom the press belongs. Hundreds of members have volunteered their time, energy, and skills to building the professional literature and helping their peers improve what they have written so that it can contribute to the knowledge base of the profession. Each new journal editor, each new book committee chair, each new editorial board has brought a fresh perspective and new ideas that advance publishing in social work and beyond.

The idea for *Professional Writing for the Human Services* emerged in a Book Committee meeting during which members reviewed a dozen proposals that could not be accepted. Concerned about the lack of skills they were seeing, members noted the need for a new reference work that would help authors improve their writing and understand the publishing process. In November 1990, the Book Committee formally requested that staff develop a reference work that would include contributions from members and staff.

As we considered the contents and structure of the book, we tried to offer materials that would help authors who wish to be published, as well as professionals who need help in improving their general writing and research skills. Consequently, we hope that parts I and III will be useful to readers, regardless of whether they want to be published. Parts I and III address writing techniques, research, graphic presentation, and the mechanics of spelling, punctuation, statistics, and so forth. The mechanics, which are taken from the NASW Press's internal style guide, were assembled to provide a reference for the problems we see most frequently. Part II and most of the appendixes look specifically at publication in professional books and journals. These chapters focus on peer review, submission for books and journals, and actual production procedures.

Throughout the book, although we often use NASW Press journals and books as examples, contributors have tried to provide information that applies to professional publications in many disciplines. (The details on submissions for NASW Press books and journals can be found in appendixes E and F.)

I believe that *Professional Writing for the Human Services* is an unusual book, both in the collaboration between staff and members and in its focus on the author. We did not want to have editors talk to each other about the esoterical aspects of peer review or publishing professionals describe new production techniques to each other, for example. Instead, we have attempted to give authors practical information that will help them write and publish. All of us who worked on the book hope that readers will find it useful.

Linda Beebe

acknowledgments

Many people helped produce this book. I gratefully acknowledge the creativity, the knowledge, the commitment, and the hard work of the following individuals:

▶ The Book Committee, 1990–92—Judy Davenport, Chair; Ann Abbott; Leon Ginsberg; and Tony Tripodi. They formulated the idea for this unique collaboration between staff and other authors and encouraged all of us to complete it.

▶ Constance Williams—Chair of the Communications Committee—whose sage counsel was invaluable, as always.

▶ Ann Hartman—Editor-in-Chief of *Social Work*—who wrote "Many Ways of Knowing" and whose philosophy on professional publishing inspired major portions of this book.

▶ Nancy Winchester—Director, Editorial Services—whose superlative management and production skills made impossible deadlines possible.

▶ Hyde Loomis—Senior Editor—whose editorial acumen is evident in this book's structure.

▶ Contributors (in addition to staff)—Ann Abbott, William Butterfield, Howard Goldstein, Henry Mendelsohn, and Trudi Jacobson—who wrote superb articles promptly.

▶ Editorial staff contributors—Lisa Braxton, Christina Davis, and Stephen Pazdan—who, with Hyde Loomis and Nancy Winchester, generously shared the knowledge they use daily to help authors improve their work.

▶ Wendy Almeleh—Editor—who is without a doubt one of the most talented editors in this field.

ix

▶ Laurel Rumpl—Editor—who also shared her considerable talents in formatting the "Quick Guide to Mechanics."

▶ Marie Flowers—Administrator for the Communications Division—who used her administrative skills to help me carve out time to complete the book.

▶ Hank Beebe and Marc Beebe—whose helpful feedback and suggestions, loving support, and forebearance about impingement on our time made it possible for me to do this book.

Linda Beebe

1 *many ways of knowing*

Ann Hartman

The development and dissemination of knowledge and the provision of opportunities for the exchange of ideas and information are major roles of a professional organization. The National Association of Social Workers (NASW) fulfills this mission by sponsoring professional meetings and conferences and stimulating a number of other efforts in the building, storage, and exchange of information. NASW develops knowledge through its publications program, which includes an extensive book list, audiovisual materials, a newspaper and pamphlets, and four professional journals.

This volume was written to help authors who want to disseminate their ideas and knowledge in the professional social work literature—in NASW Press books and journals, in materials produced by other publishers, and in less formal publications. But first, it is important to establish a framework, to explore some questions that underlie all knowledge development and dissemination, to look more carefully at the role of professional publication, and to establish the broad parameters that define social work knowledge and research.

For the past 15 years, the profession has been involved in a vigorous debate on the nature of truth, the development of knowledge, and the utility and appropriateness of different research methods for the profession. At times reasoned, often passionate, and sometimes even abusive, this ongoing discussion has raised much more than methodological issues. It has surfaced the major epistemological, ontological, and value questions that are a continuous challenge in any human enterprise, in any practice, and certainly in any search for knowledge. The following questions have been explicitly or implicitly asked: What is truth? How may we know it? Or, even, is there such a thing as truth, and may we ever know it?

Social workers are not alone in asking these questions. Intellectual leaders in the sciences and the social sciences, as well as in the other helping professions, are challenging each other over similar issues. The discussions have spawned a new set of "isms." Constructivism, deconstructionism, modernism, postmodernism, and even feminist postmodernism have joined the more familiar "isms"—pragmatism, utilitarianism, relativism, positivism, and empiricism—which have often been rediscussed and evaluated.

Why should authors, journal editors, and members of editorial boards be concerned with these demanding, abstract, and highly theoretical discussions? Some years ago, Znaniecki (1968), in his classic sociological study *The Social Role of the Man of Knowledge*, explored the social processes involved in the definitions of knowledge and in the boundary-maintenance and gatekeeping functions of those "men," and now, it is hoped, women too, who select materials for publication and presentation. More recently, in social work, Karger (1983), in a provocative analysis, reminded us that at the heart of the debate about research and the nature of knowledge is a struggle for "the political control of the direction, leadership, and the future of the profession" (p. 202). He wrote: "Those who define the questions to be asked define the parameters of the answers, and it is the parameters of the questions and the ensuing answers that function as the lens by which people view reality" (p. 203).

In the tradition of Znaniecki, Karger (1983) pointed out that "Dialogue and debate are allowed within certain parameters, with the ultimate referee being the means of communication—the social work journals. It is precisely the boundaries determined by the journals—which if not totally controlled, are at least seriously influenced by the academicians—which also limit the boundaries of the debate" (p. 204).

Thus, every time an article is accepted or rejected, the editor makes a decision that not only is part of the process of defining the profession and its truth, but also has political implications in the distribution of intellectual leadership, power, and status and, in these days of publish or perish, implications for the careers and even the incomes of academicians (Kirk & Corcoran, 1989). Furthermore, the norms of the journals can even shape the direction of inquiry in that the articles and books they have published suggest to aspiring authors the kinds of explorations that will be most likely to appear in print.

It is important for authors to know that the members of editorial boards and consulting editors of most professional journals (as well as of professional organizations that publish books) assume this responsibility with seriousness. They are aware that they have individual epistemological positions, either implicit or explicit, that guide their selection, shape the journal or other type of publication, and thus contribute to the definition of the particular profession and its truths and to the distribution of status and power. It is important for these convictions to be made as explicitly as possible. It is also important that those who shape the journals, and thus the information disseminated to the profession, represent a wide spectrum of interests, world views, and areas of expertise.

There are many truths and many ways of knowing. Each discovery contributes to a profession's knowledge base, and each way of knowing deepens professionals' understanding and adds another dimension to their view of the world.

The social work profession needs large-scale studies in which variables can be reduced to measurable units and the results translated into the language of statistical significance. It needs in-depth "thick" descriptions, grounded in context, of a single case, a single instance, or even a brief exchange. For example, large-scale studies of trends in marriage furnish helpful information about a rapidly changing social institution. But getting inside one marriage, as in *Who's Afraid of Virginia Woolf?*, richly displays the complexities of one relationship, leading to new insights about the pain, joys, expectations, disappointments, intimacy, and ultimate aloneness in relationships. Both the scientific and the artistic illuminate ways of knowing. In fact, as Geertz (1983) pointed out, innovative thinkers in many fields are blurring the genres, finding art in science and science in art and social theory in all human creation and activity.

There are indeed many ways of knowing and many kinds of knowers: researchers, practitioners, clients. Some seekers of truth may take a path that demands distance and objectivity, whereas others rely on deeply personal and empathic knowing. Some will find the validation of their findings through statistical analysis and probability tests, whereas others will find it through the intensity and authenticity of "being there" (Geertz, 1988) or through public and shared consensus on what has been called practice wisdom (Siporin, 1989). Some truth seekers will strive to predict, whereas others will turn to the past for an enhanced understanding of the present. We social workers must not turn our backs on any opportunities to enhance our knowledge—through the examination of correlations or the explication of myths that, according to Rein and White (1981), align "rational action with normative ideals and historical commitments" (p. 16). We must attend to the theoretical advances presented by our scholars and academicians, but also gather and listen to the "stories that rise up out of practice [that] confront, challenge, confirm, or deny the stories that 'come down' from the distal citadels of the profession" (Rein & White, 1981, p. 19).

We must listen to our clients and bring forth their wisdom, their lived experience, their visions of the world. Because many of our clients are powerless and oppressed, their knowledge has been subjugated, and their insights have been excluded from the discourse by those who are empowered to define the "truth"— experts, professionals, and editorial boards. All these sources are essential to our profession and should enrich the pages of our professional literature.

Our profession needs survey research—large-scale studies that discover trends and identify needs. It needs program evaluations, so we may know more about what seems to work. It needs outcome studies that may call upon a range of ways of knowing through a single case study, experimental designs, or longitudinal reviews that reflect on the consequences of events or conditions or interventions. It needs phenomenological studies that may lead the explorer on uncharted paths, naturalistic and ethnographic studies that are familiar but more disciplined extensions of the practitioner's case study (Rodwell, 1987). And it needs heuristic approaches whose goal is utility, rather than certainty, as well as hermeneutical and interpretive investigations that lead us to decipher the meaning of events to clients, to significant others, and to ourselves (Scott, 1989).

We can enhance our understanding by listening to and reporting the narratives, the stories that make order and sense of human experience and "organize [them] into temporarily meaningful episodes" (Polkinghorne, 1988, p. 7). We can attend to the myths that link values and action, and we must respect the tacit knowledge and practice wisdom that is "inductively derived from experience and shapes the practitioners' cognitive schema" (Scott, 1989, p. 40).

Now that authors, editorial boards, and the profession are more open to exploring and receiving many ways of knowing, we must be ever aware that each way is grounded in and an expression of certain ontological, epistemological, and value assumptions. These assumptions must be made explicit because knowledge and truths can be understood and evaluated only in the context of the framing assumptions. Theories can both illuminate and obscure our vision (Scott, 1989, p. 48). They also "constitute moral intervention in the social life whose conditions of existence they seek to clarify" (Giddens, 1976, p. 8). We must be clear about the nature of these interventions.

The boundaries of our profession are wide and deep, and our literature must reflect this extensive territory. We are concerned about the nature of our society, about social policy, about social justice, and about social programs. We are concerned about human associations—about communities, neighborhoods, organizations, and families. We are concerned about the life stories and the inner experiences of the people we serve and about the meaning of their experiences to them. No one way of knowing can explore this vast and varied territory. In the chapters that follow, several ways of knowing, several paths to knowledge are presented. We hope that this volume will be helpful to those wishing to contribute to the profession's literature and that as more social workers engage in knowledge development and dissemination, these contributions will enrich our understanding of our clients, ourselves, and our world.

references

Geertz, C. (1983). Blurred genres: The refiguration of social thought. *Local knowledge: Further essays in interpretive anthropology.* New York: Basic Books.

Geertz, C. (1988). *Works and lives.* Stanford, CA: Stanford University Press.

Giddens, A. (1976). *New rules of sociological method.* London: Hutchinson.

Karger, H. J. (1983). Science, research and social work: Who controls the profession? *Social Work, 28,* 200–205.

Kirk, S. A., & Corcoran, K. J. (1989). The $12,000 question: Does it pay to publish? *Social Work, 34,* 379–381.

Polkinghorne, D. E. (1988). *Narrative knowing and the human sciences.* Albany: State University of New York Press.

Rein, M., & White, S. H. (1981). Knowledge for practice. *Social Service Review, 55,* 1–41.

Rodwell, M. K. (1987). Naturalistic inquiry: An alternative model for social work assessment. *Social Service Review, 61,* 231–246.

Scott, D. (1989). Meaning construction and social work practice. *Social Service Review, 63,* 39–51.

Siporin, M. (1989). Metamodels, models, and basics: An essay review. *Social Service Review, 63,* 474–480.

Znaniecki, F. (1968). *The social role of the man of knowledge.* New York: Harper & Row.

PART I

preparation

for writing

2 basic writing techniques

Linda Beebe

Something happens to people's ability to write at some point between eighth-grade English and the end of graduate school. There often seems to be an inverse relationship between a person's level of knowledge and the ability to communicate it clearly. As we acquire more knowledge, we also acquire the notion that we must dress it up—put it in fancy language, so those who hear us speak or read our writing will understand that we are grown up and full of knowledge. The result can be incomprehensible. But you can achieve other results. The lessons you learned in elementary school about English and writing are still valid. If you use them to convey your professional knowledge, you will enhance your communications skills.

This chapter is not intended to be a treatise on writing. Instead, I hope that it will help you apply some of the basic lessons you learned in elementary school to your professional writing. Although I use the primary journal article as an example throughout, you can apply most of the techniques to any form of writing. Professionals write reports, case records, letters, memorandums, and other informal communications more often than they write journal articles; all can be improved with more attention to basic writing skills.

If you are serious about writing, nothing will help you more than to read good writing. Read everything you can in your specialty. Also read fiction and literature. (I have no patience with those pompous souls who declaim, "*I* never read fiction," as if anyone who does has cotton balls for brains. I believe that good mysteries, poetry, and science fiction are especially helpful because of their clarity and logic, but then that's what I like to read.) Finally, read what writers have to say about their craft. The suggested readings at the end of this chapter include some materials that I think are good examples.

what is good writing?

Good writing stirs the reader; it persuades or enlightens. Good writing is strong and vigorous, and it displays the humanity of the writer. Because good writing is the demonstration of clear, logical thought, a good writer can communicate the most complex subjects so clearly that an educated layperson can understand them. Good writing is honest, and it is in touch with reality.

Many editors and writers would tell you that good writing is the opposite of the writing encouraged by academia. Kidder (1991) had this to say about academic writing:

> Academic writing is convoluted, jargon-ridden, and isolated from the messy realities of the world . . . young scholars don't know any better. The examples set before them inculcate certain rules. Don't use the first person. Say as much as you can on any given subject. Repeat and rephrase (but don't necessarily trim) if you don't get it right the first time. Bolster your arguments with references to those of others. Climb the ladder of abstraction to the topmost rung and stay there. Use long, complex sentences. Wherever possible, find the polysyllable. And never, *never* be "anecdotal," a word almost always preceded by "merely."
> (p. B1)

Ignore the many bad examples and model your writing on the work of the superlative writers who grace every field. Good writing, in academia or in practice, is trim and vigorous, not flabby with abstractions and polysyllables.

Zinsser (1988, p. 43) described five hallmarks of good writing:

- ► clarity
- ► common sense
- ► logic
- ► plausibility
- ► precision.

Most of all, you must have something important to communicate. Your writing should enlighten the reader or add to the development of knowledge in some way, whether you write for one individual or thousands.

get started

Writing signifies mystery and danger to many people. When they sit down to write, panic sets in, and all the ideas that previously were so clear to them are either gone or seem muddied and un-workable. Becker (1986) suggested that writers, even professional ones, are stymied because they look for the one "right" way. They think that if they can just get the perfect opening sentence—the *right* way to begin—everything else will fall into place. Every writer falls into that trap at some point, and it is guaranteed to fail.

First, you have to realize that writing is work that is as difficult as any other you will ever do. Gene Fowler (as quoted in Fitzhenry, 1987) is reported to have said, "Writing is easy: all you do is sit staring at the blank sheet of paper until the drops of blood form on your forehead" (p. 394). But writing brings enormous rewards, not the least of which is what we ourselves learn from it. Zinsser (1988) noted how writing and learning are connected:

> Writing organizes and clarifies our thoughts. Writing is how we think our way into a subject and make it our own. Writing enables us to find out what we know—and what we don't know—about whatever we're trying to learn. Putting an idea into written words is like defrosting the windshield: The idea, so vague out there in the murk, slowly begins to gather itself into a sensible shape. (p. 16)

Successive writing and rewriting demonstrate what we know and teach us what we do not know.

Once you realize that there is no right way, that all writers must rewrite what they first set down, it is easier to break the logjam and start sorting out what you know and do not know. You may find some of the following techniques helpful.

Mapping is a powerful tool for unleashing your imagination. You write a central concept in the center of a blank page, then spin off related thoughts, branching them as subordinate relationships occur to you. The weblike outline you generate in this sponta-neous, almost random process often stimulates ideas you do not realize you have. Listing random thoughts is another technique that works. Do not make any judgments about those thoughts or try to assemble them in any logical order—that comes next; just write down any thought that comes to mind. Finally, if all else fails, type nonsense until the brain takes over from the fingers.

All these techniques open you to what artists and writers have described as "visitors from the unconscious mind." Once you free your unconscious, your memory and intuition begin working to help you formulate your ideas on paper.

organize your work

You cannot, of course, simply tumble your thoughts onto paper and think you're finished. Every written document, a one-page memo or a 400-page book, must be organized coherently. How you organize your writing will depend on the subject matter, the potential audience, the type of document—journal article, brief report, grant proposal, or book chapter, for example—your purpose in writing, and the style of working that suits you best.

ORGANIZING METHODS

Often, we stumble from one paragraph or word to another until we eventually write approximately what we thought we would. A plan of work helps smooth the process. There have been many variations on the following seven-step plan:

1. Brainstorm your ideas. Use mapping or lists of random thoughts to generate many ideas.
2. Limit the subject. Determine what is really important and group like thoughts together. If you produced a list of random thoughts, use different-color highlighters to identify those that fit together. Then develop an outline.
3. Write the introduction.
4. Plan the components of the body of text.
5. Plan the conclusion.
6. Write the paper.
7. Revise and rewrite.

These seven steps clearly define the tasks that must be done, but you may not want to take them in exact order. Writing is linear and sequential. You must write one word, then one sentence, then one paragraph until you have finished what you want to say. Still, you need not write those elements in the order the reader will read them. For example, because writers often find the introduction the most difficult, some guides suggest that you write the introduction last, when you know not what you intended to write, but what you actually wrote.

For me, as for many people, the most important organizing tool is an outline. Once I know what I want to accomplish, I outline all the major components I need to achieve my objective and as many of the subordinate components as I know. First, I type the outline and print it out, so I will have a clean reminder of where I intend to proceed. Then I use the outline components as subheads to organize my writing. The wording of the subheads and even their organization may change as I revise and rewrite, but I have a clear structure to work within. A good outline frees me to skip around in my first draft, writing the sections that seem to be the easiest first and building from them. My outline reminds me where I'm headed, and rewriting takes care of faulty transitions.

Drafting a title first can also help crystallize your thoughts and ideas. What is your purpose in writing? What do you want readers to expect from your article? The ideal title describes the content accurately and precisely with the fewest possible words.

ORGANIZING FORMATS

How will you organize your writing so that readers can understand the content and utility of what you have written? Almost any document requires a beginning (introduction), a middle (discussion), and an end (conclusions). Generally, the beginning sets the stage, defines the problem, or describes the issue at hand. The conclusion ends the work by summarizing, providing implications, or pointing toward the need for future work. The middle is elastic; its size and shape depend on the information your readers need to find your conclusion plausible. The following are two different organizational formats.

IMRAD

This acronym stands for Introduction, Methods, Results, and Discussion. The IMRAD system of writing developed in U.S. scientific journals between the late 1800s and the 1950s. As the United States poured more money into scientific research, scientists wrote more and more papers. As the papers proliferated, journal editors demanded more efficient and less verbose papers and instituted IMRAD to establish organizational consistency. Day (1988) described the IMRAD system as follows:

> The logic of IMRAD can be defined in question form: What question (problem) was studied? The answer is the Introduction. How was the problem studied? The answer is the Methods. What were the findings? The answer is the Results. What do these findings mean? The answer is the Discussion. (p. 7)

You will find variations of the IMRAD system in most quantitative research reports. (For more on research reports, see the two chapters "The Quantitative Research Report" and "The Qualitative Research Report" in this volume.)

Variations on the Wall Street Journal Formula

The *Wall Street Journal* has been acclaimed for its strong, clear reporting. Widely adapted for use in other media, the newspaper's formula is designed to pique the reader's interest and hold it as the story unfolds to a logical conclusion. First, the lead paragraph sets the scene for the reader. Next, the "billboard" paragraph advertises what's coming. Once the reader knows what to expect, the "nut" paragraph tells him or her what the article is about and why it is important. Then the body of the article is proof that supports the significance of the message in the "nut" paragraph. Every sentence must tie back to the "nut" paragraph while it leads to a logical conclusion.

However you structure your writing, remember these keys:

▶ Put the issue in context.
▶ Tell the reader what to expect.
▶ Define the issue and its importance.
▶ Develop the proof.
▶ Lead to a logical conclusion.

Strong organization provides a road map to help readers understand what you say and how that message is important to them.

DOCUMENTATION

Documentation, painful though it may be, is essential to the scholarly endeavor. Carter (1987) noted three purposes of references: (1) to demonstrate how the new contribution advances knowledge previously reported in the literature, (2) to provide information already substantiated by others, and (3) to direct the reader to sources of additional information. The author's handling of documentation demonstrates his or her attention not only to scholarly rigor, but to ethical standards. You must document all statistical data and credit the work—words, thoughts, and findings—of others. Although some authors tend to overreference, it is far better to cite a source than to risk committing plagiarism.

Gathering and organizing the documentation is never easy. Many teachers recommend using index cards to create a bibliographic card for each source you may use. If you are careful to write all the information you may need (see the section on References in part III for details), you can then sort the cards in the order you need for the final reference list. You will also need to keep careful notes on the material you want to use. Whenever the references are brief enough, I tend to retain photocopies marked with all the bibliographic information and filed according to subject.

Gibaldi and Achtert (1988) recommended that you maintain your references in a bibliographic file in word processing as you do your research. Just set up a self-explanatory file label (such as refs, bibl, or bibliog) and type in the references with full information as you acquire them. Then you can add or delete as you proceed. Gibaldi and Achtert also suggested that you establish a separate file for notes and especially for quotations, which you can then retrieve as needed directly into your document.

write the first draft

You have decided your purpose. You know who your audience is, or at least the medium you will use to try to reach your audience. You have a clear plan to achieve your purpose. You probably have notes in various forms—in a computer file, on index cards, or in a notebook. Now it is time to write the first draft of what will resemble your final product.

First drafts are supposed to be messy, ungrammatical, and disconnected. Believe it or not, most writers do not create elegant, pithy, clear prose on their first round. Your goal simply is to get the words and ideas written down however they come out of your mind. Do not worry about grammar. Do not worry about sentence construction or spelling. Do not worry about whether you are leaving something out or going in the wrong direction. You will probably make all these mistakes, and you can correct them all in the next round.

At this stage, you are worried only about content. Putting ideas into words is hard enough; do not make it harder by adding issues about style. If you want a sure prescription for writer's block, try to write perfect sentences when you are composing your first draft. You do not have to worry about all the errors because no one else needs to see this version. You do, though. Unless you write down your ideas, you will never fully develop the ones you have been carrying around in your head. So write until you have down as much content as you think you need. Then take a break from writing if you can.

revise and rewrite

Now it is time to worry about all the language problems you ignored when you were writing your first draft. Even the most straightforward report generally requires some reworking, and most first drafts need major revisions. Although the words *major revisions* sound ominous, the rewriting can be more rewarding and less traumatic than the original writing because you already have accomplished the difficult task of getting your initial thoughts into words. Now you need to add polish to the basic framework. Now you must go through your manuscript, word by word, sentence by sentence. Did you say what you intended to say? Are passages ambiguous? Can you clarify them so the reader will have the same understanding you do? Do the words sound right?

If you are in doubt, read the sentence out loud. Language has a cadence. Good writing has a pleasing rhythm, whereas bad writing is discordant and jarring. Most good editors rely on their ear as much as they do on rule books, and so should you.

CONSIDER VOICE AND TONE

Voice and tone should be appropriate to the audience for which the material is intended. This article, for example, would be more formal if it were written for a professional journal; instead, I deliberately selected the personal tone and voice to suit a writing guide. Some experts, however, would disagree with any personalization in a professional publication. Although the issue of third person versus first person has been debated in many arenas, no clear guidelines have emerged.

rewrite speeches

Following every major conference, the NASW Press receives several speeches with notes that say things like "everyone who heard this thought it should appear in *Social Work!*" The more diffident write, "I wonder if the journal would have any interest in this." Speeches always annoy reviewers, and reviewers always reject speeches, generally with little more comment than, "The author has some interesting things to say, but it must be rewritten in article format." You can save yourself and busy reviewers time if you rewrite a speech before you send it to a journal.

Articles and speeches are different creatures, even when they are closely related in content. Speeches are oral and articles are visual—an obvious difference, but an important one—and they have different purposes. Generally, you seek a different level of awareness about the same material.

A speech is more informal, and it requires courtesies that an article does not. Phrases like "Thank you for inviting me" or "This morning I'm going to talk about" are not germane to an article. The speech that inspires us is apt to sound too breezy and too opinionated when it is in print. When you are translating a speech to an article, you need to go beyond excising the courtesies. That is not to say that the journal article must be stiff or dull, just that it should be more formally presented than a speech.

The organization probably needs to be revised. In a speech, you may skip around to be sure you cover the salient points and to encourage interaction with your audience. In an article, you must

Scientists originally developed the protocol of writing professional papers in the third person because they were seeking objectivity. The idea was that removing the author's person from the article would focus attention on the content, rather than on the author's opinion, and therefore would ensure objectivity. Unfortunately, the result often was a convoluted focus on the author; instead of saying "I found that" the author now says, "the author found that" or—worse, "it was found that." The first phrase tells us clearly and succinctly who did what. The second gives us the same information in more words; the third phrase not only adds words, it confuses the reader because now he or she is no longer clear about who did what.

Unfortunately, journal editors do not agree on whether the use of the first person is acceptable. Journals in the natural sciences generally use the first person. In the human services, however, journal editors vary considerably in their attitudes. Use of the first

structure the information to flow logically from one point to the next. Whereas the structure of a good speech is transparent to the audience, the structure of a good article is clear. Because you cannot play back a speech, you reiterate. Repeating the same information in different ways helps the listener absorb the content of a speech. In an article, which can be reread, repetition becomes redundant and boring.

At the same time, articles require a greater level of detail. In a speech, you are apt to concentrate on a few main points because you cannot give details. You abbreviate what you know about a subject to avoid putting your audience to sleep. Remember that readers cannot ask you questions about how you know something or what you did to discover it. You need to tell them. Your audience may have asked questions that will help you incorporate the content you need to add. Folly though it is, many of us neglect to write down specific citations when we are researching information for a speech. You can save yourself a lot of trouble if you compile all the detailed citations as you write a speech, but whether you did your homework originally or not, you must add citations to an article.

Speeches stimulate interest and create awareness. The same material written in more formal language and organized with greater detail can give the reader a solid piece to work from and to cite in future work. If people like what you say in an oral presentation and tell you it is valuable, rework your material and send it to a journal. But rewrite it first.

person in a quantitative research report is rare; on the other hand, qualitative research reports require the author's voice. Some journals seek articles that reveal the author's voice; others reject articles written in the first person as not scholarly.

Regardless of the voice you select, you should concentrate on your content, rather than on you. A steady stream of "I think," "I considered," "I developed," "I believe" raises doubts about the author's basis for the content.

MAKE THE PASSIVE ACTIVE

Overuse of the passive voice is the most common language problem among professionals who are writing for their peers. Writers use the passive voice because they think they have to write in the third person and maybe because they think the extra words and complex phrases make them sound scholarly. The truth is that the passive voice adds a lot of what Zinsser (1990) called "clutter and noise." In that noisy environment, the reader cannot hear what the author is saying. You need to strip away the clutter, so the reader can hear your message.

One way to deliver your message is to use powerful verbs that will capture the reader's attention. Zinsser (1990) noted the importance of verbs: "Verbs are the most important of all your tools. They push your sentence forward and give it momentum. Active verbs push hard; passive ones tug fitfully" (p. 109). Active verbs paint images. They dazzle, launch, swagger, gallop, produce, seduce, denounce, poke, work, fight. Passive verbs are weak and flabby: they are, he was, it could have been.

Unrestrained use of the passive voice has two outcomes, both unpleasant. First, the passive construction takes the life out of what you are saying and usually makes it longer. Just changing passive phrases to active ones will strengthen your writing.

Passive	Active
It was reported by Brown.	Brown reported.
It is evident that *a* produced *b*.	*a* produced *b*.
It was thought that the agency's cash flow situation would have been improved if the paydays were to be staggered.	Jones thought he could improve the agency's cash flow by staggering paydays.
The reason he left the agency was that he wanted to go into teaching.	He left the agency to teach.
The emphasis was placed on. . . .	We emphasized. . . .
He was regretful that he had chosen his words with less care.	He regretted his hasty words.

The second problem with passive verbs is that they bury the reality of what you are saying. Brown (1988) pointed to the "secret agents" in the passive voice. We know something was done—the last cookie was eaten or the last beer was drunk—but we do not know which agent ate the cookie or drank the beer. Sometimes you may not know the agent or be at liberty to say who it is; then you must resort to the passive voice.

Authors also use the passive voice, Brown (1988) noted, to appeal to the generic person. "It is understood" or "it is widely known" or "it is thought" are signals that the author is trying to slip something past the reader. Who understands? Who knows? Who thinks? Unless you are trying to obfuscate, avoid passive construction. The active voice is always stronger, almost always shorter, and usually more honest.

CUT THE JARGON

Every profession, every field, every distinct specialty has its own jargon. Used properly and sparingly, jargon is an important tool, one that permits specialists to communicate precisely. Too frequently, however, professionals expand their use of jargon into a pretentious language that interferes with communication, rather than enhances it.

The first definition of *jargon* in *Webster's Ninth New Collegiate Dictionary* (1987) is "confused unintelligible" language. Subsequent definitions include "strange, outlandish, or barbarous"; "technical terminology"; and "obscure and often pretentious." Barzun (1986) said this about jargon:

> The newer sciences, influenced by science and journalism, have produced, on the whole, poor jargons. They have been seduced into the manufacture of bad Greek and Latin compounds or equally pretentious English, deplorably vague. . . . In the new specialties one finds also a pseudo jargon, that is, ways of speech not required by special facts, tools, or actions, but used on the contrary to avoid the definite and the particular. (pp. 73–74)

I sometimes see 20-page papers that contain almost nothing but jargon and are so convoluted that even the authors' colleagues cannot understand them. Reviewers who are specialists in the area write to the editor, "I could not comprehend what the author was trying to say." The following examples from Lutz's *Doublespeak*, (1989, pp. 19, 20, 22, 229) demonstrate how we distort our language.

Jargon	Meaning
soft wheel infrastructure system	highway
negative side of a competency scale	criminally negligent
major incident response vehicle	ambulance
career offender cartel	organized crime

(continued)

Jargon	Meaning
home plaque removal instrument	toothbrush
negative patient care outcome	death
therapeutic misadventure	death
social expression products	greeting cards

Although most of these examples come from governmental direc-tives, one sees similar distortions and pomposities in the human services literature every day.

Zinsser (1990) discussed another recent phenomenon, the tendency to string buzzword nouns together with no action verbs to help the reader know what is going on. The example he used was "communication facilitation skills development intervention." Only an insider—or a code breaker—would know that the words describe a program to help improve writing skills.

Much of this language is preposterous, what Bernstein (1969, pp. 480–482) called "windyfoggery," but there is a great danger in distorting the language. Writers like Brown, Zinsser, and Lutz remind us of the moral function of language, which can be a tool or a weapon. As professionals who are concerned with human well-being, you especially should be concerned that your words stimulate—not limit—thinking.

Jargon shuts out the uninitiated. If you wish to share your knowledge and help others understand what you know, do not allow your writing to be infected with jargon. For all but the most technical material, cut out the jargon and replace it with clear, simple English.

PARE DOWN

You write to communicate ideas and facts. To do so, you must frame the message as explicitly and succinctly as possible. Clobber-ing your reader with verbiage is not only sloppy writing, it is rude behavior. If you are kind to your readers by weighing your words and organizing your thoughts, they will comprehend your message and maybe even agree with it. In 1918, William Strunk, Jr. (quoted in Strunk & White, 1979) gave the most valuable advice on brevity ever written:

> Vigorous writing is concise. A sentence should contain no unnecessary words, a paragraph no unnecessary sentences, for the same reason that a drawing should have no unnecessary lines and a machine no unnecessary parts. This requires not that the writer make all his sentences short, or that he avoid all detail and treat his subjects only in outline, but that every word tell. (p. xiv)

If a word or phrase does not add to what you are trying to communicate, cut it out. Pruning helps a journal article or report as much as it does a flowering shrub. Once you get rid of the deadwood, the framework is clear and the ideas burst forth. First, eliminate all excess words like the following:

Redundant	Simplified
has been engaged in a study of	studied
an example of this is the fact that	for example
has the capability of	can
the question as to whether	whether
it is worth pointing out in this context that	note that
it is often the case that	often

Use adjectives and adverbs carefully. These indispensable parts of speech are composites, words formed from nouns and verbs to modify our language. Used sparingly, they clarify and enhance the nouns and verbs that give our writing strength and color. All too often they are redundant and weakening. An excessive use of modifiers is a hallmark of stream-of-consciousness writing that was not revised.

Excessive Modification	Rationale
successfully avoided	Avoidance is an absolute; either one avoids or one does not.
ongoing progress	Progress is forward movement.
very spectacular	Either the object being described is spectacular or it is not.
particularly unique	Unique is singular, unparalleled.

Another way to weaken your words and ideas is to qualify them with many modifiers, such as *rather, very, seems to,* and *sort of.* Cut every unnecessary modifier and let your work stand on its own.

CHECK THE GRAMMAR

Although glaring grammatical errors may be a result of haste, not of ignorance, readers are nonetheless put off by them. Check to be sure that all your singular verbs are matched with singular nouns and your plural verbs with plural nouns. Determine what tense—present, past, future—the verbs should be in each sentence and make certain that all verbs are in the same tense. Try to make like elements—clauses or lists, for example—as parallel in their construction as possible.

INSERT YOUR HUMANITY

You most likely are writing about people, their problems, and solutions to those problems. Are the people there? Can I recognize their pain? See how they are helped? Know that you care? Or do you talk instead about concepts in terms so lofty and pretentious that the people disappear? If you want to inform your colleagues or stir them to action, you need to make the people alive in your writing.

To bring life to your writing, strip away any pretentions and concentrate on the message. If you have changed from the passive to the active voice, cut out the jargon, and eliminated excess words, you have taken major steps to simplify your writing so that the content and the humanity are visible. But take another look. Substitute short, active verbs for all those nouns puffed up into verbs like *prioritize* and *operationalize*. Be sure you are using a fair number of strong Anglo-Saxon words instead of relying only on Latin words. Use *woman* instead of *female*, *die* instead of *perish*, *murder* instead of *homicide*, *help* instead of *aid*. Although Latin words are essential to our language, it is the Anglo-Saxon words that convey our emotions and our humanity.

Do not be afraid of words that convey the emotions of the people you are writing about. If you can portray the people vividly and truthfully, you probably can succeed in communicating the problems and the solutions.

CORRECT PECCADILLOS

Peccadillos are minor sins that really do not interfere with comprehension and that can be corrected easily in editing. Unfortunately, they sometimes get in the way, and the author receives a less-than-useful critique because a reviewer focuses more on the minor sin than on the substantive issues that need changing. The following are peccadillos that I have seen stir reviewers' ire.

Singular ''Data''

The word *data* generally is considered to be a plural noun; therefore, it requires a plural verb. Examples: the data were conclusive, the data indicate, the data reveal.

Misuse of ''While'' and ''Since''

While and *since* are adverbs that refer strictly to time, but they often are mistakenly substituted for *although* or *whereas* or *because*. Both although and whereas are used to contrast two unlike elements. Because denotes a rationale. The following demonstrates some incorrect and correct usages.

Incorrect	Correct
Since the agency already pays rent on this office, hosting the committee did not increase expenses.	Because the agency already pays rent on this office, hosting the committee did not increase expenses.
John complained about workloads since he worked Saturdays and David did not.	John complained about workloads because he worked Saturdays and David did not.
Agency B offers services to adolescents, while Agency C offers services only to adults.	Agency B offers services to adolescents, whereas Agency C offers services only to adults.
While the WIC budget has increased, it has not kept pace with inflation or needs.	Although the WIC budget has increased, it has not kept pace with inflation or needs.

This is not to say that *while* or *since* should be excised from your vocabulary. For example, you may say, "Mr. Jones stayed with the children while his wife was at work," or "Since October, the agency has doubled its caseload."

"That" versus "Which"

So many people are confused about the use of these two pronouns to introduce clauses that some have suggested they be treated as interchangeable elements. Purists (who include many reviewers and almost all editors), however, insist on the differentiation. *That* introduces clauses that are essential to the sentence. If the clause was eliminated, the sentence would not work. *Example:* The political races that women won were all in rural areas. *Which*, on the other hand, introduces clauses that are not essential to the meaning of the sentence. They are parenthetical rather than necessary. *Example:* Women's issues, which often are ignored in political races, cut across party lines.

Misplaced and Dangling Modifiers

This minor sin is a little more serious because it can interfere with the reader's comprehension, as you can see in the following examples. However, the professional literature is riddled with other examples.

Misplaced or Dangling Modifier	Corrected
Besides causing lung cancer, our data suggest that. . . .	Our data suggest that cigarettes, besides causing lung cancer. . . .
Marc was accepted at Rutgers, which greatly pleased his grandfather.	Marc's acceptance at Rutgers greatly pleased his grandfather.

(continued)

Misplaced or Dangling Modifier	Corrected
To test well on vocabulary, good books must be read.	To test well on vocabulary, one must read good books.
A program was established that helped aspiring writers.	We established a program that helped aspiring writers.

review critically

Once you have removed the clutter and noise, you can review the content critically. Look carefully to be certain that you have said what you intended to say and that it is worth saying. Ask yourself, Is it true? Important? Comprehensible? New? in reviewing your writing.

IS IT TRUE?

Presumably, you started with valid findings. Be certain, then, that the information you provided supports your conclusions. Sometimes, the body of an article is so vague that the reader cannot tell how the author moved from the hypothesis to the conclusion. You need to discuss the results in sufficient detail so the conclusion is as logical to the reader as it is to you. Do not make assumptions about the reader's knowledge. Some facts that appear self-evident to you, the expert, may need to be clarified for the reader.

Describing how others may use your findings—the implications section—is standard practice. Remember that knowledge is built little by little. Will your findings change the entire field of child welfare? Or will they make the more modest contribution of simplifying intake? Do not make claims you cannot substantiate. Readers, starting with the reviewers, will take your work more seriously if you are not grandiose about your contribution.

If you have used the words and thoughts of others, have you documented them? So much reading is required to write an article that it is easy to forget who said what. "Did I think this or read it?" is a common concern. Nonetheless, using someone else's work without attribution is plagiarism, which is unethical and illegal. Markman, Markman, and Waddell (1989, pp. 119–126) described four forms of plagiarism:

1. *Word-for-word plagiarism* occurs when words or sentences or longer passages are quoted verbatim without attribution.
2. *Patchwork plagiarism* occurs when most of the words and constructs in a passage are quoted without attribution, but the words may be changed or the sentence structure altered.

3. *Lifting out the perfect phrases* is a more subtle form of patchworking. Phrases written by someone else are inserted into the author's own sentence construction without documentation.
4. *Paraphrasing* is also plagiarism if you do not credit the original author for the thoughts and ideas.

Remember, too, that if you cite an article or a book, you are telling the reader that you have read it. Inserting references you gleaned from a literature search, but have not read, is not being truthful.

IS IT IMPORTANT?

Space in professional journals and the time of the journal's readers are too precious to waste on inconsequential matters. Because discoveries of monumental importance are rare, most journal articles inch us forward, rather than propel us to great heights. Yet each contribution should have some impact on the human condition. It is possible to write a beautiful account of perfectly accomplished research that will make no difference to anyone. If your results are trivial or if they cannot be used by others, then the paper is not important. Learning the difference between an important contribution and a trivial one is a difficult lesson for anyone.

IS IT COMPREHENSIBLE?

You have accomplished a large part of this task by cleaning up your language. That work may reveal the need for a different organizational scheme. Does the paper flow from an interesting beginning to a logical and justifiable conclusion? If not, try rearranging the text. "Cutting and pasting" are mercifully easy with word processors. Just copy your article to a new file and play with it until you are happy with the arrangement. Once you are satisfied with the results, you can delete the first copy, but it is good insurance to retain it until you are certain. You may also need more transitions to help the reader understand your content.

IS IT NEW?

Remember that primary journals publish only original materials. Can you specify how your material takes the knowledge in your field beyond its present state? Are your findings new, or have you pulled yet one more little subset of data from a larger study? The least publishable unit (LPU) is not a recent phenomenon. In 1981, Broad described the LPU as a euphemism for the fragmentation of data and one way of squeezing more papers out of a research report. Although large-scale studies often yield several articles, some authors stretch them out to twice the number justified. Do not repackage your own work or the work of others.

ASK FOR CRITICISM AND HELP

Asking someone to criticize your work—and then using the comments you receive appropriately—calls for a mix of self-confidence and objectivity that is not easily come by. The risk involved in sharing your work—the writing that came as much from your soul as from your brain—may seem monumental. But compare that risk with sending an article off for anonymous review and waiting four months to be told "This is not yet ready for publication," which is a favorite line from reviewers who are confronted with a manuscript that should have gone through three more revisions. Worse still, imagine a seriously flawed article getting into print and reading a torrent of letters tearing it apart.

Although I have not always been gracious about accepting help, I have always believed it is far better to learn that I have not achieved my objective before it gets into print, not after. Most of us do not write solely for our own pleasure. At some point, therefore, we must make that writing public. Going public is easier when you do it first with a small audience of trusted colleagues.

Some environments are more conducive to this kind of sharing than are others, but you can encourage collegial exchange if you seek it out and if you reciprocate by providing the kind of feedback you would like to receive. If your comments in general are constructive and kind, you will usually receive like comments. Pamela Richards, writing in Becker (1986), talked about the importance of trust:

> This problem of trust is critical because it undermines the kind of emotional and intellectual freedom that we all need if we are to create. Who can you trust? . . . You have to trust these people not just to treat you right (not to be competitive with you, not to tell tales when you mess up), but also to tell you the truth. I must believe absolutely that if I write crap or think idiotic thoughts they will tell me. If I can't trust them to tell me the truth, then their feedback will not help me trust myself. (pp. 115–117)

The writing–feedback–rewriting loop helps us learn. Substantive feedback teaches the author who is open to being helped in two ways. First, the fresh perspective of knowledgeable colleagues can give you insights into your subject matter. Your colleagues' feedback can help you identify gaps. Did you miss an important connection? Did you skip over an area because you did not have the data you needed? Maybe you have included all the necessary information, but you have not presented it clearly enough. The second important function of feedback is to identify flaws in the writing. If your colleagues do not understand what you said, your article needs to be revised, no matter how well written you thought it was.

A formal mentoring program is an alternative. Sometimes, working with a professional editor on one or two articles gives authors enough confidence to be comfortable sharing their work with their colleagues. However you go about it, seek feedback and look for tough, honest responses. Then use those responses to polish and refine your writing.

conclusion

Writing is hard work; for most writers, its difficulty is compounded by a lack of time. Berger (1990) pointed out that neither practitioners nor academics have sufficient time for writing. Most agencies do not reward practitioners for publishing, nor do they provide time or resources to support writing. Academics, on the other hand, are expected to publish if they want to be assured promotion or even continued employment. Yet they, too, are often overloaded with work responsibilities and undersupported with resources.

Even if your employer does not compensate you directly, writing is enormously rewarding. We learn through the act of writing. The knowledge you can acquire by writing about your work is, in itself, a reward, as is the camaraderie you can develop with your colleagues. When you are published, the sense of making a contribution to your field is greatly fulfilling. And every author, no matter how well published, gets a thrill from seeing his or her work in print.

Writing, like all professional endeavors, requires skills, training, and practice. If you received a competent elementary school education, you have the basic skills. The way you learn to write is by writing and rewriting. I hope that the basic techniques outlined in this chapter will help you improve your skills and find pleasure in the difficult task of writing.

references

Barzun, J. (1986). *A word or two before you go.* Middletown, CT: Wesleyan University Press.

Becker, H. S. (1986). *Writing for social scientists: How to start and finish your thesis, book, or article.* Chicago: University of Chicago Press.

Berger, R. M. (1990). Getting published: A mentoring program for social work faculty. *Social Work, 35,* 69–71.

Bernstein, T. (1969). *The careful writer.* New York: Atheneum.

Broad, W. (1981). The publishing game: Getting more for less. *Science, 211*, 1137–1139.

Brown, R. M. (1988). *Starting from scratch: A different kind of writer's manual.* New York: Bantam.

Carter, S. P. (1987). *Writing for your peers: The primary journal paper.* New York: Praeger.

Day, R. A. (1988). *How to write and publish a scientific paper* (3rd ed.). Phoenix: Oryx Press.

Fitzhenry, E. (Ed.). (1987). *Barnes & Noble book of quotations.* New York: Harper Perennial.

Gibaldi, J., & Achtert, W. S. (1988). *MLA handbook for writers of research papers.* New York: Modern Language Association of America.

Kidder, R. M. (1991, January 30). Academic writing is convoluted, jargon-ridden, and isolated from the messy realities of the world. *Chronicle of Higher Education, 37,* B1.

Lutz, W. (1989). *Doublespeak: From "revenue enhancement" to "terminal living": How government, business, advertisers, and others use language to deceive you.* New York: Harper & Row.

Markman, R. H., Markman, P. T., & Waddell, M. L. (1989). *Ten steps in writing the research paper.* Hauppauge, NY: Barron's Educational Series.

Richards, P. (1986). Risk. In H. S. Becker, *Writing for social scientists: How to start and finish your thesis, book, or article.* Chicago: University of Chicago Press.

Strunk, W., & White, E. B. (1979). *The elements of style* (3rd ed.). New York: Macmillan.

Webster's ninth new collegiate dictionary. (1987). Springfield, MA: Merriam-Webster.

Zinsser, W. (1988). *Writing to learn.* New York: Harper & Row.

Zinsser, W. (1990). *On writing well: An informal guide to writing nonfiction* (4th ed.). New York: Harper & Row.

suggested reading

If you are interested in the art of writing, many authors have written about the subject. The following are some of my favorites.

Barzun, J. (1986). *A word or two before you go.* Middleton, CT: Wesleyan University Press.
> A selection of Barzun's writing on language between 1943 and 1986 is collected in this volume. Barzun writes incisively about the damage that educated writers do to the English language.

Becker, H. S. (1986). *Writing for social scientists: How to start and finish your thesis, book, or article.* Chicago: University of Chicago Press.
> A sociologist, Becker uses his own professional experiences to describe the traumas and rewards of writing.

Brown, R. M. (1989). *Starting from scratch: A different kind of writers' manual.* New York: Bantam.
> Although she addresses people who want to write fiction, Brown's chapters on the evolution and preservation of the English language are superb references for any writer.

Rosen, M. J. (Ed.). (1989). *Collecting himself: James Thurber on writing and writers, humor and himself.* New York: Harper Perennial.
> Thurber's essays and cartoons reveal how he wrote and who influenced his writing.

Thomas, L. (1983). *Late night thoughts on listening to Mahler's ninth symphony.* New York: Viking Press.
> Although only a few specifically address writing, these lucid and witty essays are models for writing about any science.

White, E. B. (1962). *The points of my compass: Letters from the East, the West, the North, the South.* New York: Harper & Row.
> Perhaps the most civilized and accessible writer of English in the 20th century, White should be required reading for all writers.

Zinsser, W. (1988). *Writing to learn.* New York: Harper & Row.
> Zinsser says he wrote the book to relieve two prevalent fears: the fear of writing and the fear of subjects for which readers have no aptitude. He uses excellent writing from many disciplines to demonstrate that a scientist who can think clearly can write clearly enough to engage any reader.

Zinsser, W. (1990). *On writing well: An informal guide to writing nonfiction* (4th ed.). New York: Harper & Row.
> In this essential reference, Zinsser emphasizes how the good writer continues to learn about his or her craft.

3 *the library literature search*

Henry N. Mendelsohn and Trudi E. Jacobson

The starting point for performing most research is to conduct a formal systematic search of the literature. The aim of the literature search is to discover what has been written about a topic, so the researcher can avoid duplicating extant research; build on, succinctly present, and critique previous findings; and point out why the current research adds to the knowledge base of the discipline. In writing a dissertation, the doctoral student conducts a literature search to identify the topical literature and to aid in mastering a subject.

Established researchers and scholars who are working in a familiar field may know the literature well enough to cite previous works without conducting such a search or may discover them serendipitously from references in the literature they read. However, given the huge number of scholarly journals and the myriad social science disciplines conducting research on similar topics, it is difficult for even the most knowledgeable scholar to keep abreast of all the relevant literature in his or her discipline, let alone in related or allied disciplines.

Knowing how to conduct a literature search in a systematic manner is an important skill. Unfortunately, few researchers in the social sciences have a sound knowledge of how to do so. This chapter presents a succinct and systematic way to perform a literature search, using resources and services available in most mid-size to large college and university libraries, as well as in many large public libraries.

organization and services of libraries

Libraries vary greatly in size, resources, purposes, and abilities. Large libraries are complex, bureaucratic institutions that collect, organize, store, and make publicly available the knowledge and culture of a society.

Libraries are divided along functional lines. Technical services "marks and parks" (catalogs and stores) books and other materials that the acquisitions department has acquired. The public services department handles the circulation of materials, as well as reference and research services.

PUBLIC SERVICES

Most libraries help users gain access to their holdings. Reference librarians aid in the use and interpretation of tools (secondary sources) that help one find the primary literature, such as research reports, journal articles, and government publications. Reference librarians will explain the card or online public access catalog, recommend the best indexing or abstracting service to meet one's needs, find reference sources, and so on.

College, university, and large public libraries often employ librarians who serve as subject specialists. In addition to their degrees in library science, subject specialists may also have master's degrees in other areas, such as sociology, English, or biology. Subject specialists who also purchase many of the books and other materials are referred to as bibliographers.

When you conduct a comprehensive literature search, you will probably need to consult a reference librarian, especially, if one is available, a subject specialist. With the rapidly changing technology of information storage and retrieval, even the most sophisticated library user may be surprised to find that procedures change from year to year.

NETWORKS AND INTERLIBRARY LOANS

Libraries have been overwhelmed by the information explosion and by rapid technological advances and have been hindered by inflation, coupled with declining financial support and staff shortages. The huge body of information produced today can inundate even the largest library. The Library of Congress, for example, has tens of millions of items waiting to be processed for public use, and many libraries cannot afford to purchase all the materials that are published.

To cope with these problems, most libraries have formed networks to help classify, catalog, and share their materials. Libraries also provide electronic access to myriad databases in remote locations.

One result of these networks is interlibrary loan, which is often a separate department or office within public services that helps users obtain needed materials from other libraries or sources when their own library does not have them. Libraries are linked electronically through "bibliographic utilities" that readily identify who owns what and send materials back and forth through the mail. Although most libraries are generous in what they lend, they often do not lend old and rare materials, rather restricting their use to the library building and permitting them to be used only under supervision.

encyclopedias, handbooks, and dictionaries

Students who are unfamiliar with a discipline may want to start with these secondary sources. There are a number of general and specialized options for all three.

ENCYCLOPEDIAS

Encyclopedias are secondary sources that provide systematic summaries of information. A universal or general encyclopedia popularizes scholarship and knowledge for a general audience. A specialized encyclopedia treats a subject more broadly than does the research literature, which tends to focus on narrow, specific problems or questions, and presents generalizations drawn from research. It states what is known about a subject within a unified organizational framework. It may also define terms and interpret and place information within a larger framework.

Encyclopedia articles are authoritatively written and conclude with bibliographies of works that the author who was consulted to write the article recommends for further reading. The references are usually to primary sources, such as articles that present original research and government documents that provide statistical data. There are a variety of specialized encyclopedias for social work and related fields, as well as numerous others for just about every academic discipline. However, they may not always be up-to-date.

Therefore, it may be necessary to augment the information they offer with more current references.

Encyclopedia of Social Work

The National Association of Social Workers publishes the *Encyclopedia of Social Work* (Minahan, 1987). It is the only encyclopedia devoted exclusively to social work. Currently in its 18th edition, it presents materials on the entire range of activities in social welfare and social work. Its two volumes contain 225 articles, all of which were written specifically for that edition, together with 99 biographies of persons who made important contributions to social welfare and social work.

The 26 readers' guides identify related articles on a topic. For example, under the general topic of poverty and income support, there are 12 articles, such as "Child Support" and "Income Distribution." Each article also contains cross-references to related articles.

A supplementary third volume presents a statistical overview of social welfare and socil work and includes 21 updated articles (Ginsberg, 1990). Much of the data comes from the government, but other sources were also used. References to original sources are given because the data that are presented are probably only part of a much larger body of data in the original source.

Behavioral and Social Science Encyclopedias

Borgatta's *Encyclopedia of Sociology* (1992) is a four-volume set covering 370 topics of importance to the study of sociology and social problems. Examples of topics of interest to social work are drug abuse, deviance, divorce, ethnicity, family roles, family violence, race, and social work.

Kuper and Kuper's *The Social Science Encyclopedia* (1989) presents over 700 in-depth entries that are concerned with theories, issues, methods, and biographies for the major social sciences. Arieti's six-volume comprehensive *American Handbook of Psychiatry* (1984) is organized around the foundations of psychiatry: child and adolescent psychiatry, sociocultural and community psychiatry, adult clinical psychiatry, organic disorders and psychosomatic medicine, treatment, and new psychiatric frontiers. Psychoanalytic concepts are covered in Eidelberg's *Encyclopedia of Psychoanalysis* (1968). Wolman's *International Encyclopedia of Psychiatry, Psychology, Psychoanalysis, and Neurology* (1977) covers psychology and many related fields.

Romanofsky's *Social Service Organizations* (1978) lists, in alphabetic order, 293 national and prominent local organizations, current and historical, that have had a major impact on the social services. Each organization is sketched historically.

The *Encyclopedia of Associations,* although really more of a directory, contains a section on Social Welfare Organizations. Each entry includes when the organization was founded, the number of members, number of staff, budget, a description of its purpose, and a list of its regularly issued publications. Addresses and phone numbers are also included.

Several other encyclopedias may be useful: Corsini's *Encyclopedia of Psychology* (1984), Heyel's *Encyclopedia of Management* (1982), Kadish's *Encyclopedia of Crime and Justice* (1983), Kruskal and Tanur's *International Encyclopedia of Statistics* (1978), and Woody's *Encyclopedia of Clinical Assessment* (1980).

HANDBOOKS

Handbooks are compendiums of one or more subjects on a basic or an advanced level. They are arranged for the quick location of facts and may be carried, unlike a multivolume encyclopedia. Handbooks may supply answers to specific questions, such as statistics, rules, or quotations. Some also organize and summarize a body of basic information about a field of study. In many cases they supplement encyclopedia articles.

Numerous handbooks are of use to social workers. One that most social workers will be familiar with is the American Psychiatric Association's *Diagnostic and Statistical Manual of Mental Disorders, Third Edition—Revised* (1987). Other handbooks devoted to assessment are Ciminero, Calhoun, and Adams's *Handbook of Behavioral Assessment* (1986), which addresses numerous topics in behavioral assessment; Goldstein and Husen's *Handbook of Psychological Assessment* (1984); Groth-Marnet's *Handbook of Psychological Assessment* (1984); and Kellerman and Burry's *Handbook of Psychodiagnostic Testing: Personality Analysis and Report Writing* (1981).

DICTIONARIES

Dictionaries contain the words of a language or the terms of a subject arranged in some definite order, usually alphabetic, with explanations of their meanings, pronunciations, etymologies, and syntactical and idiomatic uses. They may either describe how words are used in everyday discourse or prescribe the proper use of words.

A dictionary devoted to a particular subject often considers the meanings of terms in relation to a larger body of knowledge. It not only defines words but attempts to place them within the broader concepts of a field or within a particular school of thought.

Social work and other social and behavioral sciences often use
everyday words but assign different meanings to them or use them
in specific contexts. When you write any type of paper, it is important to define what you mean by your usage of a particular term
or concept. Encyclopedias may also provide definitions of terms.

The National Association of Social Workers published the second
edition of *The Social Work Dictionary* in 1991 (Barker, 1991). The
dictionary defines 5,000 terms frequently used in social work.
Both the *Dictionary of Social Services, Policy and Practice* (Clegg, 1980)
and *Dictionary of Social Welfare* (Timms & Timms, 1982) define
social work and social policy terms and concepts as used in Britain.
Clegg also refers to British laws and acts of Parliament. Because
social work borrows from and utilizes research and terminology
from related social and behavioral sciences, Mitchell's *A New
Dictionary of Sociology* (1979) is useful for locating concise definitions
of sociological terms. Two additional sociological dictionaries are
the *Encyclopedic Dictionary of Sociology* (1986), which provides
definitions and brief articles on nearly 1,400 entries, and *Harper-
Collins Dictionary of Sociology* (Jary, 1991), which contains 1,800
entries with charts and graphs. *The Dictionary of Mental Health*
(Fisher, 1980) presents numerous definitions of mental health
terms and concepts. Another useful publication is the American
Psychiatric Association's *American Psychiatric Glossary*, 6th edition
(Stone, 1988).

HOW TO FIND

When searching a card catalog or online public access catalog to
find out what encyclopedias, dictionaries, or handbooks your
library owns, you may have to use Library of Congress subject
headings, which many but not all online public access catalogs
use. Library of Congress subject headings are published in a three-
volume set appropriately entitled *Library of Congress Subject Headings*. Because the subject headings may not always use commonsense or popular terminology, it is best to consult these guides. For
example, the *Encyclopedia of Social Work* is listed under the broader
subject heading "Social Service—Yearbooks," and *The Social Work
Dictionary* is listed under the heading "Social Service—Dictionaries." There is no subheading for handbooks.

journals

After you find an encyclopedia article that provides an overview of
a subject, the next step is to locate books and journal articles.

Books or monographs (publications on single subjects) may present original research. However, scholarly books take a great deal of time to write and usually a year or more to edit and publish. Increasingly, research findings are presented in scholarly journals devoted to a discipline or subject area. In the natural sciences almost all original research is published in journals. In the social sciences, journals are rapidly becoming the primary source for presenting research.

Another reason for the importance of journals for presenting research findings is that each article (its methodology, organization, findings, and conclusions) is carefully screened before publication by reviewers (members of a journal's editorial board or persons chosen by the journal editor for their expertise). The reviewers determine whether an article is worthy of publication. Articles must be original, make a contribution to the discipline's literature, and meet commonly agreed-on standards of scholarship.

In social work, at least three dozen journals are devoted to some aspect of the discipline, and hundreds more are published in such related and allied fields as sociology, psychology, economics, and public administration. Because there are so many journals, it is difficult to perform a literature search without approaching the task systematically. Merely browsing through a few journals will not suffice.

HOW TO FIND: PRINT GUIDES

Indexes

An index is a systematically arranged list that gives enough information about each item that it can be identified and located. Indexes collect and arrange references to articles, documents, and books on many subjects and academic disciplines to help you retrieve information. Some indexes are devoted to a specific discipline, whereas others are multidisciplinary and still others are subject oriented. Some indexes are published by professional associations, but many are issued by commercial publishers.

An index presents the basic bibliographic information needed to find an article, document, or book. Bibliographic information for a journal article includes the author or authors, the title, the name of the journal, the volume and issue number of the journal, the pages of the article, and the year of publication.

Brower, A. M., & Garvin, C. D., "Design Issues in Social Group Work Research." *Social Work with Groups*, 12(3): 91–102, 1989.

Two examples of multidisciplinary indexes are the *Social Sciences Citation Index* and the *PAIS International in Print* (devoted to public policy issues). Other indexes and abstracts (described next) are listed in the bibliography at the end of this chapter.

Abstracts

An abstracting journal goes one step further than an index. It provides a summary, or abstract, of each (or at least most) of the articles it indexes. Reading the abstract first will save time because you will know exactly what the article is about. Knowing what an article is about is important, especially in the social sciences, where titles of articles may not be precise. A bibliographic citation with an abstract looks like this:

> Brown, A., "British Perspectives on Groupwork: Present and Future." *Social Work with Groups*, 13(3): 53–65, 1990.
>
> This study comments on some selected issues with respect to group work issues in Great Britain. The discussion locates some current group work trends in Britain in their political context and comments on organizational issues facing British group workers as they enter the 1990s.

Although indexes and abstracts vary in organization and content, one need merely consult the preface to find out the publication's scope and arrangement. Because there are many indexes and abstracts, it may be best to consult a reference librarian for advice on where to begin.

The primary source of articles on social work and social welfare, as well as on related fields, is *Social Work Research & Abstracts*, published quarterly by the National Association of Social Workers (NASW). About 450 journals are reviewed each year and around 500 abstracts and bibliographic citations are included in each issue, arranged in subject categories. The December issue contains the annual subject and author indexes. In addition to the abstracts, the journal publishes a number of research articles in each issue.

Social Planning/Policy & Development Abstracts, produced by Sociological Abstracts, Inc., is another indexing and abstracting source. It covers the applied social sciences, including policy studies, welfare administration, evaluation research, social work, health care administration, and community organization.

Additional abstracting services include *Psychological Abstracts*, which covers the world's psychological literature, and *Sociological Abstracts*, which does the same for sociology. Some abstracting services are devoted to specific topics. Examples include *Women Studies Abstracts, Child Development Abstracts and Bibliography, Criminal Justice Abstracts,* and *Sage Public Administration Abstracts: An International Information Service.*

books

Scholarly books and monographs generally focus on specific subjects. A monograph, such as a technical report issued by a research institute, is on a single subject, usually detailed in treatment but not extensive in scope. Books and monographs that report research findings are likely to be wider in scope and to have greater detail than journal articles. Social work practice methods and techniques are often published in book form. Social work libraries also have numerous how-to books that describe methods and techniques.

HOW TO FIND

Online public access catalogs (OPACs) are computerized databases that serve as indexes to what a library owns. In theory they contain the same information as an old-fashioned card catalog. In practice they may not be as sophisticated as the card catalog or they may be far more complex and sophisticated.

With the sophisticated OPACs, you may search by author, title, subject, call number, and various combinations. Some OPACs may also allow you to search by key word, combinations of author and titles, and if they are powerful enough, by Boolean logic. Some OPACs indicate information on holdings for more than just the library in which they are located. For example, if the OPAC for a public library is countywide, it lists not only its own books but those for all the area libraries; it may also show whether a book is on loan or on the shelf.

It is easy to find books by author or title, but it is more complicated to locate books by subject. Pertinent books are often missed because proper subject headings have not been used. For example, books on child abuse may be found under "Child Abuse," but they may also be listed under "Abused Children," "Child Welfare," and "Child Molesting."

To locate proper subject headings, consult the latest edition of the *Library of Congress Subject Headings,* which lists not only the correct terms, but cross-references, broader and narrower terms, and terms that are not used. Small libraries that do not follow the Library of Congress system may use *Sears List of Subject Headings* for their catalogs. These subject lists may also indicate terms that might be used in other indexes. However, no standardized terminology is used in all indexes.

If a library does not own a particular book, it may be able to obtain it for you through interlibrary loan. Because interlibrary loan takes time, you should not wait until the last minute to begin your library research.

computerized databases

The proliferation of journals, books, technical reports, and other materials has necessitated the development of ways to electronically collect, store, and retrieve information.

Electronic databases became available to the public in the early 1970s. There are now hundreds of publicly available databases that cover the academic and business literature. Today's computerized databases are referred to as *online systems*.

Database producers select items, such as journal articles, technical reports, patents, books, conference papers, annual reports, newspaper and magazine articles, government publications, theses, dissertations, and bibliographies, for inclusion in their databases. Many bibliographic databases contain abstracts, and some include statistical data. Others provide the full text of journal and newspaper articles. Some legal databases provide the full text of legal cases, statutes, and other legal information.

EXAMPLES

Social Work Abstracts is a good example of a small but specialized online database. Produced by NASW, it covers the social work journal literature from 1977 to the present. It closely corresponds to the printed index and abstracting journal but does not include the full text of journal articles. One may search the database to produce a bibliography of articles gleaned from social work journals.

PsycINFO, produced by the American Psychological Association, is a much larger online database that complements *Social Work Abstracts*. Its coverage of the psychology, psychiatric, and social work literature and the literature of related disciplines extends back to 1967. *PsycINFO* contains bibliographic records and abstracts of more than 650,000 journal articles and doctoral dissertations. It is international in scope and comes close to being comprehensive in its coverage of the psychological literature. However, it does not cover the social work literature as comprehensively as *Social Work Abstracts*. A researcher who needs a thorough review of the literature should perform a computer search in both databases.

Numerous other databases are relevant to social work and social welfare. In the field of education, there is *ERIC*, the database of the Educational Resources Information Center. Other pertinent databases are *Alcohol Use and Abuse, American Statistics Index, Child Abuse and Neglect, MEDLINE,* and *Social SciSearch*. Many more databases are described in the bibliography.

HOW TO SEARCH

A manual search of the literature would take hours, if not days, whereas an online search can be performed in minutes and the resulting bibliography can be printed on the spot. Tens of thousands, in some cases hundreds of thousands, of bibliographic or full-text records can be swiftly accessed, searched, and narrowed down to the requirements of the researcher in just seconds.

Computerized literature retrieval has several powerful features. First, each part of the bibliographic record, including the author, title, abstract, key words, and index terms (often referred to as "descriptors") can be searched either separately or in combination.

Second, Boolean logic can be applied. The searcher may ask for a combination of subjects by using the Boolean operator "and." The operator "or" may be used to ask for one subject or the other. A third operator, "not," can be used to ask for one subject but not another. For example, one may search for articles about depression *and* cognitive therapy; depression *and* either cognitive therapy *or* group therapy; or depression in adults but *not* in children.

Third, proximity operators allow the searcher to indicate whether the terms that are being searched should be adjacent to one another or whether both should simply appear in a particular field, such as the abstract. The use of proximity operators increases the precision of a search.

Database producers may be either commercial or professional organizations. Searchers can gain access to the hundreds of commercially produced databases, in most cases, through a commercial vendor, which loads the datatapes into its computers and allows the public access via telecommunications links. Searches are performed using the vendor's software. A vendor has different databases, and different vendors use different software to search their systems. Most libraries have librarians who are trained to perform online database searches and to provide advice on which databases to search. It is common for a subject specialist to perform a search at the request of a researcher or student. Commercial vendors also offer access to their databases to people who have their own computers and modems.

The fees for using databases vary considerably and include charges for every hour of access time, for telecommunications costs, and often for every item that is printed. Libraries and private information search companies also charge fees for conducting a search.

compact disk databases

Another option for searching electronically is to use CD-ROMs (compact disk–read only memory, the latter part meaning that one can only read what is "written" on the disk and cannot alter the data). CD-ROMs look like music compact disks, but contain digital full text (the complete text of encyclopedia articles, for example) or numerical data (for instance, census data), graphics (such as maps), and bibliographic data (periodical indexes with citations and perhaps abstracts).

A single CD-ROM can hold the equivalent of 275,000 double-spaced typed pages. The information is contained right on the disk, so there is no need to connect with a database vendor's computer to gain access to the information. CD-ROMs are used on micro-computers equipped with, or connected to, compact disk drives.

Indexes and abstracts in this format provide most of the advantages of an online search without the attendant costs to the user. As in an online search, all parts, or fields, of a bibliographic record can be searched. Search strategies can take advantage of the power of Boolean and proximity operators.

The period covered by a particular CD-ROM database will not always correspond to what is available online, and there will be even less correspondence between the CD-ROM version and the printed version of a particular tool. Some CD-ROM databases extend as far back as the online versions, while others may include only the most recent three or five years. Many CD-ROM databases are updated quarterly, whereas online databases may be updated monthly or even more frequently. If you know what years a CD-ROM covers, you can determine whether an online or manual search is needed to pick up earlier or the most recent citations. For example, *PsycLIT* goes back only to 1974 on CD-ROM, but the online coverage began in 1967 and the printed index started in 1927. The CD-ROM database is updated quarterly, whereas the online database is updated monthly.

EXAMPLES

The following CD-ROMs are especially useful for social work research.

Social Work Abstracts Plus. A compilation of two databases: *Social Work Abstracts* and the *Register of Clinical Social Workers. Social Work*

Abstracts covers 1977 to the present. It describes more than 23,000 journal articles and other citations in the social work literature, and over 600 major social work books. You can search by a number of fields: author, article title, source (journal), address, dissertation address, hard copy (citation in the printed *Social Work Research & Abstracts*), descriptor or subject term (the complete list of descriptors is in the database), classification code, and free-text words.

You can combine search statements using the Boolean "and," "or," and "not." You can also run new search criteria against a set you have already created. For example, if you have retrieved all records that include "adoption" in the abstract, you can then limit these records to articles that appeared in *Social Casework*. Records can be displayed, printed, or downloaded in three formats: citation, citation and abstract, or complete bibliographic record.

PsycLIT. Provides access to the worldwide literature, including journal articles, technical reports, and dissertations, in psychology and related disciplines, from 1974 to the present. It includes citations with abstracts of literature reviews, surveys, discussions, translations, theories, conference reports, panel discussions, case studies, and descriptions of apparatus and tests.

Sociofile. Offers abstracts and citations covering such topics as social welfare, social planning and policy, groups, family, and other aspects of sociology from 1,800 journals published worldwide. It covers 1974 to the present.

MEDLINE. The bibliographic database of the National Library of Medicine. Contains references from more than 3,200 journals, primarily in the biomedical literature, from 1966 to the present with annual cumulations. It is international in scope, but about 75 percent of the citations are published in English.

ERIC. Offers abstracts and citations for the U.S. literature in education from 1966 to the present. It includes both documents (research and technical reports, conference presentations, instructional and curriculum materials, project and program descriptions) and articles from over 775 journals.

PAIS on CD-ROM (Public Affairs Information Service). Provides worldwide coverage of the public policy aspects of economics, business, government, law, public administration, political science, international relations, legislation, demography, and other social sciences, with citations to articles in periodicals, government documents, books, pamphlets, reports, yearbooks, and directories. It covers 1972 to the present.

Statistical Masterfile. Includes three indexes: *American Statistics Index* (1973 to the present), which indexes government statistical publications from over 500 federal agencies; *Statistical Reference Index* (1980 to the present), which indexes statistical information from leading American sources outside the U.S. government, including business and commercial publishers, state governments, and independent and university research centers; and *Index to International Statistics* (1983 to the present), which covers statistics published by international intergovernment organizations such as the United Nations and the European Community.

Government Documents Catalog Service. Indexes all government documents cataloged by the U.S. Government Printing Office, including publications from most federal government agencies. It covers 1976 to the present.

HOW TO SEARCH

Because CD-ROM searches are not ruled by the "time is money" constraint of online searches, the researcher can perform his or her own search fairly readily. Most CD-ROMs are designed to be more user friendly than online databases. However, the apparent transparency of the search software may be deceptive. Although it is possible to enter one or two terms and obtain citations, a researcher needs to know how the database is structured and how Boolean and proximity operators work to do an adequate search.

A well-thought-out search strategy is vital, and a librarian will often be available to help construct it. Inquire about the availability of a list of descriptors or index terms, called a thesaurus, for the CD-ROM database you intend to use. Although you can search using your own terms (a free-text search), you can perform a more precise search using these official subject headings. Using descriptors or index terms will save you the trouble of identifying all synonyms and variant spellings of a term. But if a concept is new and not yet included in a thesaurus, a free-text search is appropriate.

Beyond the necessity of knowing how to construct a tight search strategy, there is also the vexing problem of having to learn several systems to work with the different search software used by CD-ROM publishers. Some software is more powerful than others and allows for more flexibility in searching. Although every search system includes ways for a researcher to perform basic functions—enter search terms, show records, and print records—each system does it differently. If you have learned how to search *Sociofile*, which is published by SilverPlatter, you will also be able to use Silver-Platter's *SWAB (Social Work Abstracts)* or *PsycLIT.* However, *Social Scisearch,* published by the Institute for Scientific Information (ISI), has different options and requires different commands. For example, the F2 function key is used to search for terms in the Silver-Platter databases, whereas the F3 function key is used in ISI's databases.

CD-ROM databases are obtained by subscription, and libraries usually absorb this cost without passing it on to users. Unlike online searches, there is no additional cost for time spent searching the CD-ROM. CD-ROM subscription rates can be expensive, and a library's budget will determine how many CD-ROM databases the library can afford. Because CD-ROMs are phenomenally powerful, and therefore popular, you may need to sign up in advance to use one.

Fledgling users need to be instructed in how to use CD-ROMs to the best advantage. Libraries may address the need for CD-ROM instruction in a number of ways. Most provide one-on-one assistance as needed while a search is being done and often provide printed instructions. Some libraries also offer CD-ROM classes, either introductory or database-specific sessions, or both. Many CD-ROM databases also provide assistance through help screens or tutorials.

Once you have performed the search to your satisfaction, you can print out the results on the spot. Or you can download your results in machine-readable form onto a disk and then manipulate them using a word-processing package. Many researchers find downloading less time-consuming—for example, in compiling a bibliography—than rekeying all the information. Some CD-ROM software packages allow you to customize the format of the citations for printing or downloading.

public documents

Social workers and other human services personnel frequently need to consult publications from the federal, state, and local governments. Public documents may be in print, on microform, in a machine-readable datafile, or on CD-ROM.

The federal government is the largest publisher of information in the world. Many federal documents are printed by the U.S. Government Printing Office (GPO). Any document bearing the GPO imprint is in the public domain, that is, available to the public without copyright restrictions. Research reports, technical reports, evaluation studies, annual reports, statistical compendiums, and "how-to" pamphlets are among the types of GPO publications. The topics covered include population, health and nutrition, welfare, education, law enforcement, courts and prisons, elections, financial and employment data on all levels of government, the labor force, employment and unemployment, earnings and income, expenditures and wealth, communications, energy, and agriculture.

GPO's Office of the Superintendent of Documents has many functions, one of which is to distribute public documents to designated libraries that serve as depositories. However, any library may order public documents. Individuals may also purchase documents directly from GPO.

Not all federal documents are available from the Superintendent of Documents. The National Technical Information Service (NTIS) was created to improve access to data files and scientific and technical reports produced by federal agencies and their contractors. It is the central source for the public sale of U.S. government-sponsored research. Much of the research is oriented toward engineering and science, but there is an abundance of behavioral and social science research, much of it relevant to social work. Many large libraries collect NTIS documents. The main source for identifying NTIS documents is the *Government Reports Announcements and Index,* an indexing and abstracting service containing current citations for publications received by NTIS. Users can purchase items directly from NTIS.

NATIONAL PUBLICATIONS

Directories

The basic reference source on the federal government, found in most libraries, is the *United States Government Manual.* This annual publication from GPO describes the programs and activities of the legislative, judicial, and executive branches of government and contains organizational charts and descriptions of programs and activities.

The following directories are commercially produced. The *Washington Information Directory,* published annually, provides information on agencies of the executive branch, Congress, and nongovernment organizations in Washington, DC. The *Federal Yellow Book* is a loose-leaf service, updated bimonthly, that presents directory information on about 27,000 federal employees. The *Federal Executive Directory* contains an alphabetic index of names in the executive branch and a key word index of agency names. The *Federal Staff Directory* publishes biographical and directory information on key staff in the executive branch. The *Encyclopedia of Governmental Advisory Organizations* is a guide to 5,000 permanent, continuing, and ad hoc U.S. presidential advisory commissions, congressional advisory commissions, task forces, and so on.

Congressional Information

A standard index to Congress, the *Congressional Index,* can be used to locate House and Senate bills and resolutions. "Status of House

Bills" reports House measures from the time hearings are held on them to their final enactment or rejection. The *Congressional Record,* the official proceedings of Congress, consists of four parts: "Proceedings of the House," "Proceedings of the Senate," "Extensions of Remarks," and "Daily Digest." The biweekly index to the *Congressional Record* has a section on History of Bills and Resolutions, which provides information on a bill's status from its introduction to its enactment or veto. DIALOG Information Services has a database entitled *Congressional Record Abstracts,* which provides comprehensive abstracts covering each issue of the *Congressional Record.*

Congressional Information Service (CIS), a commercial publishing company, publishes the *CIS Index to Publications of the United States Congress.* It is a comprehensive listing of bibliographic data and brief abstracts on current congressional documents. A companion volume, *CIS Legislative History Service,* presents legislative histories—summaries of testimony, committee reports, and the like—that indicate the history and intent of new laws. The *United States Code, Congressional and Administrative News* also publishes the full text of these histories and of public laws.

Additional information about Congress is contained in the *Congressional Quarterly Weekly Report,* which provides detailed coverage of Congress, the presidency, the Supreme Court, and national politics. The *Congressional Quarterly Almanac,* published after each congressional session, presents a summary of the session. The annual *Official Congressional Directory* contains biographical information on each member of Congress, information on committees and subcommittees, and statistical data on Congress. The *Congressional Staff Directory,* an annual publication, focuses on the staffs of the congressional members, congressional committees, and subcommittees. The *Congressional Yellow Book* gives directory information on senators and representatives, their offices, committee staffs, and so on.

Office of the President

A particularly important publication from the Office of the President is the *Federal Register.* Published daily, Monday through Friday, the *Federal Register* consists of rules, proposed rules, and notices issued by executive departments, agencies, and independent utilities, as well as executive orders and proclamations. The index to this publication is called the *Federal Register Index.* After a new rule or regulation appears in the *Federal Register,* it is eventually added to the compilation of rules and regulations entitled the *Code of Federal Regulations.*

New laws are passed by Congress and signed into law by the president. They are compiled into the *United States Code,* the laws of the United States. Once a law is enacted, the regulatory agencies interpret the law and write the rules and regulations, which are first published in the *Federal Register* and then compiled in the *Code of Federal Regulations.*

Statistics

The U.S. Bureau of the Census produces *CENDATA,* which contains selected statistical data. It is available for public access through DIALOG Information Services. The U.S. Bureau of the Census will release the 1990 census on compact disk to depository libraries. In addition, much information is contained in the databases of individual departments, agencies, and offices of the federal government. Although these databases are not publicly available, researchers may gain access to them by contacting the issuing agency.

The GPO publishes several reference books that present summary statistics and serve as guides to primary sources. The best-known publication is the annual *Statistical Abstract of the United States: National Database and Guide to Sources,* the standard summary of quantitative data about the United States. This publication presents tables and charts of data gleaned from original sources, including population data extracted from the voluminous decennial census; vital statistics; and data on health and nutrition, education, law enforcement, state and local governments, social insurance, and the human services. It footnotes each entry to lead users to the original source, which may contain much more information, both statistical and textual. An appendix includes a "Guide to Sources of Statistics," which lists statistical series arranged by subject.

Other similar reference books are the *State and Metropolitan Area Data Book;* the *County and City Data Book;* and *Historical Statistics of the United States, Colonial Times to 1970.* These three publications, along with *Statistical Abstracts,* provide a great deal of statistical information about the United States.

However, not all statistical information is covered in these four sources. Additional indexes that are commercially produced index statistical publications of federal, state, and international government bodies and organizations. The *American Statistics Index (ASI)* is a monthly with annual cumulations that attempts to be a master guide and index to all the statistical publications of the U.S. government, particularly those that contain primary data of research value. The reports are arranged by department. Thus, one need only look under the Department of Health and Human Services for an idea of the vast number of statistical reports issued by the federal government.

Whereas the GPO's *Monthly Catalog of U.S. Government Publications* indexes all federal documents, *ASI* indexes only statistical studies and publishes detailed abstracts of each study. *ASI* makes all the documents publicly available on microfiche. Thus, a large library may own the documents either as paper copy or on microfiche. If not, the fiche can be ordered from the publisher, CIS.

CIS also publishes two companion sets: the *Statistical Reference Index: A Selective Guide to American Statistical Publications from Sources Other Than the U.S. Government* and the *Index to International Statistics: A Guide to the Statistical Publications of International Intergovernmental Organizations*. Both are reasonably comprehensive and make it easier to locate such data. Again, CIS issues the original documents on microfiche.

United States Budget

Information on the funding of social programs is found in one of the most important presidential documents—the *Budget of the U.S. Government*—which contains the president's budget message and presents an overview of his budget proposals. Spending programs are explained in terms of national needs, agencies, missions, tax programs, and the like.

A related and important publication for social workers is the *Catalog of Federal Domestic Assistance,* which presents information on federal assistance programs. Descriptions of programs are indexed by the names of departments and agencies, eligible applicants, functional classifications, popular names, and deadlines.

STATE AND LOCAL PUBLICATIONS

State and local governments generate a large volume of materials. However, these materials are not as carefully controlled as are federal documents, so it is more difficult for libraries to acquire them. State libraries are often the best places to find state publications. One example of a state publication is a state's handbook. Such handbooks are often referred to by their color—for instance, red or blue books—and are usually published annually. They contain basic information on state governments and may include descriptions of departments and agencies and biographies of elected and appointed state officials.

HOW TO FIND

Many libraries maintain federal publications as separate collections. Because of their volume, these public documents are not always cataloged and entered into card catalogs or online catalogs. The documents are usually organized according to the SuDocs Classification System, devised by the Superintendent of Documents. SuDocs is an alphanumeric system based on the principle of provenance: The publications of any government department, bureau, agency, or office are grouped under like notations. It is not a subject arrangement, but rather reflects the organization of the federal government. Letters are used to indicate the parent agency. For example, "Ju" is used for the Judiciary, "Pr Ex" for the Office of the President, and "He" for the Department of Health and Human Services. Subordinate bureaus and offices are denoted by numbers, followed by decimals to note the type of publication, such as annual report, law, press release, or handbook. Additional letters and numbers may reflect the authors, edition, and year of publication.

The primary aid for identifying federal government publications is the *Monthly Catalog of U.S. Government Publications,* which indexes publications issued by all branches of the federal government. The entries are grouped alphabetically by agency, with the monthly indexes cumulated semiannually and annually. The catalog uses Library of Congress subject headings and provides full bibliographic details for each item, but no annotations or abstracts. There are author, title, subject, and series/reports-number indexes. The bibliographic information also includes the SuDocs classification number for each item, which allows users to find the document in libraries that use the SuDocs system. Most libraries have the GPO's monthly catalog. It also exists as an online database and as a CD-ROM. The electronic versions are powerful tools for quickly sorting through hundreds of thousands of federal government publications to locate relevant items.

Publications of municipal and county governments and organizations are even more difficult to identify and obtain than are state publications. Fortunately, the *Index to Current Urban Documents* represents a systematic effort to identify local government publications. It lists documents geographically by state and city or county and then by government agency and contains a detailed subject index. The publisher of the index collects the documents and makes them available on microfiche. Some libraries may subscribe to documents from selected cities and counties. Individual documents may be ordered from the publisher, Greenwood Press.

legal documents

Because social workers work within a framework of federal, state, and local laws and ordinances, it may be necessary to include legal information in the literature search. Social workers should have at least a minimal familiarity with how laws are made and how to find out about them. Legal research can be confusing and time-consuming, but if it is approached systematically and with patience and an awareness of how the literature is organized, it need not be overwhelming. A librarian can lead you through the process and provide such aids as a handbook of legal research, as well as legal dictionaries and encyclopedias.

LAWS

Federal Laws

Federal laws are first published in chronological order in *United States Statutes at Large*. They are later topically arranged in the *United States Code*. West's *United States Code Annotated (USCA)* not only gives the law, but provides numerous annotations and cross-references to other legal publications, such as the *Code of Federal Regulations (CFR)*. Thus, one can find the law in *USCA* and then locate the rules and regulations in *CFR*. The annotations in *USCA* may refer to court decisions that have cited and interpreted the statute. The lawyers' edition is entitled *United States Code Service*.

State and Municipal Laws

The organization and publication of state and federal laws are similar. Each state legislature publishes all laws, generically called session laws, passed during the current session. Like the *United States Code*, state laws are compiled in codes. The laws that local governments (often called municipalities) enact are referred to as ordinances, which are codified like state and federal laws.

Legislative Histories

Finding out why a law was passed is important, particularly for a literature review. A legislative history may contain primary documents, even research reports, that discuss why a law was needed and what it is meant to accomplish. Finding legislative histories for federal laws is relatively easy. Two sources that were previously mentioned in the section on Public Documents are the *United States Code, Congressional and Administrative News* and the *CIS Legislative History Service*. The former actually reproduces relevant documents within the text, whereas the latter provides bibliographic information that enables users to find the documents in a library that contains federal publications. There are no such publications for state laws, making it difficult at best to find their legislative histories. Some state libraries may maintain archival materials on significant state laws.

COURT DECISIONS

Federal Courts

The federal court system consists of three main divisions: the Supreme Court; the courts of appeals; and the district courts, where trials first occur. All written opinions of the Supreme Court and most appellate court decisions are published, but not all district court decisions are. Unpublished cases are often available through the court clerks.

The official version of Supreme Court cases is the *United States Reports*. The lawyers' edition is *United States Supreme Court Reports*. West Publishing Company publishes the *Supreme Court Reporter*.

The Supreme Court hears only a few selected cases that have been appealed to it. If it refuses to hear a case, the case remains as it was decided in the lower court. Most of the work of the federal courts occurs in the district courts (trial courts) and the courts of appeals.

West Publishing Company is the primary publisher of cases that originate in district courts and are referred to appellate courts. Cases before 1880 are contained in a series entitled *Federal Cases*. Cases after 1880 are contained in two series. Appellate court cases are reported in the *Federal Reporter*, which reports only selected cases because of the large number of cases. Even fewer district court cases are reported. Those that are published are contained in the *Federal Supplement*.

If you cannot find a case, consult a reference librarian. Specialized law services, called loose-leaf reporters because of their format, report on cases that are concerned with specific topics. For example, there are the *Criminal Law Reporter* and *Women's Rights Law Reporter*. A case may be included in a loose-leaf reporter but not published in West's hardbound reporter series.

State Courts

The primary reporting service for state cases is the National Reporter System by West Publishing Company. This series includes seven regional reporters that report state cases: the *Atlantic Reporter, North Eastern Reporter, North Western Reporter, Pacific Reporter, South Eastern Reporter, South Western Reporter,* and *Southern Reporter*. The reporters publish the full text of the cases.

Digests

Digests arrange cases by subjects. They are similar to abstracting services for journal articles in that they present summaries of the indexed cases and citations to where the full text of cases may be found. West Publishing Company divides the law into several hundred topics and subtopics. Cases are arranged by topic and subtopic within the digests. Once the system of arranging cases and providing cross-references is understood, it is fairly easy to find relevant cases.

Periodicals

One way to find cases is first to find articles about significant cases. Articles in law journals are usually written by law school professors, students, and scholars in related fields. They are considered secondary sources in that they generally discuss the primary sources—the cases—as well as societal issues and jurisprudence. The *Harvard Law Review* is an example of a law school review, and the *ABA Journal* is an example of a publication by a professional association (the American Bar Association).

Index to Legal Periodicals and *Current Law Index* both index law journals. They are available on CD-ROM and as electronic databases. In its electronic database form, *Current Law Index* is entitled *Legal Resources Index*, and in its CD-ROM form, it is entitled *LegalTrac*. Neither provides abstracts.

Shepard's Citations

One way to find if a case is still good law or was overturned is to consult *Shepard's Citations*, a set of publications, each of which is devoted to specific series of law books. For example, there is a *Shepard's Citations* to Supreme Court cases and another for federal appellate courts. In these publications you can look up a given case to determine if it has been appealed to a higher court and affirmed or reversed; if it was cited in another case, which may help you find cases on similar topics; and if and how the decisions of one case were treated in subsequent cases. The publications also provide judicial histories of a case and its treatment by later decisions. The best way to learn to use *Shepard's Citations* is to read the instructions in the preface and to consult it regularly.

Computerized Law Services

One way to search the legal literature quickly is to use an electronic service. There are two major vendors of computerized legal databases. West Publishing Company produces *Westlaw*, which contains the full text of the court cases in the West reporting system and enables one to consult *Shepard's Citations* electronically. *Westlaw* also contains indexes to legal periodicals, statutes, and many specialized databases. Mead Data Central produces *Lexis*, also a full-text online database. Both are powerful, sophisticated legal research systems.

HOW TO FIND

Many legal publications have both official and unofficial versions. In addition to official versions published by government bodies, at least two unofficial versions are published by commercial publishers. Two of the most frequently encountered commercial legal publishers are the West Publishing Company and the Lawyers' Cooperative Publishing Company. When you use a collection of legal materials, it is important to know to which publisher the library subscribes. Both West and the Lawyer's Cooperative have devised systems that enable the legal researcher to perform research systematically. Each system provides editorial features and annotations to aid the researcher. Consult a librarian to find out which set of materials is available. The librarian can explain the editorial features and how best to use them.

conclusion

The key to conducting a successful literature search is to be systematic. If you are new to a discipline, you will want to start with encyclopedias, handbooks, and dictionaries and then consult books and journal articles. You may also find it necessary to locate statistics that describe the problem under investigation and to peruse public documents. Depending on the nature of the problem, you may need to explore the legal dimensions as well.

Information technology will help you perform the literature search expeditiously. Frequently, more than one technological option exists to search the same body of literature. A reference librarian will be able to steer you through this maze of technology to retrieve what you need. If you approach it systematically and with patience, you will find a literature search to be a beneficial learning experience.

bibliography

ENCYCLOPEDIAS

Arieti, S. (Ed.). (1984). *American handbook of psychiatry* (2nd ed., 6 vols.). New York: John Wiley & Sons.

Borgatta, E. F. (Ed.-in-Chief). (1992). *Encyclopedia of sociology.* New York: Macmillan.

Corsini, R. J. (Ed.). (1984). *Encyclopedia of psychology* (4 vols.). New York: John Wiley & Sons.

Eidelberg, L. (Ed.-in-Chief). (1968). *Encyclopedia of psychoanalysis.* New York: Free Press.

Encyclopedia of associations (annual). Detroit: Gale Research.

Ginsberg, L., et al. (Eds.). (1990). *Encyclopedia of Social Work* (18th ed., 1990 suppl.). Silver Spring, MD: National Association of Social Workers.

Heyel, C. (Ed.-in-Chief). (1982). *Encyclopedia of management* (3rd ed.). New York: Van Nostrand Reinhold.

Kadish, S. H. (Ed.-in-Chief). (1983). *Encyclopedia of crime and justice* (4 vols.). New York: Free Press.

Kruskal, W. H., & Tanur, J. M. (Eds.). (1978). *International encyclopedia of statistics* (2 vols.). New York: Free Press.

Kuper, A., & Kuper, J. (Eds.). (1989). *The social science encyclopedia.* Boston: Routledge & Kegan Paul.

Minahan, A. (Ed.-in-Chief). (1987). *Encyclopedia of social work* (18th ed., 2 vols.). Silver Spring, MD: National Association of Social Workers.

Romanofsky, P. (Ed.). (1978). *Social service organizations* (2 vols.). Westport, CT: Greenwood Press.

Wolman, B. B. (Ed.). (1977). *International encyclopedia of psychiatry, psychology, psychoanalysis, and neurology* (12 vols.). New York: Van Nostrand Reinhold.

Woody, R. H. (Ed.). (1980). *Encyclopedia of clinical assessment* (2 vols.). San Francisco: Jossey-Bass.

HANDBOOKS

American Psychiatric Association. (1987). *Diagnostic and statistical manual of mental disorders* (3rd ed., rev.). Washington, DC: Author.

Ciminero, A. R., Calhoun, K. S., & Adams, H. E. (Eds.). (1986). *Handbook of behavioral assessment* (2nd ed.). New York: John Wiley & Sons.

Goldstein, G., & Husen, M. (Eds.). (1984). *Handbook of psychological assessment.* New York: Pergamon Press.

Groth-Marnet, G. (1984). *Handbook of psychological assessment.* New York: Van Nostrand Reinhold.

Kellerman, H., & Burry, A. (1981). *Handbook of psychodiagnostic testing: Personality analysis and report writing.* New York: Grune & Stratton.

DICTIONARIES

Barker, R. L. (1991). *The social work dictionary* (2nd ed.). Silver Spring, MD: National Association of Social Workers.

Clegg, J. (1980). *Dictionary of social services, policy and practice* (3rd ed.). London: Bedford & the National Council of Social Service.

Encyclopedic dictionary of sociology (3rd ed.). (1986). Guilford, CT: Dushkin Publishing Group.

Fisher, R. B. (1980). *The dictionary of mental health*. New York: Granada.

Jary, D. (1991). *HarperCollins dictionary of sociology*. New York: Harper Perennial.

Mitchell, G. D. (1979). *A new dictionary of sociology*. London: Routledge & Kegan Paul.

Stone, E. M. (1988). *American psychiatric glossary* (6th ed.). Washington, DC: American Psychiatric Press.

Timms, N., & Timms, R. (1982). *Dictionary of social welfare*. Boston: Routledge & Kegan Paul.

INDEXES AND ABSTRACTING SERVICES

Child Development Abstracts and Bibliography. (1927 to the present). Chicago: Society for Research in Child Development.

Criminal Justice Abstracts. (1977 to the present). Monsey, NY: Willow Tree Press.

Current Index to Journals in Education. (1969 to the present). Phoenix, AZ: Oryx Press.

Current Law Index. (1980 to the present). Menlo Park, CA: Information Access.

Index to Legal Periodicals. (1926 to the present). Bronx, NY: H. W. Wilson.

Psychological Abstracts. (1927 to the present). Washington, DC: American Psychological Association.

PAIS International in Print (previously *Public Affairs Information Service Bulletin*). (1915 to the present). New York: Public Affairs Information Service.

Resources in Education. (1966 to the present). Washington, DC: U.S. Government Printing Office.

Sage Family Studies Abstracts. (1979 to the present). Beverly Hills, CA: Sage Publications.

Sage Public Administration Abstracts: An International Information Service. (1974 to the present). Beverly Hills, CA: Sage Publications.

Social Planning/Policy & Development Abstracts. (1979 to the present). San Diego, CA: Sociological Abstracts.

Social Sciences Citation Index. (1969 to the present). Philadelphia: Institute for Scientific Information.

Social Work Research & Abstracts. (1965 to the present). Washington, DC: National Association of Social Workers.

Sociological Abstracts. (1952 to the present). San Diego: Author.

Women Studies Abstracts. (1972 to the present). Rush, NY: Author.

BOOKS

Library of Congress subject headings. (15th ed.). (1992). Washington, DC: Library of Congress.

Sears list of subject headings. (14th ed.). (1991). Bronx, NY: H. W. Wilson.

COMPUTERIZED DATABASES

Alcohol Use and Abuse. (1968 to the present). Contains information on treatment evaluation, chemical dependence, family therapy, and alcoholism in various populations. Minneapolis: University of Minnesota, College of Pharmacy, Drug Information Services.

American Statistics Index. (1973 to the present). Provides a comprehensive listing of the statistical publications from most agencies of the U.S. government. Washington, DC: Congressional Information Service.

CENDATA. From the U.S. Bureau of the Census. Palo Alto, CA: DIALOG Information Services.

Child Abuse and Neglect. (1965 to the present). Includes a variety of literature in various formats on child abuse and neglect. Washington, DC: Clearinghouse on Child Abuse and Neglect Information.

Congressional Records Abstracts. (1981 to the present). Provides comprehensive abstracts for each issue of the *Congressional Record.* Bethesda, MD: National Standards Association.

ERIC. (1966 to the present). Covers the literature on education. Includes journal articles and technical and research reports. Washington, DC: National Institute of Education and Educational Research and Information Center.

Family Resources. (1970 to the present). Covers the interdisciplinary literature related to the family. Minneapolis: Council on Family Relations.

Health Planning and Administration. (1975 to the present). Covers the nonclinical literature pertaining to health care planning, organization, financing, management, and human resources. Bethesda, MD: National Library of Medicine.

Legal Resource Index. (1980 to the present). Indexes law books, journals, and newspaper articles on legal subjects. Menlo Park, CA: Information Access.

Lexis. (1920s to the present). Presents the full text of legal cases. Dayton, OH: Mead Data Central.

MEDLINE. (1966 to the present). Provides comprehensive coverage of the medical literature. Bethesda, MD: National Library of Medicine.

Mental Health Abstracts. (1969 to the present). Covers the international mental health literature. Bethesda, MD: National Institute of Mental Health.

Monthly Catalog of U.S. Government Publications. (1976 to the present). Includes all documents published by or under the direction of the U.S. Government Printing Office. Washington, DC: U.S. Government Printing Office.

National Criminal Justice Reference Service. (1972 to the present). Covers all aspects of law enforcement and criminal justice. Washington, DC: National Institute of Justice, National Criminal Justice Reference Service.

National Technical Information Service. (1964 to the present). Indexes all U.S. government–sponsored research reports and studies on all subjects, including the behavioral and social sciences. Washington, DC: National Technical Information Service.

PAIS International. (1972 to the present). Covers the social and public policy literature, including public administration, social welfare, and law. New York: Public Affairs Information Service.

Social Planning/Policy & Development Abstracts. (1979 to the present). Indexes and abstracts the applied social science literature, including policy studies, welfare administration, evaluation research, social work, health administration, and community organization. San Diego: Sociological Abstracts.

Social SciSearch. (1972 to the present). Indexes the most significant social science journals, as well as many books. Includes bibliographies from indexed journal articles. Philadelphia: Institute for Scientific Information.

Social Work Abstracts. (1977 to the present). Covers the social work and social welfare journals. Washington, DC: National Association of Social Workers.

Sociological Abstracts. (1963 to the present). Provides international coverage of the sociological literature. San Diego: Sociological Abstracts.

Westlaw. (1920s to the present). Contains the full text of most law cases. St. Paul, MN: West.

COMPACT DISKS

Dissertation Abstracts OnDisc. (1861 to the present). Ann Arbor, MI: University Microfilms International.

ERIC. (1976 to the present). Dublin, OH: OCLC.

ERIC on SilverPlatter. (1966 to the present). Boston: SilverPlatter Information.

DIALOG OnDisc: ERIC. (1966 to the present). Palo Alto, CA: DIALOG Information Services.

Government Documents Catalog Service. (1976 to the present). Pomona, CA: Autographics.

Government Publications Index on InfoTrac. (1976 to the present). Menlo Park, CA: Information Access.

GPO on SilverPlatter. (1976 to the present). Boston: SilverPlatter Information.

Index to Legal Periodicals. (August 1981 to the present). Bronx, NY: H. W. Wilson.

LegalTrac. (1980 to the present). Menlo Park, CA: Information Access.

MEDLINE. (1966 to the present). New York: CD Plus.

MEDLINE Knowledge Finder. (1983 to the present). Andover, MA: Aries Systems Corp.

MEDLINE on SilverPlatter. (1966 to the present). Boston: SilverPlatter Information.

DIALOG OnDisc: MEDLINE(r). (1984 to the present). Palo Alto, CA: DIALOG Information Services.

PAIS on CD-ROM. (1972 to the present). New York: Public Affairs Information Service.

PsycLIT. (1974 to the present). Boston: SilverPlatter Information.

Social Sciences Citation Index Compact Disc Edition. (1981 to the present). Philadelphia: Institute for Scientific Information.

Social Sciences Index. (February 1983 to the present). Bronx, NY: H. W. Wilson.

Social Work Abstracts Plus. (1977 to the present). Boston: SilverPlatter Information.

Sociofile. (1974 to the present). Boston: SilverPlatter Information.

Statistical Masterfile: American Statistics Index (1973 to the present), *Statistical Reference Index* (1980 to the present), *Index to International Statistics*

(1983 to the present). Washington, DC: Congressional Information Service.

PUBLIC DOCUMENTS

Budget of the U.S. government. (annual). Washington, DC: U.S. Government Printing Office.

Catalog of federal domestic assistance. (annual). Washington, DC: U.S. Government Printing Office.

CIS index to publications of the United States Congress. (monthly). Washington, DC: Congressional Information Service.

CIS legislative history service. (annual). Washington, DC: Congressional Information Service.

Code of federal regulations. (reissued as regulations are updated). Washington, DC: U.S. Government Printing Office.

Congressional index. (twice weekly). Chicago: Commerce Clearing House.

Congressional Quarterly almanac. (annual). Washington, DC: Congressional Quarterly.

Congressional Quarterly weekly report. (weekly). Washington, DC: Congressional Quarterly.

Congressional record. (daily; permanent edition issued after each session). Washington, DC: U.S. Government Printing Office.

Congressional records abstracts (database). Bethesda, MD: National Standards Association.

Congressional staff directory. (annual). Mount Vernon, VA: Congressional Staff Directory.

Congressional yellow book. (annual). Washington, DC: Washington Monitor.

Encyclopedia of governmental advisory organizations. (biannual). Detroit: Gale Research.

Federal executive directory. (annual). Washington, DC: Carrol.

Federal register. (daily). Washington, DC: U.S. Government Printing Office.

Federal register index. (monthly). Washington, DC: U.S. Government Printing Office.

Federal staff directory. (annual). Mount Vernon, VA: Congressional Staff Directory.

Federal yellow book. (annual). Washington, DC: Washington Monitor.

Government reports announcements and index. (biweekly). Springfield, VA: National Technical Information Service.

Index to current urban documents. (quarterly). Westport, CT: Greenwood Press.

Monthly Catalog of U.S. Government Publications. (monthly). Washington, DC: U.S. Government Printing Office.

Official congressional directory. (annual). Washington, DC: U.S. Government Printing Office.

United States code. (issued every six years, with an annual supplement). Washington, DC: U.S. Government Printing Office.

United States code, congressional and administrative news. (annual, with supplements). Washington, DC: U.S. Government Printing Office.

United States government manual. (annual). Washington, DC: U.S. Government Printing Office.

United States statutes at large. (irregular). Washington, DC: U.S. Government Printing Office.

Washington information directory. (annual). Washington, DC: Congressional Quarterly.

STATISTICS

American statistics index. (monthly with annual cumulations). Washington, DC: Congressional Information Service.

Index to international statistics. (monthly with annual cumulations). Washington, DC: Congressional Information Service.

Statistical reference index. (monthly with annual cumulations). Washington, DC: Congressional Information Service.

U.S. Bureau of the Census. CENDATA (database). Palo Alto, CA: DIALOG Information Services.

U.S. Bureau of the Census. (1988). *County and city data book.* Washington, DC: U.S. Government Printing Office.

U.S. Bureau of the Census. (1975). *Historical statistics of the United States, colonial times to 1970.* Washington, DC: U.S. Government Printing Office.

U.S. Bureau of the Census. (1991). *State and metropolitan area data book.* Washington, DC: U.S. Government Printing Office.

U.S. Bureau of the Census. (annual). *Statistical abstract of the United States: National database and guide to sources.* Washington, DC: U.S. Government Printing Office.

LAW

ABA Journal. (monthly). Chicago: American Bar Association.

American jurisprudence (2nd ed.). (1962). Rochester, NY: Lawyer's Cooperative Publishing.

Atlantic Reporter. (weekly with annual cumulations). St. Paul, MN: West.

Black, H. C. (1990). *Black's law dictionary* (6th ed.). St. Paul, MN: West.

California Reporter. (weekly with annual cumulations). St. Paul, MN: West.

Corpus juris secundum. (1936). Brooklyn, NY: American Law Book.

Criminal Law Reporter. (weekly). Washington, DC: Bureau of National Affairs.

Current Law Index. (monthly with annual cumulations). Menlo Park, CA: Information Access.

Decennial Digests. (every 10 years). St. Paul, MN: West.

Federal Cases. (1894–1897). St. Paul, MN: West.

Federal Reporter. (1880–1925). St. Paul, MN: West.

Federal Reporter, 2d. (1925 to the present). St. Paul, MN: West.

Federal Supplement. (1932 to the present). St. Paul, MN: West.

Harvard Law Review. (8 times a year). Cambridge, MA: Harvard Law Review Association.

Index to Legal Periodicals. (1926 to the present). Bronx, NY: H. W. Wilson.

LegalTrac. (every 6 months). Menlo Park, CA: Information Access.

New York Reporter. (weekly with annual cumulations). St. Paul, MN: West.

North Eastern Reporter. (weekly with annual cumulations). St. Paul, MN: West.

North Western Reporter. (weekly with annual cumulations). St. Paul, MN: West.

Pacific Reporter. (weekly with annual cumulations). St. Paul, MN: West.

Shepard's Citations. (semiannual with annual cumulations). Colorado
    Springs, CO: Author.

South Eastern Reporter. (weekly with annual cumulations). St. Paul, MN:
    West.

South Western Reporter. (weekly with annual cumulations). St. Paul, MN:
    West.

Southern Reporter. (weekly with annual cumulations). St. Paul, MN: West.

Supreme Court Reporter. (weekly with annual cumulations). St. Paul, MN:
    West.

United States Code Annotated. (annual). St. Paul, MN: West.

United States Code Service. (annual). Rochester, NY: Lawyer's Cooperative
    Publishing.

United States Reports. Washington, DC: U.S. Government Printing Office.

United States Supreme Court Reports. (biweekly with annual cumulations).
    Rochester, NY: Lawyer's Cooperative Publishing.

Westlaw. St. Paul, MN: West.

Women's Rights Law Reporter. (weekly). Newark, NJ: Rutgers University
    Law School.

4 the quantitative research report

Ann A. Abbott

The underlying motivation for writing research articles for publication should be the desire to share the findings of empirical investigations and the outcomes of program evaluations that could have an important impact on the development of theory or the delivery of human services (Gottlieb & Berger, 1984; Meyer, 1983). Frequently, the desire to share findings via publication is stifled by "social workers' [human services workers'] well-documented aversion to research, as producers or as consumers, and a companion reluctance to put ideas in print" (Gordon, 1984, as cited in Williams & Hopps, 1987, p. 373). It is hoped that this chapter will minimize that aversion by providing helpful guidelines; summarizing the process; and, above all, encouraging would-be and already published writers to accept the challenge and responsibility of sharing research findings through the professional literature. In referring to the preparation of research publications, Becker (1986) noted that "no one learns to write all at once"; rather, "learning . . . goes on for a professional lifetime" (p. 91). In the same vein, Berger (1990), a strong supporter of mentoring as a vehicle for writing and publication, reminds us of the saying of a Chinese sage that "a journey of 1,000 miles begins with a single footstep" (p. 3). The time to begin is now. I hope the following discussion facilitates your journey.

research versus statistics

Many potential writers equate research and statistics. It is important to clarify that *statistics* are tools used for analyzing data in the

63

process of conducting *research*. To undertake the process, the researcher must understand both research design *and* basic statistics, knowledge of which is defined as foundation content by the Council on Social Work Education, the accrediting body for social work educational programs. Given that priority for accreditation, this chapter first provides general guidelines for developing and preparing research manuscripts and then presents a review of the most frequently used basic research methods and elementary statistics. A solid grasp of the guidelines should be transferable to the reporting of results based on less frequently used procedures for analyzing data.

The bulk of social work research is applied, rather than basic, research. Under most circumstances, the researcher reports observations about data that have been collected systematically and objectively under conditions reflecting a wide range of manipulation and control. In some cases, greater control is built into the research design; in other cases, greater control is introduced via the statistical method. Many times the relevance of the findings is discovered only after the data have been collected. Under those circumstances, the researcher's control over the design may have been minimal. Frequently, the very nature of the human services precludes the rigid control of subjects and the selective distribution of services (interventions). It is under such conditions that the researcher is forced to operate.

format of a research manuscript

Although some journals indicate specific formats for research manuscripts, their suggestions are more likely to designate preferred styles for references, margins, and line spacing. The majority of human services journals adhere to the guidelines of the *Publication Manual of the American Psychological Association* (American Psychological Association [APA], 1983). (See Mendelsohn, 1992, and Markle & Rinn, 1977, for specific requirements for most journals. In addition, these sources summarize the editorial aim or focus of each journal.) In most cases, the following format for research reports is standard (Arkava & Lane, 1983; Dorn, 1985; Huck, Cormier, & Bounds, 1974; Williams & Hopps, 1988):

▶ abstract
▶ introduction
▶ method

- ▶ results/findings
- ▶ discussion and implications.

ABSTRACT

The abstract is a summary of the article. Usually around 150 to 200 words, it provides information about the purpose of the study; the methodology used, including a description of the subjects; the results; and conclusions.

INTRODUCTION

The introduction should include a review of the literature, a statement about the purpose of the study (the research question to be answered), a brief statement about how the study was conducted, and what the researcher hoped to uncover. Chapter 3 of this book, "The Library Literature Search," provides comprehensive information about how to conduct a review of the literature. In writing the introduction, you should select articles from the literature review that are directly related to the study being described. Review only those studies that have directly influenced the research being presented, not every article you read. The review of the literature places the study in its historical–theoretical context. The statement of purpose illustrates how the identified information has influenced your thinking in developing and then operationalizing the current study. This section should culminate in a delineation of the research questions (propositions or hypotheses) to be tested or examined.

METHOD

The method section should be comprehensive but reported succinctly and simply. It should describe the type of study; the general design, including the format of intervention; the type of sample and the subjects; and the instruments and the statistical methods that were used—all of which are discussed in the review of research methods and statistical procedures in the next section of this chapter, which also includes examples of the presentation of various methods.

  The method section should spell out in detail the manner in which the study attempted to examine the research question or questions that were raised in the introduction. It should present the study design in sufficient detail to enable another researcher to carry out a comparable study. With regard to statistics, it is not necessary to cite references for statistical tools that are in common usage (APA, 1983).

Subjects and Sample

With regard to the subjects, the reader will want to know the general sampling plan, the population from which the subjects were drawn, how well the sample represents the population, the size and type of sample, problems that arose in drawing the sample, the overall response rate, and specific demographic details. In some cases, it is important to highlight the differences between respondents (participants) and nonrespondents (dropouts). If the study was conducted in connection with a human services agency, information about the study site should be provided.

It is important to describe the sample in detail because various statistical procedures require specific types of samples and the generalizability of the findings to the larger population rests on the nature of the sample. For example, because of the applied nature of social work research, inferences are frequently made about the generalizability of data generated from nonrandom samples—a practice the reader should be warned about.

Variables

The description of the study design should include a detailed accounting of one or more *independent variables* (or interventions) and one or more *dependent variables* (or outcome measures). It should also identify the intervening variables and a plan for controlling for their impact and present a brief description of the instruments and procedures that were used. Consideration should be given to the level of measurement (nominal, ordinal, interval, ratio) because it will have a bearing on the statistical procedures that were used to analyze changes in the dependent variables.

The independent variables, or those that were manipulated, should be defined in sufficient detail for replication. It is important to note the degree of actual control that was used and to indicate how outcomes were measured and the degree of precision of measurement. You should mention reliability (the degree that the instrument consistently detects changes or differences in what is being measured) and validity (the extent to which the instrument measures what it claims to measure). Usually, researchers indicate why they chose particular independent variables and present the rationale behind the identified dependent variables and the means for measuring them.

RESULTS—FINDINGS

Use this section to present findings based on the method designated in the previous section, including findings derived from the statistical tools used to analyze the data generated by the study. Again, bear in mind the audience for whom you are writing. Although brevity is important, the reader must be given a complete picture of the findings that emerged. For example, when the primary statistics are inferential, it is usual to report the descriptive statistics (means, standard deviations) used in the inferential analyses (APA, 1983).

Although simplicity may not seem to do justice to sophisticated research skills, it will do much to advance the purpose of the manuscript: to present the findings in a concise, understandable fashion. Keep this purpose in mind when deciding whether to present findings in graphic or textual format. If tables or figures are used, they should present a comprehensive picture that is easier to convey in that format than in the text. There is no need to present detailed findings in both formats simultaneously. Some general statement about the most important findings contained in the table should be made in the text, but all the details need not be repeated. Chapter 6, "Graphics," provides specific suggestions about the development of tables, graphs, and other figures.

DISCUSSION AND IMPLICATIONS

In addition to summarizing and tying together the entire manuscript (research project), the discussion section discloses the implications for practice and suggests modifications of theory based on the findings, together with modifications of the design for the further examination of the research question. The discussion should flow from the original intent of the study in light of the projected and identified findings. Some speculation is allowed, but it should be based only on the nature of the population. For example, if the sample comprised a group of women, speculation can be made about other women, but not about men. One way to address the issue of men would be to suggest that men as a group be examined in a future study.

review of research methods and statistical procedures

Overall, the design of research studies is based on a scientific method involving various degrees of systematic control over the process (Arkava & Lane, 1983; Grinnell & Williams, 1990; Miller, 1991). Although many statistical methods can be used with a broad range of research designs, experimental control or statistical control determines the strength of the research findings. The very nature of social work lends itself more readily to applied, rather than basic, research; however, the researcher, when given options, should strive for a greater approximation of a true experimental design. In a carefully controlled experiment, greater credibility can be assigned to the causal relationship between the independent variable (intervention) and the dependent variable. Also of concern is the utilization of random sampling, which expands the possibility of generalizing the findings to other populations or settings. The former deals with the manipulation and control of variables (internal validity); the latter is more directly related to sampling issues (external validity). Both are concerned with the actual experimental design of the study and ultimately with the soundness of the findings (Huck et al., 1974).

TYPES OF EXPERIMENTAL DESIGN

To facilitate discussion of the selection of statistical methods, this section describes the major types of experimental design. For the purposes of illustration, it is preferable to break down design into categories; however note that the categories actually reflect a continuum from true experimental design to preexperimental design. The continuum reflects the degrees of experimental control, thus affecting internal and external validity.

True experimental design is considered by most to be more powerful because of the use of randomization, control, and comparison measures (pretests, posttests). The three primary variations in design include pretest–posttest, posttest only, and the Solomon four-group design (Arkava & Lane, 1983; Huck et al., 1974). Variations include expansion of these primary designs to include multiple variables, such as those involved in the Solomon six-group design and various factorial designs (Huck et al., 1974).

Quasi-experimental designs do not satisfy all the requirements or conditions of true experimental design. Subjects are not assigned randomly, and the researcher has less control over independent variables and the use of comparison groups. The major variations include nonequivalent control groups, separate sample pretest–posttest designs, time-series designs, and ex post facto designs (Arkava & Lane, 1983; Campbell & Stanley, 1963; Cook & Campbell, 1979; Huck et al., 1974; Spector, 1981).

At the opposite end of the continuum are what are often referred to as *preexperimental designs*. These designs, which are frequently used because of the nature of social work research, include one-shot case studies, one-group pretest–posttest studies, and static-group comparison studies (Huck et al., 1974). Because of limited control in these studies, the researcher cannot always determine the relationship between the independent and dependent variables with much certainty; however, in many cases, statistical control can make up for a variety of defects in the design if experimental control is impractical. Some additional concerns (known as threats to internal validity) surrounding the use of pseudo- or preexperimental designs include the history (events other than the independent variable that have an impact on the dependent variable; thus, a project designed to study the impact of a new welfare delivery system on clients' behavior may be seriously influenced by recent news coverage about the withdrawal of benefits to clients who do not comply with regulations); the reactivity of the instrument (the instrument itself may affect the level of response); and the unreliability or invalidity of the instruments. Other concerns involve the change of the instrument over time, the differential loss of subjects (attrition may not be random, but may reflect a particular bias), bias in assigning subjects to conditions, Hawthorne effects (modification or change in the behavior of subjects because of their awareness of their role under the "microscope"), and nonrepresentative samples (which definitely affect the generalizability of findings) (Spector, 1981).

Up to this point, I have addressed primarily between-group, intersubject comparison designs involving a single independent variable and a single dependent variable. Most studies in the real world of social work involve several independent variables and their effects on the dependent variable. This being the case, it is important to draw special attention to *factorial designs*, which involve more than one independent variable and more than one level of measurement (Spector, 1981) and that focus on the effects of interactions among independent variables.

A word should be said about *single-subject* or *single-system designs*, which are realistic alternatives to using the more traditional between-group research designs (Arkava & Lane, 1983; see Bloom & Fischer, 1982, for a comparison of single-system and experimental-control designs). In single-subject or single-system design, each subject or a single subject serves as his or her own control. In other words, the researcher uses intrasubject comparisons, consisting of before-and-after measures or an expansion similar to that of time-series design. This format is particularly useful in social work, given the limited resources devoted to research in most practice settings.

HYPOTHESIS TESTING

This review of *hypothesis testing* is included only as an aid to the reader in understanding the research process. The usual protocol suggests that it is insulting to the consumer of research to include such elementary content about the acceptance or rejection of the null hypothesis in an actual manuscript (APA, 1983, p. 27).

Frequently, the research process entails comparing two or more groups to determine their comparability. In most cases, the researcher believes that the group or groups receiving the prescribed intervention (tentative solution) will be different because of the intervention. To test this difference, the researcher examines the null hypothesis, which assumes that there is no difference between or among the groups being examined. Statistical analyses provide the researcher with evidence to accept or reject the null hypothesis. If the evidence indicates that the null hypothesis should be rejected, the research supports the idea that the groups being compared are different (or that the tentative solution was effective); if the evidence indicates that the null hypothesis should be accepted, the research does not support the idea that the tentative solution was effective or that differences exist.

Once the researcher states the solution in hypothesis form, the next step is to select a level of significance, the two most common ones being .05 and .01, although .001 is frequently selected and .1 is occasionally chosen. The smaller the level of significance selected, the smaller the probability of making a Type I (false rejection) error or rejecting the null hypothesis when it is actually true. A Type II (false acceptance) error involves accepting the null hypothesis when it is false (accepting the idea that there is no difference among groups when differences actually exist). The researcher can seldom determine the presence of a Type I or Type II error. However, he or she can set levels of confidence (levels of significance) that minimize the likelihood of such errors; generally, the higher the level, the greater the possibility of a Type I error, whereas the lower the level, the greater the possibility of a Type II error (Henkel, 1976; Kachigan, 1986). Unlike a Type I error, there is no simple relationship between the level of significance and a Type II error (Huck et al., 1974); however, on the whole, the lower the confidence level, the greater the possibility of a Type II error.

A number of other factors should be taken into consideration when addressing the probability of a Type II error. For example, the probability of a Type II error decreases when the size of the sample increases and when the difference between the hypothesized and true value of a parameter increases. The probability of a Type II error increases for populations with larger standard deviations. In general, when selecting levels of significance, the researcher should ask which is of greater consequence: rejecting the null hypothesis when it is true (a Type I error) or accepting the null hypothesis when it is false (a Type II error).

SUBJECTS

"Subjects" can be broadly defined. In the case of program evaluation, the subject may be the agency being evaluated, a group of service providers, or a group or sample of clients. In an experimental study, the subjects may include a sample or subgroup of the larger population or all the available subjects.

The most desirable type of sample is the *random sample,* or one in which all members of the larger population have an equal chance of being included. Occasionally, the researcher may find it preferable to select a *stratified sample,* or one that guarantees a certain level or percentage of representation by specific constituencies, on the basis of such traits as gender, ethnicity, income, or intelligence quotient. Stratified samples may include the random selection among categories or the convenience or purposive selection of available subjects.

A frequent question concerns the size of the sample. A general rule of thumb is to use as large a sample as possible. The larger the sample, the smaller the error or deviation from the population; the smaller the sample, the larger the error or deviation from the population. Larger samples are better because they give the principle of randomness a greater opportunity to work (Arkava & Lane, 1983; Kerlinger, 1964; Siegel, 1956). Generally, the power of a statistical test increases with the size of the sample (Siegel, 1956).

Examples of Random and Stratified Samples

Jayaratne, Davis-Sacks, and Chess's (1991) study is an example of one that used a random sample. In their report of the study, the researchers included the type of sample (random), the size of the sample, the response rate, information about how data were collected, and the limitations of the sample:

> The data reported here are based on two separate samples drawn from the *NASW Membership Directory* in 1985. The first is a simple random sample of 1,159 members drawn from the *NASW Membership Directory.* The second is a random sample of 300 members who designated themselves in the *NASW Membership Directory* as being in full-time private practice. All respondents were mailed a 10-page questionnaire, a cover letter explaining the nature of the study, a stamped return envelope, and a response confirmation postcard. The respondents were instructed to mail the postcard separately from the questionnaire to maintain confidentiality. All respondents who did not mail back the

response confirmation postcard were mailed a second package containing all of the items noted above.

The response rate from the first sample was 66.6 percent ($n = 772$), and the response rate from the private practice sample was 54.7 percent ($n = 164$). The analyses here are restricted to workers who were working full-time in an agency setting or full-time in private practice and who had an active caseload. Agency administrators who did not carry cases and agency practitioners who had part-time private practices had been excluded from the analyses. These exclusionary criteria result in a more homogeneous sample of job characteristics that may be more similar than dissimilar. The resulting analytic sample consisted of 160 private practitioners and 486 agency practitioners. The differential response rates from the two samples may indicate different response biases; therefore, the findings should be interpreted with some caution. It is difficult to explain why those in private practice had a lower response rate. (p. 225)

Another study (Kingson et al., 1988) used a stratified sample in research on the health, employment, and welfare histories of older recipients of General Assistance. In addition to describing their sampling procedures, the authors included details about the size of the sample and response rates, together with the limitations of the sample:

To develop a profile of the older general assistance client, 155 Maryland GPA clients aged 50 to 64 were interviewed in 1983. Additionally, data on welfare and medical assistance histories were drawn from client records. A stratified sampling procedure was used to identify a sample representative of older GPA recipients statewide. Accordingly, clients were selected at random from a large city (Baltimore), an urban county (Montgomery, outside of Washington, D.C.), and a rural county (Harford), the three types of jurisdictions in Maryland. The goal was to interview a sample of 150 GPA recipients representative of the distribution of older GPA recipients in each type of locale statewide (Baltimore City, 75 percent; Montgomery County, 17 percent; and Harford County, 8 percent). This strategy was used as an alternative to the more costly approach of sampling older GPA recipients statewide. . . .

Those sampled and subsequently interviewed represent 35 percent of the total number of eligible subjects. It is clear that they represent the group most willing to be part of the survey. To the extent that this group differs from other older GPA clients in Maryland, then the results are biased. Still, those interviewed enable an initial description of this difficult-to-study population. The major biases introduced as a result of a low response rate are that: the transient, hard-to-reach clients are underrepresented, although special efforts were made to locate them; women are overrepresented; and longer-term clients are overrepresented. This is consistent with the greater difficulty encountered in arranging interviews with male participants and in locating people who moved frequently. Unfortunately, survey research does not always yield ideal samples, particularly of hard-to-reach populations. In considering the findings and implications of this exploratory study, it is important to recognize both the limitations of these data and the new information provided about an obscure group. (p. 106)

In many cases, details about the demographic characteristics of samples are presented using frequency distributions.

VARIABLES

The two primary types of variables described in most research studies are independent and dependent variables. *Independent variables* are those that are thought to influence or cause a certain response, behavior, or change in the dependent variable. *Dependent variables* are those that are thought to be influenced by the action of the independent variables. In some studies, other extraneous or intervening variables are also identified (Rosenberg, 1968). They include those variables that are not easily recognized, measured, or manipulated but that may affect the impact of the independent variables on the dependent ones. The recognition of these variables is important in understanding the true relationship between the independent and dependent variables.

Examples of Descriptions of Variables

Long and Miller (1991) presented a detailed description of the dependent and independent variables they used in their study on suicidal tendency and multiple sclerosis. They used the specific subheadings "dependent variable" and "independent variables" and further subdivided the latter category into three subcategories—support systems, physiological variables, and psychological variables, as follows:

Dependent Variable
Certain methodological problems occur when examining suicide. For example, a conceptual distinction among attempted suicide, lethal suicidal behavior, and suicidal ideation is well-documented in the suicide literature. Additionally, questions arise as to whether people with multiple sclerosis demonstrate greater tendencies toward suicide than other people. [Some authors] . . . suggested that such comparisons are difficult to make. Lethal or attempted suicide may be underreported because of the misclassification of suicide-related behaviors.

This study measures serious thought (suicidal ideation) or contemplation of suicide. One might question why suicidal tendency was used, rather than attempted or lethal suicide. If practitioners hope to identify and predict suicidal behavior for prevention through intervention and related services, measures of suicidal tendency appear more appropriate than any ex post facto measure. In this study, suicidal tendency is measured by a Likert-type scale. . . .

Independent Variables
Support Systems. . . . Several variables measuring the presence of social support systems for respondents were examined. Family support was measured by a five-item scale . . . examining the amount of perceived support from a respondent's spouse, children, and family.

Support from friends was measured by a three-item scale . . . examining the availability of friends or others for encouragement. Support from clergy and the Multiple Sclerosis Society [was] measured by single items.

Physiological Variables. . . . In this study, age, progression of disease, and self-perceived functional limitations were examined in relationship to suicidal tendency.

Psychological Variables. Several psychological factors were examined as predictors of suicidal tendency. Traditionally hopelessness (despair) has been identified as a predictor of suicidal risk. . . . In this study, fear of premature death . . . , fear of the dead . . . , fear of the dying process . . . , and fear of the unknown . . . were examined in relation to suicidal tendency.

. . . In this study, self-perceived religiosity, belief in a supreme being, and religious orthodoxy were examined in relationship to suicidal tendency. (pp. 105–106)

The previously mentioned study by Jayaratne et al. (1991) presented the independent and dependent variables in a different fashion. The two samples represented the independent variable (private practice versus agency setting). The dependent variables were categorized as follows under the general heading Study Variables: Measures of Psychological Strain, Measure of Physical Health, Measures of Performance, and Measure of Life Satisfaction:

Study Variables

This study included several measures of psychosocial strain, physical health, work performance, and life satisfaction. . . . All measures are self-reported and perceptual. . . .

Measures of Psychological Strain

Five measures of psychological strain were included in this study . . . anxiety, depression, . . . irritability, . . . depersonalization and emotional exhaustion. . . .

Measure of Physical Health

A . . . 12-item index of somatic complaints was used (for example, poor appetite, having trouble getting to sleep). Responses indicate frequency of occurrence of each complaint. Higher scores indicate fewer instances of somatic complaints. . . .

Measures of Performance

Two measures of perceived job performance were used. On each, higher scores indicate higher perceived performance. Personal accomplishment, an eight-item index, measures an individual's sense of achievement with clients. . . .

Performance success, a single item . . . measures perceived success on a rating scale of one to seven.

Measure of Life Satisfaction

. . . A single item was used as a global measure of life satisfaction. . . . Higher scores indicate greater satisfaction with life. (p. 225)

SELECTION OF STATISTICAL METHODS

The type of research design, including the nature of the sample and the degree of control, should strongly influence the type of statistical method or methods selected for analyzing the data. The following discussion presents guidelines for selecting some commonly used statistics.

To answer the research question, data are collected and analyzed using various statistical procedures. Two general types or categories of statistics are used in analyzing data: *descriptive statistics*, or those that summarize pools of data, and *inferential statistics*, or those that allow the researcher to generalize from one situation or sample to the larger population.

DESCRIPTIVE STATISTICS

Descriptive statistics are useful in summarizing findings or characteristics about a group. The following methods are used to describe single variables. They are used most frequently as the primary statistical method in applied behavioral research, including designs classified as preexperimental, although they may be used in conjunction with more sophisticated methods (see the section on Inferential Statistics) to describe the nature of the sample. The primary classifications of descriptive statistics are measures of central tendency and measures of variability.

Measures of Central Tendency

Measures of central tendency (or best numerical descriptor) include the following:

▶ the *mean*, or arithmetic average, which is determined by adding all the scores and dividing by the total number of scores added
▶ the *median*, or the point in a distribution of scores, where one half fall below and the other half above
▶ the *mode*, or the number that occurs most frequently in the given series of numbers being examined.

Measures of Variability

Measures of variability (or the degree of dispersion among a set of numbers) include these:

▶ *range*, or the difference between the highest and lowest scores. It can be presented either as a single number representing the difference or as two numbers, the actual highest and lowest values.
▶ *variance*, which is based on the degree that each score deviates from the mean (the formula for calculation is given in every elementary text on statistics).
▶ *standard deviation*, or the square root of the variance.

Whereas the foregoing statistical methods are used to describe single variables, the following are used to describe the relationship between two or more variables. These methods can be classified as *measures of the strength or nature of the relationship* (or the degree that two variables covary). These measures include correlation and regression.

Correlation

Correlation indicates the degree of the relationship; however, it is important to remember that the degree of correlation should not be construed as reflecting a causal relationship. Many times a third variable may be contributing to the indicated correlation between two variables. Correlation coefficients reflect the degree of linear relationship between two variables. Actual correlations range in value from -1.0 to $+1.0$. The closer a correlation is to 1.0, the more accurately a researcher can predict the value of one variable from the known value of another (Jaeger, 1990). Several different types of correlations can be computed:

The *Pearson product-moment correlation* is a parametric statistical method used to describe the continuous linear relationship between two variables presented in continuous data form.

A *partial correlation* using the Pearson product-moment correlation is useful in determining the degree of relationship between two variables while controlling for the influence of a third variable.

Spearman's rho is a nonparametric method used to describe the relationship between two rank-order variables (it can be used with ordinal data). There is no partial correlation analog for Spearman's rho.

Correlation matrix can be used to present intercorrelations between many variables. As many correlations are presented as there are combinations of variables. Variations (such as point-biserial correlation, biserial correlation, eta correlation, phi coefficient, and tetrachoric correlation) are available on the basis of the nature of the data. Details of these variations are presented in a wide range of books on statistics, such as Bohrnstedt and Knoke (1988), Huck et al. (1974), and Jaeger (1990).

Regression and correlation are closely related in as much as both are concerned with the association–relationship among variables and with prediction. However, regression deals with the nature of the relationship and correlation deals with the strength of the relationship. Conceptually, regression precedes correlation analysis.

Stepwise regression is a popular form of regression that indicates the importance of predictor variables in descending order based on the amount of variance explained. The reader is reminded that it is the computer, not the researcher, that selects the variables in order of their importance.

It is impossible to compare the actual regression coefficients because they represent different predictor variables with different metrics. Therefore, the regression coefficients are converted to standardized beta weights, which have a common metric—the standard deviation unit. The predictor variable with the largest beta weight has the greatest predicting power in relation to the criterion or dependent variable. Conversely, the predictor variable with the smallest beta weight contributes the least to predicting the criterion.

Frequently, for purposes of cross-validation, the researcher randomly divides the sample into two groups. The first group is used to develop the predictor equation, and the second group is used to predict a criterion score for each subject in it. These generated scores are then correlated with the actual score to determine the accuracy of the prediction equation.

Causal models and *path analysis* are expansions of the regression model. These techniques are used to represent causal relationships among variables via graphic presentations and structural equations (see Bohrnstedt & Knoke, 1988, for the underlying assumptions for their usage). Borden (1991) is an example of the presentation of findings analyzed through path analysis.

The researcher is often confronted with nominal-level data. *Discriminant function analysis,* a regression variation, is a tool when nominal dependent variables are being analyzed (the main version of multiple regression requires continuous data). Many computer-assisted statistical packages provide for the inclusion of nominal independent variables in the form of dummy variable regression (which artificially converts the nominal level of measurement to more sophisticated levels of measurement). Although regression and correlation are descriptive methods, they can be accompanied by statistical tests that allow the researcher to make inferences. In this regard, they are discussed in more detail under the section on Inferential Statistics.

Frequency distributions are useful in describing the general characteristics of a group. Such distributions can be expanded via *bivariate cross-tabulations* to illustrate the relationship between two variables (Bohrnstedt & Knoke, 1988).

Examples Using Descriptive Statistics

The following examples illustrate the use of descriptive statistics. Frequently the examples include a combination of descriptive and inferential methods, which reflects the real world of research. The comments, however, will highlight the use of descriptive statistics.

Most studies use measures of central tendency and variability to describe preliminary findings, especially in relation to the subjects. Rosenthal, Groze, and Curiel (1990) used means and standard deviations in describing the average age of adoptive children and their parents in a study that compared minority and racially mixed adoptive families to their white counterparts. They used frequency distributions, together with percentages, to summarize additional characteristics about the families being studied. Martinez-Brawley and Blundall (1991) found the median and range useful in summarizing the demographic characteristics of the farm households in their study of beliefs and attitudes about the need for rural social services. Pawlak and Flynn's (1990) use of frequency tables and percentages in describing the political activities of executive directors of human services organizations highlights the importance of tables in consolidating findings in an easy-to-read format. Edelstein, Kropenske, and Howard (1990) used means and range in their study of the evaluation scores of trainees regarding the usefulness of specific didactic curricular topics, including format and relevance, as well as the style used by the instructor in presenting the material.

In addition to using means and standard deviations to describe social indicators (dependent variables), such as low birthweight, infant mortality rates, crime rates, arrest rates for drug violations, and other measures associated with poverty, Coulton, Pandey, and Chow (1990) used a correlation matrix to illustrate the strength of the relationship among the indicators they examined. They used an inferential statistic—multiple analysis of variance with repeated measures—to test the hypothesis that

> (1) the types of poverty areas (for example, traditional, new, emerging, and low) would differ on these indicators, with areas that have been poor for the longest time being most extreme; (2) these indicators would have changed during the 1980s; and (3) the amount of deterioration on the indicators during the 1980s would be greatest in emerging poverty areas because these areas are the ones that moved into concentrated poverty status during that period. (p. 12)

A study of stress and competence as predictors of the behavioral problems of children (Vosler & Proctor, 1990) is another good example of the use of a correlation matrix, in addition to the Pearson product-moment correlation and stepwise multiple regression.

INFERENTIAL STATISTICS

Inferential statistics include both *parametric* and *nonparametric* types. The two categories reflect different underlying assumptions about the populations from which the data were collected. Parametric statistics assume that the sample came from a population with a normal distribution of characteristics and with homogeneity of variance. It should be noted that these assumptions are frequently ignored. Studies such as that of Boneau (as reported in Hardyck & Petrinovich, 1969, p. 173) strongly suggest that these criteria are not as important as they were once thought to be.

Nonparametric statistics can be used with nominal data gathered from samples that do not meet the criteria of normal distribution and homogeneity of variance. Because of the greater strength or power offered by the various parametric statistics, most researchers prefer to use them unless the criteria for their usage absolutely cannot be met. Power, in this situation, means increased sensitivity to differences among groups of subjects being compared and the minimized possibility of making a Type II error. It is important to keep in mind that inferential statistics rule out only fluctuations in the sample and not other threats to the soundness of the findings.

Researchers use *inferential statistics* to generalize (infer from) the characteristics of a smaller group (the representative sample) to a larger group (population). This ability is based on the quality of the sample being examined. A random sample, or one in which all members of a population have an equal chance of being selected, is preferred. A nonrandom sample, whether it is a convenience or purposive sample, is at a greater risk of being nonrepresentative of the larger population that it purportedly represents. By selecting various levels of significance, you can minimize the possibility of erroneously determining that the sample is reflective of the population.

The following are typically used parametric inferential statistical methods. (Note the underlying assumption of parametric statistics: homogeneity of variance and the normal distribution of the population.)

t-test

Although it can also be used to test whether a correlation coefficient is significantly different from zero, the *t*-test is used primarily to examine the difference between the means of *two* samples to determine the comparability of the two populations from which the samples were drawn. The *t*-test uses the means of the two samples, their variances, and their respective sample sizes to determine a *t*-value that the researcher compares to a table of critical *t*-values. The critical *t*-value selected is determined by the degrees of freedom, which is equal to the number of subjects minus 2, and a chosen level of significance (usually .01 or .05 or occasionally .001). If the derived *t*-value is larger than the critical value, the researcher concludes that there is a significant difference between the means of the two groups. There are several variations of the *t*-test: the one just mentioned for independent samples and another, for nonindependent samples, which takes into account the contamination generated by multiple test taking, repeated exposure to conditions, or matched pairing.

The study by Evans, Burlew, and Oler (1988, Table 1) is an excellent illustration of the use of the *t*-test for independent samples (parents with children who have sickle-cell anemia and parents with comparable-aged children who do not have sickle-cell anemia). The researchers also compared differences between single-parent families and two-parent families within the sample of parents of children with sickle-cell anemia (Evans et al., 1988, Table 2).

One-Way Analysis of Variance

One-way analysis of variance, or ANOVA, is similar in intent to the *t*-test (to compare group means); however, it is designed to be used for *two or more* groups to compare means along one dimension—one and only one independent variable. Using ANOVA, the researcher attempts to determine how much of the total variation in the dependent variable is related to the independent variable and how much is left unexplained (Bohrnstedt & Knoke, 1988). ANOVA can be used with experimental data and with nonexperimental data; obviously, it is much more difficult to draw causal inferences from the nonexperimental data or those that were not generated from random samples that meet the criteria for statistical inference. ANOVA is used to test the null hypothesis that two or more groups come from the same, rather than different, populations. If the null hypothesis is not true, the next effort is to show how the means differ from one another. The method involves calculating a value and comparing it to a designated critical value. If the value generated is greater than the critical value, the null hypothesis is rejected.

Once a significant difference has been identified, it is important for the researcher to determine where the significant differences lie. Several analyses are designed specifically to locate the source of significant difference by analyzing all possible pairs of means. The five basic multiple-comparison procedures, ranging from liberal to conservative, include Fisher's LSD, Duncan's new multiple range test, Newman-Keuls, Tukey's HSD, and Scheffe's test (the usage of each is based on slightly different circumstances) (Huck et al., 1974).

The *two-way ANOVA* is designed to examine the impact of two independent variables (the impact of the first independent variable, the impact of the second independent variable, and the impact of the interaction between these two independent variables).

The *three-way ANOVA* allows the researcher to examine the impact of three independent variables (the main effects of the three variables and four interactions: AB, AC, BC, ABC [second-order interaction]).

These two variations—two-way and three-way ANOVAs—are frequently described by the number of levels involved in each independent variable; for example, the 2 × 4 design implies a two-way ANOVA, with the first variable having two levels and the second having four levels. The question is sometimes raised, Why not use two one-way ANOVAs, rather than one two-way ANOVA, or three one-way ANOVAs, rather than one three-way ANOVA? The answer is that the two-way and three-way ANOVAs are more sensitive to differences, especially in their power to detect interactions among variables.

Many studies involve ANOVAs with *repeated measures* over time. Special variations of ANOVA have been designed to accommodate the impact of taking repeated measures. A thorough discussion of the use of ANOVA with repeated measures is presented in Huck et al. (1974).

In a study of premenstrual syndrome, Coughlin (1990) presented a useful example of one-way ANOVA, together with Scheffe's test (one of the five basic multiple-comparison procedures mentioned earlier).

As was noted, Coulton et al.'s study (1990) illustrates the use of univariate and multivariate ANOVAs with repeated measures, the findings of which are presented in tabular form and discussed in the text. In research examining the affective and behavioral responses of gay and bisexual men to HIV antibody testing, Huggins, Elman, Baker, Forrester, and Lyter (1991) reported their findings using two repeat-measure ANOVAs in the text without presenting an accompanying table.

Analysis of Covariance

Analysis of covariance is a method of statistical control used to adjust for differences among two or more groups and to prevent the contamination of findings related to these differences. It is also able to minimize differences that are not related to the independent variables. Similar to ANOVA, analysis of covariance allows the researcher to address additional concerns: to control or correct for differences between two or more samples and to control for the influences of variables that are not directly examined in the study (Jaeger, 1990).

Covariation between two variables can arise from the confounding effects of other factors, such as intervening variables. In principle, a portion of the confounding effects should be minimized by random sampling and experimental control; however, such minimization is not always guaranteed. To determine the true amount of covariance between two variables, the researcher should remove the effects of other factors. This is the primary role of analysis of covariance.

A study of an alternative program to decrease school dropout rates (Franklin, McNeil, & Wright, 1990) is an example of a quasi-experimental design using analysis of covariance. The researchers controlled for the length of time in treatment (covariate) in their attempt to examine the impact of a number of independent variables (such as group therapy). As they put it, "Analysis of covariance was used to evaluate the impact of multimodal social work treatments on outcome measures. The covariate was the number of months in the treatment program that controlled for the differential effects of different lengths of exposure to the program" (p. 186).

Nonparametric Procedures

As was previously indicated, analogous nonparametric procedures exist for most of the parametric procedures. Table 4.1 presents a comparative list of these procedures.

One commonly used nonparametric procedure is *chi-square*, a statistical test for determining the significance of cross-tabulated variables (Bohrnstedt & Knoke, 1988). Nominal data are divided to reflect specified categories. Chi-square is used to determine

TABLE 4.1 Parametric and Analogous Nonparametric Procedures

Parametric Procedures	Nonparametric Procedures
Pearson product-moment correlation coefficient *r*	Spearman's rho
t-test correlated samples	Sign test Wilcoxon matched-pair, signed-rank tests
t-test independent samples	Median test Mann-Whitney *U* test
One-way ANOVA	Kruskal-Wallis one-way ANOVA of ranks Median test
One-way ANOVA with repeated measures	Friedman two-way ANOVA of ranks
(No analogous parametric test)	Chi-square single-sample *k* independent samples

NOTE: ANOVA = analysis of variance.
SOURCE: From *Reading Statistics and Research* (p. 199, Table 10.1) by S. W. Huck, W. H. Cormier, & W. G. Bounds, Jr., 1974, New York: Harper & Row. Copyright © 1974 by HarperCollins Publishers. Reprinted by permission.

whether the data presented deviate systematically from a predetermined pattern by comparing the observed frequency of occurrence to the expected frequency of occurrence. The expected frequencies are based on the null hypothesis of no relationship. If a significant relationship is detected, the null hypothesis is rejected.

Heger and Greif (1991) used chi-square to analyze the differences between mothers and fathers who participated in survey research on the abduction of children by their parents. The previously cited research by Jayaratne et al. (1991, Table 1) used a slightly different format for presenting findings based on the use of chi-square. A third variation can be found in a study of the complications in discharge planning for Medicare patients (Proctor & Morrow-Howell, 1990, Table 2).

Inferential Components of Multiple Correlation and Regression

As was noted earlier, correlation and regression are descriptive methods. As in the case of other parametric methods, they are accompanied by a set of statistical tests, the t or F (ANOVA), that allow the researcher to make inferences from existing data to other populations. These statistics are the same t and F that were discussed earlier; however, in the context of regression, they are statements of significance related to specific parametric estimates, such as regression estimators or correlation coefficients.

Arches's (1991) study of burnout and job satisfaction among social workers illustrates the use of multiple regression (hierarchical) in conjunction with t-tests. Rosenthal's (1991) study of social workers' interest in practice in developing countries is an example of the use of multiple correlation (and of F tests).

conclusion

Sharing research findings is both a challenge and a professional responsibility. The quality of the profession depends on the dissemination of new information. It is hoped that the material presented here will serve as an invitation to authors and as a map to ease their journey to publication. For some, that path may be easier; for others, it requires grim determination; for all, it means advancement of professional knowledge.

references

American Psychological Association. (1983). *Publication manual of the American Psychological Association* (3rd ed.). Washington, DC: Author.

Arches, J. (1991). Social structure, burnout, and job satisfaction. *Social Work, 36,* 202–206.

Arkava, M. L., & Lane, T. A. (1983). *Beginning social work research.* Boston: Allyn & Bacon.

Becker, H. S. (1986). *Writing for social scientists: How to start and finish your thesis, book, or article.* Chicago: University of Chicago Press.

Berger, R. M. (1990). *Four steps to getting your paper published.* Unpublished manuscript, Getting Published Program, California State University, Long Beach.

Bloom, M., & Fischer, J. (1982). *Evaluating practice: Guidelines for the accountable professional.* Englewood Cliffs, NJ: Prentice Hall.

Bohrnstedt, G. W., & Knoke, D. (1988). *Statistics for social data analysis* (2nd ed.). Itasca, IL: F. E. Peacock.

Borden, W. (1991). Stress, coping, and adaptation in spouses of older adults with chronic dementia. *Social Work Research & Abstracts, 27*(1), 14–21.

Campbell, D. T., & Stanley, J. C. (1963). *Experimental and quasi-experimental designs for research.* Chicago: Rand McNally.

Cook, T. D., & Campbell, D. T. (1979). *Quasi-experimentation design and analysis issues for field settings.* Chicago: Rand McNally.

Coughlin, P. E. (1990). Premenstrual syndrome: How marital satisfaction and role choice affect symptom severity. *Social Work, 35,* 351–355.

Coulton, C., Pandey, S., & Chow, J. (1990). Concentration of poverty and the changing ecology of low-income, urban neighborhoods: An analysis of the Cleveland area. *Social Work Research & Abstracts, 26*(4), 5–16.

Dorn, F. J. (1985). *Publishing for professional development.* Muncie, IN: Accelerated Development.

Edelstein, S., Kropenske, V., & Howard, J. (1990). Project T.E.A.M.S. *Social Work, 35,* 313–318.

Evans, R. C., Burlew, A. K., & Oler, C. H. (1988). Children with sickle-cell anemia: Parental relations, parent-child relations, and child behavior. *Social Work, 33,* 127–130.

Franklin, C., McNeil, J. S., & Wright, R. (1990). School social work works: Findings from an alternative school for dropouts. *Social Work in Education, 12,* 177–194.

Gordon, J. E. (1984). Creating research-based principles: A model. *Social Work Research & Abstracts, 20,* 3–6.

Gottlieb, N., & Berger, R. M. (1984). Publishing research articles [Points and Viewpoints]. *Social Work, 29,* 192.

Grinnell, Jr., R. M., & Williams, M. (1990). *Research in social work.* Itasca, IL: F. E. Peacock.

Hardyck, C. D., & Petrinovich, L. F. (1969). *Introduction to statistics for the behavioral sciences.* Philadelphia: W. B. Saunders.

Heger, R. L., & Greif, G. L. (1991). Abduction of children by their parents: A survey of the problem. *Social Work, 36,* 421–426.

Henkel, R. M. (1976). *Tests of significance.* Beverly Hills, CA: Sage Publications.

Huck, S. W., Cormier, W. H., & Bounds, Jr., W. G. (1974). *Reading statistics and research.* New York: Harper & Row.

Huggins, J., Elman, N., Baker, C., Forrester, R. G., & Lyter, D. (1991). Affective and behavioral responses of gay and bisexual men to HIV antibody testing. *Social Work, 36,* 61–66.

Jaeger, R. M. (1990). *Statistics: A spectator sport* (2nd ed.). Newbury Park, CA: Sage Publications.

Jayaratne, S., Davis-Sacks, M. L., & Chess, W. A. (1991). Private practice may be good for your health and well-being. *Social Work, 36*, 224–229.

Kachigan, S. K. (1986). *Statistical analysis.* New York: Radius Press.

Kerlinger, F. N. (1964). *Foundations of behavioral research.* New York: Holt, Rinehart, & Winston.

Kingson, E., Peterson, C. S., Magaziner, J., Lopez, E. D., Joyce, C., Kassner, E., & Sowers, S. (1988). Health, employment, and welfare histories of Maryland's older General Assistance recipients. *Social Work, 33*, 105–109.

Long, D. D., & Miller, B. J. (1991). Suicidal tendency and multiple sclerosis. *Health and Social Work, 16*, 104–109.

Markle, A., & Rinn, R. C. (1977). *Author's guide to journals in psychology, psychiatry, and social work.* New York: Haworth Press.

Martinez-Brawley, E., & Blundall, J. (1991). Whom shall we help? Farm families' beliefs and attitudes about need and services. *Social Work, 36*, 315–321.

Mendelsohn, H. N. (1992). *An author's guide to social work journals* (3rd ed.). Washington, DC: National Association of Social Workers.

Meyer, C. (1983). Responsibility in publishing [Editorial]. *Social Work, 28*, 3.

Miller, D. C. (1991). *Handbook of research design and social measurement* (5th ed.). Newbury Park, CA: Sage Publications.

Pawlak, E. J., & Flynn, J. (1990). Executive directors' political activities. *Social Work, 35*, 307–312.

Proctor, E. K., & Morrow-Howell, N. (1990). Complications in discharge planning with Medicare patients. *Health and Social Work, 15*, 45–54.

Rosenberg, M. (1968). *The logic of survey analysis.* New York: Basic Books.

Rosenthal, B. S. (1991). Social workers' interest in international practice in the developing world: A multivariate analysis. *Social Work, 36*, 248–252.

Rosenthal, J. A., Groze, V., & Curiel, H. (1990). Race, social class, and special needs adoption. *Social Work, 35*, 532–539.

Siegel, S. (1956). *Nonparametric statistics for the behavioral sciences.* New York: McGraw-Hill.

Spector, P. E. (1981). *Research designs.* Beverly Hills, CA: Sage Publications.

Vosler, N. R., & Proctor, E. K. (1990). Stress and competence predictors of child behavior problems. *Social Work Research & Abstracts, 26*(2), 3–9.

Williams, L. F., & Hopps, J. G. (1987). Publication as a practice goal: Enhancing opportunities for social workers. *Social Work, 32*, 373–376.

Williams, L. F., & Hopps, J. G. (1988). On the nature of professional communication: Publication for practitioners. *Social Work, 33*, 453–459.

5 *the qualitative research report*

Howard Goldstein

In social work, the conventional view of what a research report should be tends to conform to the requirements of a physical science model of investigation. Dissertations, research articles accepted for publication in professional journals, and other research documents commonly represent the properties of this model.

By these standards, the qualitative research report may easily be seen as "unconventional" because of its *naturalistic* character. Although it does not pretend to be a "scientific" document, it can provide, in its own right, a coherent and instructive account of the natural state of the social world that is investigated. Distinguished by its own rules of internal consistency and integrity, the qualitative or ethnographic report provides an *interpretation* of a slice of life as that life presents itself. The particular "slice" may be an episode in someone's life; the activities of certain groups, communities, or institutions; cultural patterns; or other unaffected social processes. In Geertz's (1983) terms, the qualitative research report reveals "the symbolic forms—words, images, institutions, behaviors—in terms of which, in each place, people actually represent themselves to themselves and to one another" (p. 58).

It is not the purpose of the qualitative report to prove or verify selected theories, hypotheses, or experiments. In its own form, such a report summarizes new knowledge, impressions, or theoretical assumptions that were generated by the researcher's entry into a complex, real-life world. Further depth and verification are added to the report by a chronicle of the research event itself, including

The author is grateful to Edward Graham for allowing him to refer to his doctoral dissertation—an example of thorough quantitative research.

the dilemmas, mischances, discoveries, and surprises encountered in doing the study.

Qualitative inquiry is allied with the interpretive social sciences (including cultural anthropology) and the feminist critique of positivism (Davis, 1985; Farganis, 1986). This perspective observes that a more meaningful understanding of particular human circumstances arises from a careful interpretation of their real-life qualities, rather than from the analysis of quantifiable facts.

Because qualitative methods are not widely used (at least in social work), it is important to say something more inclusive about this approach to inquiry and knowledge development. The following brief overview is intended not only to inform the reader about this method, but to identify the content that is included in the research report. From the first musings about the research question to the closing of the last interview or observation, as you will see, the plans, revisions, accidents, and chance events that occur are all woven into the texture of the final report.

qualitative inquiry: characteristics and contrasts

Observing that the label *qualitative methods*—or its alternate title, *ethnography*—has no precise meaning in any of the social sciences, Van Maanen (1983) explained that

> it is at best an umbrella term covering an array of interpretive techniques which seek to describe, encode, translate, and otherwise come to terms with the meaning, not the frequency, of certain more or less naturally occurring phenomena in the social world. . . . [These techniques] attempt to reduce the distance between indicated and indicator, between theory and data, between context and action. (p. 9)

Thus, in this chapter, I present one version of the processes, stages, and methods of this mode of inquiry. The references listed at the end of the chapter offer their own variations on these themes.

In common, the different forms of qualitative inquiry suggest the analogies of journey and exploration, even saga and adventure. Such analogies may seem outlandish or inapplicable to something that is as sober as a research report. Standard versions of research that make scientific claims do not, after all, look kindly on metaphorical language that implies the intrusion of "subjectivity" or even "personal bias." Whether any form of research in the social sciences or social work can claim "objectivity" or the absence of a personal and biased view is arguable (see, for example, Goldstein, 1991; Rosenau, 1992). Qualitative research is straightforward about this question: Its findings derive from and depend on the subjective or reflexive interpretations of the people, places, and events that are investigated.

Considering the analogies of "journey" and "exploration," any researcher can be thought of as an explorer entering an uncharted terrain. To avoid getting lost or mired in this unfamiliar territory, the thoughtful explorer painstakingly prepares for the expedition: He or she devises an overall plan and set of procedures and selects certain tools and instruments to map out and analyze the domain of inquiry.

Still, there are some important differences between the preparations of researchers who use quantitative methods and those who are guided by a qualitative orientation—differences that influence how the respective final reports are written. Normally, quantitative research calls for precise and rigorous groundwork; much work is done up front to ensure that the investigation will proceed in strict accord with the initial research plan. Not the least, the object field to be studied and its pertinent variables are defined and delimited, and presumably testable explanatory theories or hypotheses are chosen. On the basis of these plans, a set of instruments or statistical devices to collect, measure, and analyze the data is designated. These systematically orchestrated preparations anticipate, in many ways, how the findings and conclusions of the quantitative investigation will be organized, that is, the form and structure of the final report.

The qualitative researcher, concerned more with discovery and explanation than with proof, cannot predict how the inquiry will unfold or what will be found. This is not to say that the inquirer is not curious or does not entertain some hunches; yet, to be sure that the outcome "speaks for itself," the researcher deliberately brackets predictions and presuppositions and holds them in abeyance.

The open-minded character of qualitative inquiry should not be confused with anything resembling a seat-of-the-pants, slipshod disposition. It is because this investigation does not proceed according to a standard formula that the researcher is obligated to set certain limits and yet not compromise the unique nature of the inquiry.

This intent is reflected in the formulation of a broad but workable research question. On the basis of this question, the researcher devises a general plan of action that generally identifies the people, places, or things that will be the focus of inquiry. A set of questions may be used to guide the study, but these questions must be sufficiently flexible and adaptable to the contingencies that are bound to arise over the course of the study. By design, the inquiry is open and receptive to whatever one encounters. As Rosenau (1992, p. 106) put it, the inquirer proposes to ''go among the people and simply let them speak for themselves'' while trying to make sense of what they are saying and doing at a particular time and within a certain context and culture. Geertz (1988, p. 10) metaphorically referred to this researcher as both a pilgrim and a cartographer exploring an unknown social terrain. In this venture, standard equipment includes notebooks, field journals, recording devices, and other means of capturing the quality and nature of the human event. Writing, therefore, is not a skill reserved for the final report; it is an art that is germane to every stage of the process of inquiry.

Let me sum up these differences for the moment if only to introduce what is involved in writing the qualitative research report. Quantitative research is a method, a set of techniques, governed by specific ground rules and protocols. The researcher usually has a dependable compass in hand and a specific objective in mind so the course is usually clear; in fact, any deviations from the course are likely to render the findings suspect. The aim is to *map* and *describe* the territory in question. In contrast, the qualitative researcher is far less sure where he or she is heading—and for good reason. First, each research enterprise is like no other to the extent that the human event to be studied is like no other. Second, the ''instrument,'' if you will, of the investigation is the interpretive talent of the reflective researcher, who, through observation, participation, questioning, and listening, strives to incorporate what is occurring in a complex social field. All the while, the inquirer is aware that what can be known and understood is always limited by the constraints of language, by where in the field the observer happens to be positioned at the particular time, by cultural differences, and by many other ambiguous factors that are typical of most human circumstances.

These differences between the two modes of inquiry lead, of course, to different orders and types of knowledge. The quantitative researcher, regulated by concerns with valid proof, ''truth,'' and measurement, renders a statistically factual but abstract version of a human event that is based on frequencies, distributions, correlations, and other quantifiable measures. The qualitative investigator, concerned with meaning and explanation, strives to capture, interpret, and present in a report the voices and felt experiences of the subjects of the study. This account is framed in a narrative mode, one that is replete with innuendos of plot, character, setting, intention, and meaning. In many ways, qualitative inquiry can be thought of as a commonsense, but highly disciplined, way of finding out people's thoughts, actions, and beliefs.

a research example

One learns about research by doing research; this is particularly true of the qualitative or ethnographic approach because its prescriptions are not specific. Let us consider a question that would be of interest to social work and consider how the qualitative researcher would proceed, taking into account that the vagaries of the inquiry shape the contents of the final report. This mode of research will stand in a clearer light if I first at least allude to the methods of the quantitative investigator. The question has to do with parents' perceptions and attitudes—in this instance, how parents think they are affected by the severity of their children's retardation. It is likely that both quantitative and qualitative researchers have similar motives and concerns as the incentive for undertaking such a study in the first place—perhaps to verify observations made in practice with similar parents or the need to refine and develop a service program. Why one or the other method is selected should reflect the purpose of research and what information is needed. If description—the "what" of the question—is sought, then statistical findings will suffice; if an explanation in some depth or the "why" and "how" is required, then the interpretive mode is appropriate.

A QUANTITATIVE APPROACH

In a quantitative approach, the researcher's first task is to delimit the scope of inquiry, to restrict it to specific variables that lend themselves to study and measurement. For example, a study seeks to determine the differences in levels of self-esteem and depression among parents of children with retardation (see Graham, 1992). As a forecast of parental reactions, the guiding hypothesis assumes in advance that the parents' depression and self-esteem are the dependent variables that are linked with levels of their children's retardation: The more severe the retardation, the more negative the effects on the degree of depression and lowered self-esteem. Depression and self-esteem in this case are defined in accord with two scales selected to measure each variable. These scales, along with other questions, form the instrument that is mailed to a sample of several hundred willing respondents, over a third of a larger list initially acquired from a state agency. The responses are coded and processed by computer-driven statistical packages. Statistical findings are carefully analyzed and described in a report that also spells out the generalizability of the findings and their implications for practice, planning, or education. To be sure, this is an abbreviated version of a far more complex and demanding investigation; it serves, however, as a basis for comparison.

A QUALITATIVE APPROACH

Given the same question, this ethnographer also is curious about the impact of the child's retardation and its meaning for the parent, but does not assume in advance what it may be. Parenthetically, if indicators of something that may be construed as depression and self-esteem—or any other construct—turn up in the findings, either or both would be framed in the parents' terms and meanings. It would be foolish to imply that the researcher does not already entertain some notions about the question; often, these preliminary musings about, or attraction to, the nature of the relationship between the parents and children foreshadow the construction of the research problem itself. However, it is the obligation of the inquirer to suspend any conjectures, to bracket and put aside any assumptions, if the intent is to evoke the voices of the parents themselves, to elicit their stories and folk wisdom to generate knowledge from the inside out.

The Research Questions

The first step toward making the research problem more explicit is the shaping and refinement of the research questions. After careful thought, the researcher narrows the focus of the study and sets some soft boundaries, as guides not only for the investigation, but for subsequent analyses of the data. Still, it is assumed that these initial questions—and perhaps even the original notions about the problem—will be reconsidered as new information is acquired along the way.

These formative questions usually are aimed at what the researcher first needs to know about the circumstances—for example, How do these parents perceive their children? How do they understand "retardation"? If there are other children in the family, is the child in question "different"? Depending on whether the inquirer is seeking the particulars of the parents' views or is inviting the respondents to tell their stories in their own terms, the schedule of questions may be focused or broadly conceived. As you will see, the method used also bears on how the questions are structured: Interviews with the respondents would require a well-organized set of questions; in participant observation, on the other hand, questions serve largely as reminders about what to observe and explore. However these questions are worked out, they need to be sensitive to and in tune with the culture and idiom of the respondents.

The Theoretical Sample

The term *sample* often is associated with such qualifiers as *stratified* or *random* that imply that the sample is representative of something or some population. This is not necessarily the case in qualitative inquiry: Theoretical sampling involves the selection of the kind of cases that will likely generate theory (Glaser & Strauss, 1967). Thus, the selection of the sample depends on the research question, that is, not only what information is needed, but who can tell you about it. The size of the sample (typically small because of the interest in the depth of the material) may be limited by the number of available respondents. If many respondents are available, the researcher can limit the size by determining when "saturation" is reached. In other words, the sample size may be open ended and the inquiry will proceed to the point where interviews or observations cease to produce new or revealing information. Other considerations bearing on theoretical sampling include the issue of the desired diversity (for instance, parents of children with severe retardation *and* parents of children with mild forms of retardation) or the homogeneity of the sample.

Access

Where will the inquiry be carried out? In the parents' homes? At a meeting? In an institution? This is no small matter for the ethnographer because the research cannot begin until he or she can gain entry into the immediate life circumstances of the respondents. Whether doing so involves gaining access to case records or finding a setting for discussion or observation, this issue is integral to the initial planning for the project and an important ingredient of the final report.

QUALITATIVE OR ETHNOGRAPHIC METHODS

On planning the study, the researcher assumes that "out there" somewhere is a field of experience that should yield what needs to be known about the question. Thus, depending on the sources of knowledge (people, places, events, documents) and their accessibility, the researcher can use a variety of methods (individually or in some combination) to penetrate that field. (Although not relevant to the research example, historical and bibliographic methods are also included in the array of qualitative methods.)

Interviewing

The interview is pertinent when firsthand impressions about the research question (in my example, the parents of children with retardation) are sought. The interview can be firmly or loosely structured, depending on whether specific details or broad impressions are needed. The questions may focus on daily routines ("What's it like caring for Johnny all day?"), critical incidents ("How do you feel or what do you do when . . . ?"), contrasts ("When is it harder . . . ?"), relationships, or any issues that will encourage the respondents to reflect on and report their experiences. The interview is not an interrogation but a discourse, a shared journey into the unexplored realms of the respondents' episodes and events of living. As an active listener, the inquirer guides the discussion with sensitivity, courtesy, and sincere interest.

Life History

Similar to the interview, the life history involves fewer respondents because of its intensity and depth. The inquirer attempts to evoke the respondents' personal accounts of their lives at a particular point and in the context of the research question. Obviously, several interviews over time are needed to stir the respondents' stories of their earlier hopes, expectations, and choices; how things worked out; their private meanings; the cultural textures of living; and other perceptions that, in my example, would deepen the researcher's understanding of the current relationship between the parents and the children.

Focus Groups

With focus groups, several parents may be convened at a home, school, or center for a series of meetings. The inquiry could start with a specific question about being a parent, or the members of the group could be encouraged to sort out issues that they think are significant. Themes, contrasts, shared and singular perspectives, and cultural and familial influences are but a few of the insights that can emerge. The focus group is also valuable at a point in the study when data have been collected but their meaning is unclear. In my example, parents who have been interviewed or, if contrast is desired, a fresh group of parents could be convened and asked to reflect on the findings and offer their impressions.

Participant Observation

Alone or together with the foregoing approaches, this method addresses the research question by directly involving the inquirer in the activities and interactions of the situation. As both an insider and an outsider, the observer in my example could spend several days with a family, be present at mealtimes or at critical times of the day, or participate in the activities of parents at a center or school for children with retardation. In this way, the inquirer could gain firsthand knowledge of the environment and its emotional climate—social interaction involving who does what, when, with whom, under what circumstances, and for what reasons; thus, the emerging patterns begin to fill the spaces of the research question.

FIELD NOTES

A valuable adjunct to these ethnographic methods and a significant precursor to the final report, field notes (in addition to any audio or visual recordings) are used to record impressions and observations. They are obviously required in participant observation and are equally helpful for taking stock of the ambience of the interview and its other nuances.

Because the ethnographic experience is so often charged with uncertainty and ambiguity, field notes also serve as a personal journal—a journey's log that helps keep track of where the inquirer happens to be at the time. It is likely that many transient ideas recorded along the way eventually may be discarded; yet any errant thought or impression may become a breakthrough in understanding, the first indicator of a possible organizing scheme, and often a signal that an original premise or question may be wrong. In any case, field notes form the keystone of the bridge to the final report.

the analysis and final report

The analysis of qualitative or ethnographic data involves the discovery of often fugitive meanings, the symbols of order, the indicators of patterns and themes that are generally diffused among the raw material. Although analysis is part of the final stage of the inquiry, it also flows through the entire process as formative impressions are sifted and compared.

The analysis of ethnographic data calls for special skills or talents. The principal task is to make sense of and find meaning in what may first appear to be a chaotic assortment of information as the basis for the final report. The researcher is now the interpreter, the individual responsible for creating a coherent and intelligible mosaic of constructs out of the blur and confusion of observations of another social world. The skill or talent required is *reflexivity,* or reflective thought.

If, as Hammersley and Atkinson (1983) asserted, all social research has a reflexive character, then a prime example is the reflexivity that is integral to qualitative inquiry. As an existential fact, we are part of the social world we study. We cannot escape this social world to study it, nor can we escape the presence of bias; working with what knowlege we have, we need to recognize that it may be erroneous and that we therefore may need to subject it to systematic inquiry. If the reflective mind of the researcher is the primary research instrument, it follows that it is also the medium by which meaning, knowledge, and theory are drawn from the fruit of the inquiry.

Reflexivity, or what Schön (1983) called "reflection-in-action," is a form of problem solving that is pertinent to questions or problems about complex human situations in which there is no guaranteeably correct solution or objective reality. Let us consider a few implications of reflective thinking for the analysis and the final report. The reader is also invited to consider for a moment how these implications may be critical to the processes of social work practice itself (Goldstein, 1991; Papell & Skolnik, 1992).

First, reflexivity stands in opposition to linear or cause–effect thinking when it comes to explaining and understanding social interaction. Applied to my example, reflective analysis illuminates patterns of interaction, what these patterns may mean to a particular parent and child, the adaptive purposes they serve, and so on. Rather than an examination of the discrete sets of behaviors and responses, an analysis of the intertextual process being worked out between a parent and a child—or the complex interwoven relationship—would be more enlightening. Even as certain constructs about this process are delineated, they would need to be qualified by conditions of time and place, context, and relation to other events. This is a complex endeavor to be sure; yet, to the extent that it echoes the ambiguous human event, it is reliable.

Second, the study and analysis of any human situation are, in effect, the study and analysis of a text or narrative. Facts, frequencies, and variables are isolated fractions of the event; stories, memories, and autobiographies are texts that, again, are expressed in some context, in relation to some occurrence, and at a particular moment in persons' lives.

Therefore, the third aspect concerns the interpretive role of the reflective inquirer. To be sure, there are systematic steps to be taken in the activities of analysis (Glaser & Strauss, 1967; Hammersley & Atkinson, 1983; Miles & Huberman, 1984). Confronted with what is usually an astonishing mass of field notes, jottings, transcripts, and tapes, the inquirer must first sort and rearrange the mass of data into logical clusters, such as time, situation, the respondents' characteristics, and the respondents' typical behaviors.

As the examination of the data proceeds, the focus shifts from the breadth of the data to its particulars, from description (what people are saying and doing) to explanation (their meanings, motives, and intentions). Still, these procedures would be superficial without the penetrating attributes of the artistry, imagination, and divergence of reflective thought. Metaphorically, a dialogue begins to take place between the researcher and the data in which the researcher begins to "hear" certain themes and messages. Or, analogously, one could say that the effort is akin to listening to unfamiliar music. With repetition, the words begin to become more distinct and understandable and the harmony and melody take form. Themes and phrases appear and reappear. A beginning, middle, and end are evident. Only as this process unfolds and comparisons are made will these explanations begin to fall into organizing constructs that, in combination, shape certain theoretical understandings of the research question.

the form and style of the report

Because there are no precise prescriptions or rules for writing the final report, the contours of the report would be shaped by a logic based on the nature of the specific inquiry and the audience to which it is directed. In my example of the study of parents of children with retardation, the following outline suggests the form the report could take if it was based largely on interviews and aimed at an academic audience. A more journalistic style would be appropriate if the report was written, say, for the citizen board of a center for mental retardation.

1. A restatement of the research questions and their implications.
2. An overview of the methodology and its rationale, including the selection of the theoretical sample. The chronology of the inquiry and how it worked out would also be pertinent.
3. Profiles of the respondents, including their characteristics and their life circumstances. Their idioms, expressions, and folk versions of their circumstances should be used freely.
4. The organization of constructs (such as attitudes, relationship patterns, and the parents' definitions of the situation), supported by excerpts from interviews that express thoughts, feelings, and outlook. Such constructs may cut across the sample or may be peculiar to specific clusters of parents.
5. A summary of the findings based on these constructs and their implications. Beyond a straightforward catalog of impressions and conclusions, it is important to show how the results conform with, contradict, or modify the literature, theories, or

understanding of the problem. Also to be noted is how the findings may suggest some new insights that would be relevant to education, practice, or the development of programs and policies. Most of these insights would, of course, be based on the acquired data. But the author should not dismiss his or her other personal impressions and reflections (and they should be clearly stated as such); intimately and in a firsthand way, the author has been involved in and therefore learned much about the details of the respondents' lives that are usually not evident to the casual observer.

6. Because the results do not pretend to be generalizable, other research endeavors suggested by the study should be indicated. For example, the study may raise new and more penetrating questions that should be asked, identify other subjects or populations who may be queried, or advise how the findings of the study can be used to design a quantitative research project aimed at a larger group of respondents.

This outline suggests the format and arrangement of the content of the report; it says little, however, about the authorship or kind of writing that will convince the reader of the true-to-life nature of the study and its findings and, correspondingly, the style of the report itself. The purpose of an ethnographic report, after all, is not only to inform the reader, but to draw the reader into the discourse. The researcher makes no claims on truth; he or she is aware that the knowledge of the world entered and explicated is always partial, situated, and subjective (Richardson, 1990). The researcher is also aware that the study and its report are not without problems; they are the consequences of many strategic choices about what to include, omit, organize, and so on. Thus, letting the reader know about the journey and its outcomes is also an invitation to debate.

AUTHORSHIP

Denzin (1989) was clear that the inquirer bears sole responsibility for the substance and conclusions of the inquiry: "Interpretive research begins and ends with the biography and the self of the researcher" (p. 12). In this project, he added, the inquirer can consult only himself or herself. And so, he concluded, "Only you can write your experiences. No one else can write them for you. No one else can write them better than you can. What you write is important." (p. 12)

This being the case, to what extent can the report be trusted as a relatively dependable interpretation of the social world in question? Is it sufficiently reliable to serve as a recommendation for specific policies or practices? For our purposes, the question can be put in another way: How should the researcher take on the role of the author in a way that enhances the authority and reliability of the report?

Geertz (1988) carefully weighed this question, wondering why the writer of an ethnography should be taken seriously in the first place. The study, after all, cannot be replicated. Although it may glisten with conceptual elegance, this is not enough to support the inquiry and its findings. Neither is the force of the theoretical argument because, as Geertz pointed out, even the proud theories of Bronislaw Malinowski and Margaret Mead lie in ruins. Geertz's answer is explicit. After a careful analysis of the works of ethnographers whose investigations stand as exemplars of superb research (Claude Levi-Strauss, Ruth Benedict, Edward Evans-Pritchard), he concluded that a "good" ethnography radiates the persuasive quality of "having been there."

The writing of a credible, compelling report therefore calls on the inquirer's talents "to persuade the readers that what they are reading is an authentic account by someone personally acquainted with how life proceeds in some place, at some time, among some group. . . . [It] is the basis upon which anything else ethnography seeks to do—analyze, explain, amuse, disconcert, celebrate, edify, excuse, astonish, subvert—finally rests" (Geertz, 1988, pp. 143–144).

STYLE

If the fidelity of the research report depends on the kind of responsible authorship that imparts the writer's exacting familiarity with the particular slice of life, then the author's style is a critical matter. The style of "conventional" research reports is determined by certain protocols and is confined by the data. The rules for empirical objectivity require detachment; the intrusion of the self of the researcher in the results and conclusions of the inquiry is avoided.

Doing qualitative research, by definition, involves using the inquirer's self as the interpretive medium, the "voice" of the process from beginning to end. Thus, keeping in mind the interests of the audience, the author must write in a style that clearly conveys his or her personal experience of having been there.

Admittedly, there is little in our professional education that encourages and supports writing that is personal, metaphorical, or interpretive—that is free of jargon and academic posturing and that corresponds with the human interests of social work. Even the writing of case records or "process recording" often is a self-conscious enterprise. The reports of interviews, particularly when they are marked by exceptionally intimate revelations or emotions, can sound pedestrian, if not trite, when they are depersonalized by use of the editorial "we" ("*We* felt empathic about. . . .") or impersonal nouns ("*The caseworker* was troubled by. . . .").

Thus, the idea of a report based on personal authorship and a literary, rather than "scholarly," style can make one uneasy. Van Maanen (1988), an experienced ethnographer of modern organization structures, calmed this unease when he urged ethnographers to experiment with and reflect on the many ways that social reality may be presented. On the basis of his own writings, he outlined, with a touch of the theatrical, possible styles or genres of writing ethnography. Among other styles, he described what he calls the *realist, confessional,* and *impressionist* forms and styles of the report. These styles are worth a brief description, as much to open the reader's thoughts to the possibility of a range of literary alternatives when it comes time to write the report as for the guidance they offer.

The "realist tale" represents a style used when the intent is to emphasize the authenticity of a cultural representation. The text is written in a dispassionate, third-person voice to place the voices of the members of the culture in the forefront, to ensure that their points of view take precedence. The report, however, is no less subjective and interpretive because it is the omniscient author who has the final word on the selection of the content and how it is interpreted and presented. The report comprises a series of theoretical constructs related to the research question, with each construct supported by a collection of cultural details derived from the field. The following excerpt is based on my fictitious study:

> Common to all these mothers of children with retardation is the tendency to avoid criticism about their maternal role. In various ways, they sidestep any discussion of any problems with the child; as Mrs. J put it, "There are some difficult times with Sam, but who doesn't have problems with their kids?" Even in casual dinner table conversation, the mother imposes silent controls when the recitation of the day's events touches on anything bearing on the child's behavior. . . .

What Van Maanen (1988) called the "confessional tale" contrasts sharply with the realist tale. Here the report is highly personalized and, in its attempt to demystify the research experience, adds the human quotient that is absent in the realist genre. This style is also in accord with a phenomenological or hermeneutical perspective that strives to capture the naturalistic characteristics of the human event.

The writer of the confessional tale does not forgo the rigor of detail of the realist mold. But to these details and analysis the writer adds an account of how he or she arrived at these findings, the vicissitudes of fieldwork, the writer's own interpretive standards, and possibly some comments on how certain errors and blunders influenced the course of the study. The report reaches for a quality of naturalness and acknowledges that there are other ways to interpret the same data because what the writer gained from the respondents were not neutral truths, but social constructions, beliefs, and myths. An example of this style is as follows:

> At first I was put off with the ways that most of these mothers kept clear of any of my questions about the kinds of discipline they ordinarily used. Mrs. J was the third mother I interviewed, and when she said that sure, she had some bad times with her child, "but who doesn't?" I began to understand that the mothers were reacting to the term *discipline* in a negative way. Basically, these mothers were hearing my question as a criticism of their parenthood. . . .

The "impressionist tale" (Van Maanen, 1988) is designed to draw the audience into an unfamiliar story world and to see, hear, and feel it as the field-worker did. By the use of dramatic forms (often involving the researcher), the story is meant to come alive. What makes the story convincing is its integrity; all the pieces fit together in ways that shape a vivid scenario in the life of the respondent. For example:

> Mrs. J and I had been talking for about an hour when she asked if I would join the family for dinner. It was not just the fact that I had missed lunch that day that led me to accept the invitation; I was also eager to get a firsthand view of how the Js got along with each other. Perhaps Sam might do something that would help me understand how Mrs. J reacted to or dealt with his impulsive behavior. I was not sure what I was looking for, but it did not take long before I was struck (literally and figuratively) with the force of Sam's frenzied reaction to the intrusion of a stranger. A cup (thankfully plastic) struck my temple just as I spooned the first mouthful of soup. Mrs. J gasped, immobilized, her face blank. . . .

researching and reporting lives

These styles may appear extreme when contrasted with conventional "rules" governing the business of doing and writing social research. Still, each style or its variations may be considered a model for writing reports for select audiences. The realist style is certainly appropriate for the ethnographic doctoral dissertation; it includes all the trappings of a respectable academic enterprise. The confessional style is equally appropriate for this purpose. But it can also serve as a medium for discourse among academics and students. Because it includes the experience of "how I did it and what I found," the study offers a measure of vicarious learning for the interested reader, and because the qualitative study does not promise absolute answers, it invites ongoing discussion and debate about various aspects of social research and its findings.

And last, the "impressionist" style provokes attention to neglected groups who may profit from the findings of qualitative research. The clearly narrative nature of this style would be appealing and comprehensible to citizens, planners, board members, and others who have some investment in the research problem.

Finally, this survey of qualitative research and report writing stirs the need to rethink the question of what social research should actually look like in the first place. Speaking about postmodern social science, Rosenau (1992) commented on its rejection of the scientific model that presumes to offer final truths and verifiable facts. Instead the interest is in "indeterminacy rather than determinism, diversity rather than unity . . . complexity rather than simplification . . . the unique rather than the general" (p. 8). These interests would be smothered by the constraints of standard "scientific" or "scholarly" styles of writing; their protocols leave little room for the human experience of research and for a reflective and imaginative style of writing that properly captures the social world in question. Considering that social research involves the entry of the inquirer into the intimate social world of the respondent, the researcher must be free to be a responsible translator of and narrator about that journey. When Geertz (1988, p. 129) asked, "Whose life is it anyway?" he appealed to researchers to preserve, with some humility, the authenticity and integrity of the human lives and circumstances they are searching to understand.

references

Davis, L. V. (1985, March–April). Female and male voices in social work. *Social Work, 30,* 106–115.

Denzin, N. K. (1989). *Interpretive interactionism.* Newbury Park, CA: Sage Publications.

Farganis, S. (1986). Social theory and feminist theory: The need for dialogue. *Sociological Inquiry, 56,* 50–68.

Geertz, C. (1983). *Local knowledge.* New York: Basic Books.

Geertz, C. (1988). *Works and lives: The anthropologist as author.* Stanford, CA: Stanford University Press.

Glaser, B. G., & Strauss, A. L. (1967). *The discovery of grounded theory.* Chicago: Aldine.

Goldstein, H. (1991). Qualitative research and social work practice: Partners in discovery. *Journal of Sociology and Social Welfare, 18,* 83–100.

Graham, E. (1992). *Differences in self-esteem and depression among parents of individuals with mental retardation.* Unpublished doctoral dissertation, Boston College Graduate School of Social Work.

Hammersley, M., & Atkinson, P. (1983). *Ethnography: Principles in practice.* London: Tavistock Publications.

Miles, M. B., & Huberman, A. M. (1984). *Qualitative data analysis.* Beverly Hills, CA: Sage Publications.

Papell, C. P., & Skolnik, L. (1992). The reflective practitioner: A contemporary paradigm's relevance for social work education. *Journal of Social Work Education, 28,* 18–26.

Richardson, L. R. (1990). *Writing strategies: Reaching diverse audiences. Qualitative research methods* (Vol. 21). Newbury Park, CA: Sage Publications.

Rosenau, P. M. (1992). *Post-modernism and the social sciences.* Princeton, NJ: Princeton University Press.

Schön, D. A. (1983). *The reflective practitioner: How professionals think in action.* New York: Basic Books.

Van Maanen, J. (Ed.). (1983). *Qualitative methodology.* Newbury Park, CA: Sage Publications.

Van Maanen, J. (1988). *Tales from the field: On writing ethnography.* Chicago: University of Chicago Press.

suggested reading

Agar, M. H. (1980). *The professional stranger: An informal introduction to ethnography.* New York: Academic Press.

Douglas, J. (1984). *Creative interviewing.* Beverly Hills, CA: Sage Publications.

Lincoln, Y., & Guba, E. (1985). *Naturalistic inquiry.* Beverly Hills, CA: Sage Publications.

Lofland, J. (1974). Styles of reporting qualitative field research. *American Sociologist, 9,* 101–110.

Lofland, J., & Lofland, L. (1984). *Analyzing social settings.* Belmont, CA: Wadsworth.

Morgan, D. L. (1988). *Focus groups as qualitative research.* Newbury Park, CA: Sage Publications.

Spradley, J. P. (1979). *The ethnographic interview.* New York: Holt, Rinehart & Winston.

Spradley, J. P. (1980). *Participant observation.* New York: Holt, Rinehart & Winston.

Watson, L. C., & Watson-Franke, M. (1985). *Interpreting life histories.* New Brunswick, NJ: Rutgers University Press.

6 *graphics*

William H. Butterfield

The essence of science is the development and extension of knowledge. However, facts, principles, and theories do not, by themselves, lead to new understandings in science. Significant advances in science come through effective communication (Johnston & Pennypacker, 1980). Effective communication helps the recipient of the information to understand the importance and significance of the scientific data. Communication is most effective when the recipient of the information can clearly see functional relationships in the data and when the data are related to existing theories and knowledge (Conant, 1951). This chapter focuses on the use of graphics for the clear and quick communication of information.

ways to show functional relationships

When Conant (1951) stated that effective communication helps the reader to understand functional relationships, he was referring to the mathematical definition of a functional relationship. In mathematics, functional relationships refer to how one variable changes when the value of another variable is changed. Common methods for communicating functional relationships are equations, rules, tables, and graphics.

The information in a table or graph can be used to construct a rule or to develop an equation. However, each way of expressing functional relationships is better suited for different purposes. This chapter focuses on graphic methods for showing important relationships in the data.

105

ADVANTAGES AND DISADVANTAGES OF USING EQUATIONS

An equation is a mathematical sentence that says that two sets of numbers or symbols are equal (Bashaw, 1969). The major advantage of equations is that they convey a great deal of information in a precise and condensed form. They are a shorthand way of representing large quantities of data. For example, the equation $X^2 = Y$ tells us that the value of Y for any value of X is equal to X times X.

Equations are not always the best way to communicate information for the following reasons:

1. Equations may accurately or inaccurately represent data. For example, a commonly used equation is the linear regression equation, which is used to predict how well a change in one variable predicts a change in a second variable. The equation yields a statistic r. When that statistic is multiplied by itself ($r \times r$), it is called the coefficient of determination (r^2). The coefficient of determination ranges in value between 0 and 1.00. A coefficient of 1.00 means that if one event occurs, the occurrence of a second event can be always predicted; a coefficient of 0 means that the occurrence of the second event cannot be predicted from the first event. So when the coefficient of determination is near 0, even though the regression equation represents the trend of the data, its ability to predict a specific data value will be low. When its predictive value is low, the equation does not accurately represent many of the data values in a set of data.

2. Equations may also convey a false belief that data sets that have identical statistics are equivalent. Equivalent regression lines or statistics can be generated from different sets of data. For example, Table 6.1 lists data sets that have identical regression equations and summary statistics. However, when the data are graphed, as in Figure 6.1, the differences in the data sets are apparent. It is unlikely that anyone looking at the graphs of the curves would argue that the data sets were equivalent. However, if only the statistics were available (as in Table 6.2), it would be easy to make that mistake. Refer to Table 6.1 and Figure 6.1 on page 107.

   A second example (Table 6.3) involving a single data set may make this situation even clearer. On the basis of the results of the equations used to compute the statistics in Table 6.3, the agency seems to have an admirable record of pay equity. However, the actual data (Table 6.4) tell a different story.

   The foregoing examples show that equations can accurately represent the data in the sense that they tell us about some

TABLE 6.1   Sample Data Sets

Data Set 1		Data Set 2		Data Set 3		Data Set 4	
X	Y	X	Y	X	Y	X	Y
10.0	8.04	10.0	9.14	10.0	7.46	8.0	6.58
8.0	6.95	8.0	8.14	8.0	6.77	8.0	5.76
13.0	7.58	13.0	8.74	13.0	12.74	8.0	7.71
9.0	8.81	9.0	8.77	9.0	7.11	8.0	8.84
11.0	8.33	11.0	9.26	11.0	7.81	8.0	8.47
14.0	9.96	14.0	8.10	14.0	8.84	8.0	7.04
6.0	7.24	6.0	6.13	6.0	6.08	8.0	5.25
4.0	4.26	4.0	3.10	4.0	5.39	19.0	12.50
12.0	10.84	12.0	9.13	12.0	8.15	8.0	5.56
7.0	4.82	7.0	7.26	7.0	6.42	8.0	7.91
5.0	5.68	5.0	4.74	5.0	5.73	8.0	6.89

SOURCE: From *The Visual Display of Quantitative Information* (p. 13) by E. Tufte, 1983, Cheshire, CT: Graphics Press. Copyright © 1983 by Graphics Press. Reprinted by permission.

FIGURE 6.1   Illustration of how data sets with identical statistics can have widely different distributions of data and how graphics make the differences apparent, whereas the data table does not

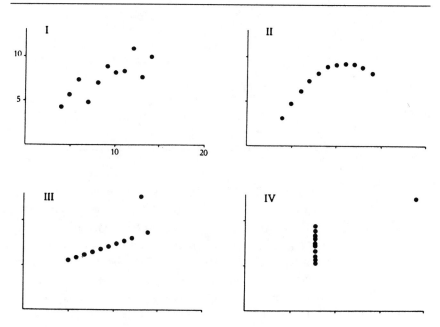

SOURCE: From *The Visual Display of Quantitative Information* (p. 13) by E. Tufte, 1983, Cheshire, CT: Graphics Press. Copyright © 1983 by Graphics Press. Reprinted by permission.

TABLE 6.2   Sample Data Set's Statistics

Number of cases = 11; Mean of X = 9.0; Mean of Y = 7.5
Regression equation: $Y = 3 = 0.5X$
Standard error of the estimate = .118
Sum of squares = 110
Regression sum of squares = 27.50
Residual sum of squares = 13.75
Correlation coefficient = .82
Coefficient of determination (r^2) = .67

SOURCE: From *The Visual Display of Quantitative Information* (p. 13) by E. Tufte, 1983, Cheshire, CT: Graphics Press. Copyright © 1983 by Graphics Press. Reprinted by permission.

TABLE 6.3   An Agency's Annual Salary Statistics for Full-time Employees

Statistic	Men	Women	Men and Women
Mean	$25,000	$25,000	$25,000
Median	$25,000	$25,000	$25,000
Mode	$25,000	$25,000	$25,000

TABLE 6.4   Actual Wages of Full-time Employees

Employee	Annual Income	Sex
1	$14,000	Female
2	$15,000	Female
3	$25,000	Female
4	$25,000	Female
5	$25,000	Male
6	$25,000	Male
7	$25,000	Male
8	$25,000	Male
9	$46,000	Female
Total	$225,000	

characteristic of the data, but they may not tell us all that there is to know about the data. The numbers that they yield represent the "best fit"—not the actual data points. Thus, we cannot use equations to reconstruct the original data.

3. Finally, if the equations are complicated, they can be understood only by sophisticated readers and thus are of little value when one is attempting to communicate with less sophisticated audiences.

ADVANTAGES AND DISADVANTAGES OF USING RULES

Rules are restatements of equations in sentence form. For example, the equation for conversion of Fahrenheit temperature to centigrade temperature is $C° = 5/9 (F° - 32)$. The corresponding rule would be this: To convert a temperature in degrees Fahrenheit to a temperature in degrees centigrade, subtract 32° from the Fahrenheit temperature and multiply the result by five-ninths. The major advantage of rules is that text can be used to explain, interpret, and evaluate the underlying data (Schmid & Schmid, 1979). But because words often convey multiple or ambiguous meanings, readers may have difficulty understanding the written explanation or deriving the actual equation from the textual material.

ADVANTAGES AND DISADVANTAGES OF USING TABLES

Tables can be used to show the actual values of dependent and independent variables or to show summarized data. Tables 6.1 and 6.4 are examples of tables that present actual values, and Tables 6.2 and 6.3 are examples of tables that present summary data. Tables can show data that are not easily represented in graphic form. Graphs, at best, can show relationships in three dimensions, whereas tables can be used to show relationships between more than three variables. However, multidimensional tables are often difficult to interpret (Zeisel, 1968). Although useful for many purposes, tables also have these disadvantages:

1. They cover limited ranges of data and thus cannot be used to extrapolate values reliably beyond the limits of the table.
2. Tabular information can conceal important relationships that are immediately apparent in graphic representations of the same data.
3. It is difficult to comprehend relationships in large tables of information. The map in Figure 6.2 would require a table measuring seven columns by 3,056 rows (Tufte, 1983, p. 19). At 60 rows a page, the table would be almost 51 pages long. It is unlikely that many readers would see the relationships that jump out on the map. Even a casual glance at the map raises questions in a reader's mind. For example, why are there high rates of stomach cancer in northern Arizona, North Dakota, Minnesota, and Wisconsin? Are lifestyles or heredity involved? Or are there chemicals in the soil? The map does not give us the answers, but it raises questions in a way that a table is unlikely to do.

This is not meant to imply that tables, rules, or equations are not valuable methods for displaying data. For some purposes, the best way to represent data is to use an equation, rule, or table. For others, graphs are much better ways to show important relationships. The remainder of this chapter focuses on the use of graphs.

FIGURE 6.2 Illustration of how area maps can be used to reveal relationships not apparent in large data tables

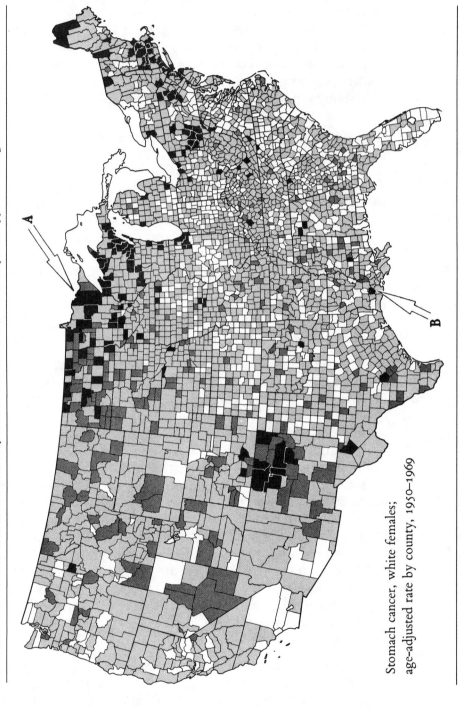

Stomach cancer, white females;
age-adjusted rate by county, 1950–1969

SOURCE: From *The Visual Display of Quantitative Information* (p. 19) by E. Tufte, 1983, Cheshire, CT: Graphics Press. Copyright © 1983 by Graphics Press. Reprinted by permission.

ADVANTAGES AND DISADVANTAGES OF USING GRAPHS

The following are the advantages of well-done graphic displays:

1. Graphs encourage the viewer to think about the substance of the relationship between the variables. They allow the observer to "see patterns and structure not revealed by other means of studying the data" (Tufte, 1983, p. 19).
2. They make complex relationships easily comprehensible by scientists and educated lay people.
3. They often efficiently communicate "complex quantitative ideas . . . nearly always of a multivariate sort" (Tufte, 1983, p. 19).
4. They present many numbers in a small space. For example, Figure 6.2 is the result of graphing 21,000 numbers (Tufte, 1983, p. 19).
5. They reveal data at several levels of detail, from a broad overview to a fine structure. For example, a graph may show a client's depression scores for a year, with the individual data points representing the client's weekly scores.

Graphic presentations also have their disadvantages. The major difficulties include these:

1. Exact values are sometimes difficult to read from a graph.
2. It is difficult to show the relationship among many variables on the same graph. Although complex relationships among several variables can be shown on a single graph (by using a common baseline and stacking several variables on the same graph), there is a limit to how many relationships can be conveyed.
3. The data presented may not cover all possible values of the variables.
4. The reader's perceptual system can lead him or her to misinterpret the data.
5. Graphs can be used to represent only two- or three-dimensional relationships, whereas tables can be used to represent multidimensional data. Even three-dimensional graphs are often difficult to understand. The three-dimensional graph presented in Figure 6.3 shows the relationship between parental income, custody, and child support payments. However, the data values are impossible to read accurately. Depending on how one estimates the scale values for the set of columns on the far right, for instance, it is possible to obtain estimates that range from somewhere around $1,950 to over $2,700. The actual values, reported in the body of the article, are $1,905 to $2,514. It is also difficult for the typical observer to figure out which bar is in which row.

FIGURE 6.3 Illustration of difficulties interpreting a three-dimensional chart

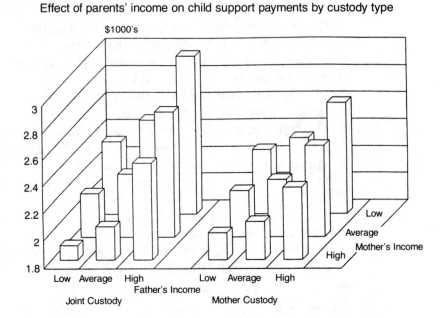

Effect of parents' income on child support payments by custody type

SOURCE: From "Legal Custody Arrangements and Children's Economic Welfare," by J. Seltzer, 1991, *American Journal of Sociology, 96,* p. 921. Copyright © 1991 by the University of Chicago Press. Reprinted by permission.

6. Graphs can show the actual data or show summaries of data. Summary graphs list values that represent some characteristic of the data, for example, the mean, median, range, slope, or variance. As is the case with tables and equations, when graphs contain summary values, the values do not tell all that there is to know about the data. That is, one cannot use summary graphics to reconstruct the original data.

In spite of these problems, graphs are powerful tools for scientific analysis and communication, although their power is often compromised, as Schmid and Schmid (1979) noted:

> Although statistical charts are often a more powerful and significant vehicle for communication than words [or equations or tables], there is a strange tolerance for poorly constructed charts. Paradoxically, the reader who is outraged by an ungrammatical sentence, an ambiguous statement, or even misplaced punctuation marks may be quite tolerant or indifferent to crudely designed, idiosyncratic, inappropriate or confusing charts. (p. 11)

The main reason that many graphs are poor is that although scientists receive a great deal of training in the mathematics of statistics, they receive almost no training in the presentation of data, no matter what the form. So, it is not surprising that many authors do not understand how to present data.

Furthermore, there are no standards for presenting graphs in the social sciences. The only standards of which the author is aware are those published by the American Society of Mechanical Engineers (1960), the Council of Biology Editors (1988), and the U.S. Army (1966). The lack of attention to the presentation of graphs in the social and life-science curricula may also be due to the belief that students know how to construct graphs. However, the proper construction of effective graphs is neither simple nor straightforward.

Three major areas should be addressed in striving for graphic excellence:

1. the proper selection of the type of graph to best represent the data
2. the mechanics of preparing good graphs
3. the impact of people's perceptions on understanding graphs.

The following sections focus on these issues. The discussion is based on the work of a number of writers, the most notable of which are Brinton (1914); Chambers, Cleveland, Kleiner, and Tukey (1983); Cleveland (1985); Council of Biology Editors (1988); Johnston and Pennypacker (1980); Schmid and Schmid (1979); Spear (1969); Tufte (1983); and Tukey (1977).

graphic excellence

Tufte (1983) called well-drawn graphics "friendly" graphics, and Wainer (1984, p. 137) noted that "the aim of good data graphics is to display [information] accurately and clearly." Table 6.5 contrasts the characteristics of "friendly" and "unfriendly" graphics.

TABLE 6.5 Friendly and Unfriendly Graphics

Friendly Graphics	Unfriendly Graphics
Accurate Presentation of Data	
1. The type of graphic used is appropriate for the data.	1. The graphical presentation is inconsistent with the type of data being used.
2. Important relationships are emphasized.	2. Important relationships are hidden or deemphasized.
3. The graphical presentation shows the natural relationships in the data.	3. The graphical presentation is inconsistent with the original data.

(continued)

TABLE 6.5 *continued*

Friendly Graphics	*Unfriendly Graphics*
4. Data are shown in context.	4. The graph presents insufficient data for the viewer to see the relationship between the data and previous or subsequent data.
Minimal Perceptual Problems	
5. Quantities are not represented by areas and volumes.	5. Quantities are represented by areas and volumes.
Emphasis on Data	
6. There is a high ratio of data to nondata.	6. Few data points are shown.
7. There is a high ratio of data ink to nondata ink.	7. The nondata ink hides the data ink.
8. Shading and cross-hatching are avoided when possible.	8. Shading and cross-hatching are used extensively.
9. Color is avoided.	9. Color is used extensively.
10. The graphic is understandable by color-deficient or color-blind viewers.	10. Red and green are used to show relationships.
Clear and Complete Presentation	
11. Labels and explanations are complete.	11. Explanations are incomplete. The data in the graph are not fully explained in the labels, legends, or explanatory headings.
12. The type and symbols are clear and precise.	12. The type is clotted and overbearing and the symbols are not clear or are difficult to read.
13. The type is upper- and lowercase with serifs.	13. The type is all capitals and has no serifs.

SOURCES: Brinton (1914), Cleveland and McGill (1984), Tufte (1983), and Wainer (1984).

Almost 80 years ago, Brinton (1914, pp. 360–361) developed a checklist for evaluating graphics. Much of his checklist is still relevant. The following, adapted from Brinton, are the relevant sections:

1. Are the data in the chart correct?
2. Has the best method been used for showing the data?
3. Are the proportions of the chart the best possible to show the data?
4. When the chart is reduced in size, will the proportion be suitable for the space in which the chart must be printed?
5. Are the proportions such that there will be sufficient space for the title of the chart when the chart has been reduced to its final printing size?
6. Are all scales in place?
7. Have the scales been selected and placed in the best possible manner?

8. Are points accurately plotted?
9. Are the numerical figures for the data shown as a portion of the chart?
10. Have the figures for the data been copied correctly?
11. Can the figures for the data be added and the total shown?
12. Are all dates accurately shown?
13. Is the zero vertical scale shown on the chart?
14. Are all zero and 100 percent lines made broad enough?
15. Are all lines on the chart broad enough to stand the reduction in size used in printing?
16. Does the lettering appear large enough and black enough when reduced to the size that will be used for printing?
17. Is all lettering placed on the chart in the proper direction for reading?
18. Is cross-hatching well made, with lines evenly spaced?
24. Does the key or legend correspond with the drawing?
25. Is there a complete title, clear and concise?
26. Is the drafting work of good quality?

Brinton (1914, pp. 362–363) also developed the following set of rules for presenting graphs, most of which are still relevant:

1. Avoid using areas or volumes when representing quantities.
2. The general arrangement of the chart should proceed from left to right.
3. Always place figures for the horizontal scale at the bottom of the chart. (See Cleveland, 1984a, 1984b, for exceptions.)
4. Always place figures for the vertical scale at the left of the chart.
5. Whenever possible, include in the chart the numerical data from which the chart was made.
6. If numerical data cannot be included in the chart, show the numerical data in tabular form accompanying the chart.
7. Place all lettering and all figures on a chart so that it can be read from the base or from the left-hand edge of the chart.
8. Arrange a column of figures relating to dates with the earliest date at the top.
9. Arrange separate columns of figures, with each column relating to a different date, with the column for the earliest date at the left.
11. For most charts, and for all curves, show the independent variable in the horizontal position.
12. As a general rule, the horizontal scale for curves should read from left to right and the vertical scale from bottom to top.
13. For curves drawn arithmetically, select the vertical scale, whenever possible, so that the zero line will show on the chart.
14. Make the zero line of the vertical scale for a curve a much broader line than the average coordinate lines.
16. For curves drawn logarithmically, set the bottom line and the top line of the chart at some power of 10 on the vertical scale. (This rule assumes that the log is to the base 10, but some charts are drawn to other bases, in which case the bottom and top lines should each be at some power of the base used.)
17. When the scale of a curve refers to percentages, make the line at 100 percent a broad line of the same width as the zero line.
18. If the horizontal scale for a curve begins at zero, make the vertical line at zero (usually the left-hand edge of the field) a broad line.

19. When the horizontal scale expresses time, do not make the lines at the left-hand and right-hand edges of a curve heavy, because a chart cannot be made to include the beginning or end of time.
20. When curves are to be printed, do not show any more coordinate lines than necessary for the data to guide the eye.
21. Make curves with much broader lines than the coordinate ruling so that the curves may be clearly distinguished from the background.
25. Make the title of a chart so complete and so clear that misinterpretation will be impossible.

using appropriate graphs

The first step in selecting an appropriate chart is to identify what relationship should be emphasized. This task seems so intuitive that many authors simply ignore it. However, it is worth making explicit.

Before I discuss the ways graphs have been used, I will describe the various types of graphs that can be used.

LINE GRAPHS

Line graphs are by far the most common types of graphs used in the social sciences. Because they are so common, I will spend considerably more time on them than on other graphs.

The most common type of line graph is the *linear coordinate graph*. Figure 6.4 will help you understand linear graphs.

Linear graphs have two axes. The horizontal axis is sometimes called the *X axis*. The *X* axis is divided into two segments. The point that divides the line is called the *origin* and is arbitrarily given the value of 0. The left half of the line is assumed to represent negative values (values less than 0), and the right half is assumed to represent positive values (values greater than 0). The vertical axis is sometimes called the *Y axis*. The *Y* axis is divided into two segments. The point that divides the line is called the *origin* and is arbitrarily given the value of 0. The bottom half of the line is assumed to represent negative values (values less than 0), and the upper half is assumed to represent positive values (values greater than 0). The *X* and the *Y* axes intersect at their origins at 90 degrees. The cross formed by the intersection of the vertical and horizontal axes divides the area covered by the coordinates into four sectors that are called *quadrants*. The quadrants are numbered counterclockwise. The first quadrant is to the right of the *Y* axis and above the *X* axis, the second quadrant is to the left of the *Y* axis and above the *X* axis, the third quadrant is to the left of the *Y* axis and below the *X* axis, and the fourth quadrant is to the right

FIGURE 6.4   Axes for constructing linear graphs

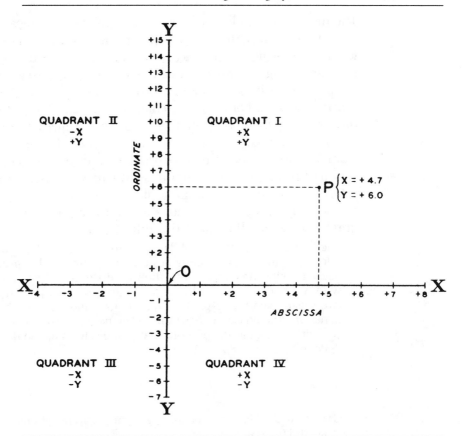

SOURCE: From *Handbook of Graphic Presentation* (2nd ed., Figure 3-1, p. 32) by C. Schmid & S. Schmid, 1979, New York: John Wiley & Sons. Copyright © 1979 by John Wiley & Sons. Reprinted by permission of John Wiley & Sons, Inc.

of the *Y* axis and below the *X* axis. Most graphs are drawn in the first quadrant, but they can be drawn in any quadrant or in several quadrants.

Several kinds of linear coordinate graphs deviate in some form from the basic principles for constructing linear graphs. They include logarithmic graphs, bar and column graphs, index graphs, and probability graphs.

Logarithmic, bar, column, and index graphs are not true linear coordinate graphs because they do not have a value of 0 at their origin. But because relationships are represented as distances on the horizontal and vertical axes, the conventions used with linear graphs generally apply. When the conventions differ, I will note the differences as I discuss these types of graphs.

LOGARITHMIC GRAPHS

The most common type of nonlinear scaling is log-linear scaling. This method of scaling uses a linear scale on the X axis and a logarithmic scale on the Y axis. The advantage of this method is that large ranges of data can be plotted in a small area and proportional changes in the value of a variable are represented as simple linear functions. For example, changes that have large absolute differences, when computed as ratios, may represent the same proportional change. That is, a change in the value of a variable from 5 to 10 has the same proportional change as a change from 500 to 1,000. Yet, the casual observer may not perceive this relationship when the data are plotted on a linear graph. The relationship becomes clear, however, if it is graphed on a log-linear graph. Figure 6.5 illustrates this difference.

> The figure shows two sets of data plotted against the familiar equal interval addition scale and invites the interpretation that great day to day variability was imposed by the introduction of the treatment along with the evident increase in the level of responding. [When] the same two sets of data are re-plotted on an equal ratio scale, in the right panel, . . . the phase to phase variability now appears to be equivalent . . . with respect to the proportional changes from day to day. (Johnston & Pennypacker, 1980, p. 349)

FIGURE 6.5   Illustration of how log-linear graphs reveal similar rates that are concealed in linear graphs

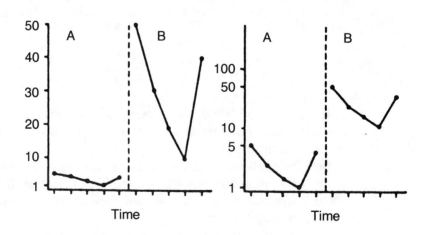

COMPARISON OF INTERVAL AND RATIO
PLOTS OF SAME DATA

SOURCE: From *Strategies and Tactics of Human Behavioral Research* (p. 349) by J. Johnston & H. Pennypacker, 1980, Hillsdale, NJ: Lawrence Erlbaum Associates. Copyright © 1980 by Lawrence Erlbaum Associates. Reprinted by permission.

One must be extremely careful, however, in using logarithmic graphs to display data. One must also be clear about what is more important: the absolute changes in values or the proportional changes. Even then it "is probably wiser to exhibit the values in actual rather than logarithmic terms. There is a possibility of misinterpretation either way" (Johnston & Pennypacker, 1980, p. 339). But a viewer of a logarithmic graph usually cannot translate the values into the raw values without replotting the data. In general, nonlinear graphics should be used for analytical purposes and "as a rule should not be a part of any dissemination effort unless the mathematical and/or theoretical sophistication of the intended audience is guaranteed" (Johnston & Pennypacker, 1980, p. 350). A useful alternative is to present both the raw and transformed data plots. This alternative allows emphasis to be given to the proportional changes while letting the reader see the original data. There were no examples of logarithmic graphs in the journals surveyed for this chapter. However, there were several cases in which such graphs might have made it easier to compare rates of change that were obscured in the original data. In these cases, the presentation of both a linear graph and a log-linear graph was probably desirable.

BAR AND COLUMN GRAPHS

Bar and column graphs use rectangular enclosed areas to show the value of whatever is being measured. They differ from true linear coordinate graphs in that only one axis represents the magnitude, frequency, or whatever is being measured. The other axis is used to separate the categories or items that are being measured. The only difference between bar and column graphs is orientation. In the bar chart, the rectangular bars are arranged so that whatever value is being measured is represented as a value on the horizontal axis. The vertical axis is used to separate things into categories and is always a nominal scale; that is, it shows only names of categories, not ranges or magnitudes.

The column graph reverses the axes. The vertical axis shows the magnitude or whatever is being measured, and the horizontal axis lists the named categories. Schmid and Schmid (1979) identified the eight most common types of bar and column graphs. Keeping with my belief that good graphs are self-explanatory, I show their graphs (in Figure 6.6 on p. 120) without further comment.

About 15 percent of the graphs listed in Table 6.6 (pp. 125–126) were either bar or column graphs. These graphs can also be drawn in three dimensions. (Figure 6.3 is an example of a three-dimensional column graph.) Bar and column graphs can be effective

FIGURE 6.6 Illustration of different types of bar charts

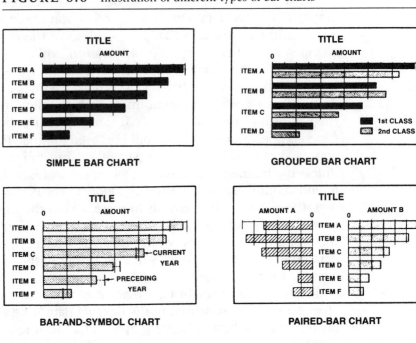

SIMPLE BAR CHART

GROUPED BAR CHART

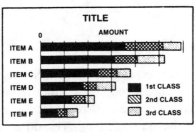

BAR-AND-SYMBOL CHART

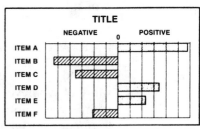

PAIRED-BAR CHART

SUBDIVIDED BAR CHART

DEVIATION-BAR CHART

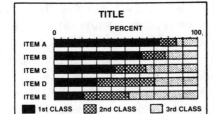

SUBDIVIDED 100% BAR CHART

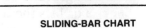

SLIDING-BAR CHART

SOURCE: From *Handbook of Graphic Presentation* (2nd ed., Figures 4-2 and 4-3, pp. 62–63) by C. Schmid & S. Schmid, 1979, New York: John Wiley & Sons. Copyright © 1979 by John Wiley & Sons. Adapted by permission of John Wiley & Sons, Inc.

ways to show the relative values of categorical data. But some of the graphs are difficult to interpret. The most difficult are the subdivided, the paired, and the sliding bar or column charts. The problem is that each of these types of graphs does not give the viewer a common scale for comparing bar values. This problem will be illustrated later.

INDEX GRAPHS

Index graphs are commonly used by the U.S. government. An example is the Consumer Price Index, issued by the U.S. Bureau of the Census. The data on the graph are compared with data for a specific date or year. The data for the base year are usually given the value of 0, or sometimes 100 percent, and changes before or after the base year are shown as a decrease or increase from the base amount or base percentage. The disadvantage of these sorts of graphs is that it is impossible to compare two graphs with different base years unless the value of the raw data for the base year is known. Figure 6.7 is an example of an index graph.

FIGURE 6.7   Illustration of an index graph

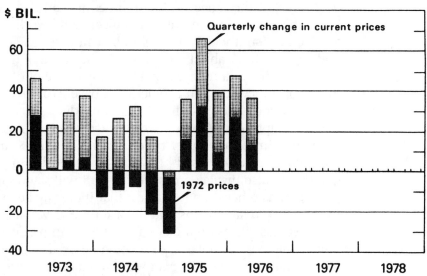

PROBABILITY GRAPHS

Probability graphs are unknown to most researchers, and I am not aware of any published examples in the social science literature. Nevertheless, they can be an effective analytic tool and may even be an effective means of showing the degree that a distribution of scores deviates from a normal distribution. Normally distributed data are represented by a straight line on these graphs. Thus, it is easy to see when a distribution is not normally distributed (see Schmid & Schmid, 1979, for an example).

POLAR GRAPHS

Polar graphs are also rare in the social science literature. They are graphs whose origin is at the center of a circle. One dimension of the graph represents the distances from the origin, which are usually shown as concentric circles. The other dimension is represented by angles and is usually expressed as degrees of rotation on a circle, but it can be expressed in other units. For example, Figure 6.8 uses a clock face to represent time.

Figure 6.8 shows the number of law enforcement officers who were killed each hour of the day from 1966 to 1975. Its impact is immediate. As I pointed out earlier, summary charts such as this one may or may not tell the whole story. The viewer cannot determine if the mean values shown on the graph are representative of all years or the ranges in the number of deaths for each hour. But if the graph is representative, officers who work the 9:00 P.M. to 3:00 A.M. shift would do well to be cautious. The graph also leads one to think about what may be the cause of the deaths. Are the deaths due to auto accidents? To the failure of officers to see that people they come in contact with have weapons? Or to the officers' fatigue and inability to react quickly?

Polar graphs can also be used to show relationships between time and almost any other type of variable. For example, a frequency plot could be used just as easily as a column graph. Polar graphs can also display areas effectively. I will say no more about polar graphs other than to suggest that they may be an effective way to show relationships that involve time or variables that can be expressed as cycles on a clock face. For example, it would be interesting to see if polar graphs could be used as substitutes for charts that plot several lines of yearly data on a horizontal axis that goes from January to December. (An example of the repeated-time-scale graph can be found in Schmid and Schmid, 1979, p. 43.)

FIGURE 6.8   Illustration of a polar graph

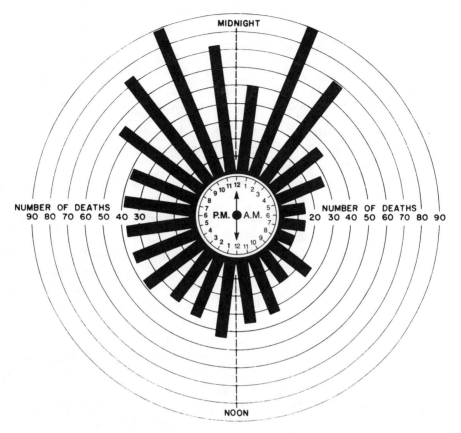

**LAW ENFORCEMENT OFFICERS* KILLED
BY HOUR OF DAY: 1966–1975†**

* DATA ON HOUR OF DAY NOT AVAILABLE FOR 8 OFFICERS WHO WERE KILLED
† TOTAL NUMBER OF OFFICERS KILLED: 1,023

SOURCE: From *Handbook of Graphic Presentation* (2nd ed., Figure 4-34, p. 92) by C. Schmid & S. Schmid, 1979, New York: John Wiley & Sons. Copyright © 1979 by John Wiley & Sons. Reprinted by permission of John Wiley & Sons, Inc.

PIE GRAPHS AND OTHER GRAPHS

Pie graphs are frequently used in magazines and newspapers. Because they use angles and area to express quantities, they are poor graphs for showing important relationships, and for that reason will not be discussed in this chapter.

The many other types of graphs are beyond the scope of this chapter. Several of the books cited earlier, such as Schmid and Schmid (1979) and Tufte (1983), contain excellent examples of these other types of charts that may well be useful in showing relationships in ways that have a high impact on the reader.

The various types of graphs used in the social sciences employ only a few common types of measures:

- counts (how many of something)
- time (duration or latencies)
- magnitude or intensity
- distance
- direction.

These measures are used to derive a number of other measures:

1. ratios
   a. percentages (the whole quantity divided into a partial quantity, times 100)
   b. rates (the whole quantity divided into a partial quantity), such as
      (1) the birthrate (the number of live births per 100,000 females)
      (2) the rate of change (the count at the beginning of a period divided by the count at the end of a period)
      (3) response rates (the number of questionnaires returned divided by the number sent).
2. frequencies (counts per unit time)
3. trends (the direction of changes over time)
4. differences (the result after two or more counts, magnitudes, frequencies, rates, or proportions are subtracted from or added to a known quantity)
5. correlations (the degree that the value of one variable predicts the value of another variable)
6. areas
7. volumes.

These basic measures have been combined in many ways. Tables 6.6, 6.7, and 6.8 present the results of my random selection of graphs from social work and psychology journals and from other sources, such as the U.S. government statistical reports, that show a variety of combinations of these basic variables and the number of graphs, out of those sampled, that used the relationship shown. The reader should not infer, however, that the more common ways of expressing relationships are better. Many of the frequently selected graphics did not highlight important relationships and therefore were inappropriate for the data.

TABLE 6.6 Relationships Found in a Survey of Linear Coordinate, Bar, and Column Graphs, with Examples of Types of Relationships

Vertical Axis	Horizontal Axis	Frequency per 100 Graphs
Count	Count	2
Income	Persons in each age group	
Count	Time	27
Number of aid applicants	Month	
Number of unemployed persons	Month and year	
Count	Name	1
Income	Source of income	
Count and range	Time	1
Median and low and high income	Year	
Magnitude	Time	8
Degree of clients' satisfaction	Weeks of treatment	
Mean count	Time	1
Mean income	Year	
Mean rate	Time	8
Cancer rates per 100,000 patients	Age	
Mean rate and range	Time	1
Mean cancer rates per 100,000 and high and low rates	Year	
Name	Time	1
Types of income	Year	
Name	Count	8
Types of income	Dollars earned	
Name	Magnitude	1
Type of alcohol consumption	Gallons	
Name	Percentage	5
Types of income	Percentage of all income	
Name	Percentage and range	1
Type of employee	Percentage of employees per 1,000 employees and the highest and lowest number across all states	
Percentage	Time	10
Percentage of each type of public welfare expenditure	Year	

(continued)

TABLE 6.6 *continued*

Vertical Axis	Horizontal Axis	Frequency per 100 Graphs
Percentage	Count	3
Percentage of rental units	Count of rental units by category	
Percentage deviation	Time	1
Percentage women's income is of men's income	Years	
Percentage (cumulative)	Percentage (cumulative)	1
Rate (ratio of two counts)	Time	5
Birthrate per 100,000 women	Year	
Rate and magnitude	Time	1
Rate and time	Time	3
Time	Magnitude	2
Time from birth	Intensity of life events	

TABLE 6.7 Relationships Found in a Survey of Index Graphs, with Examples of Types of Relationships

Vertical Axis	Horizontal Axis	Rate per 100 Graphs
Count	Time	2
Women's income	Years	
Percentage of base period	Time	3
Percentage of average rates of illness (average computed by totaling monthly frequencies for several years and dividing the total by the number of years)	Months	
Percentage of base period	Name	4
Percentage change over several time periods	Years of schooling completed	

TABLE 6.8 Relationships Found in a Survey of Area Graphs, with Examples of Types of Relationships

Variables Compared		Rate per 100 Graphs
Count	Area	1
Number of births	Census tracts	
Name	Area	1
Predominant ethnic groups	City wards	
Percentage	Area	1
Percentage of students completing high school	States	
Rate	Area	2
Rate of illness	County	

selecting the type of graph

Schmid and Schmid (1979, p. 31) pointed out that it would be difficult, if not impossible, to present a simple generalized categorical prescription for the use of any form of graph. In selecting a particular graphic form for portraying data or statistics, one should consider primarily the *meaning of the data* and the *audience to whom the chart is directed*.

Once the audience for the graph and the meaning of the data have been established, the next step is to select a specific type of graph. Schmid and Schmid (1979) noted that in many cases several graphic forms are acceptable and that the final decision is a matter of preference. Because they and other authors, such as Spear (1969), Tufte (1983), and Tukey (1977), devoted whole volumes to describing the various types of graphs that can be used, the reader is referred to those works. Space precludes the use of more than a sample of the common types of graphs in this chapter.

THE MEANING OF THE DATA

As was pointed out earlier, data are multidimensional. For this reason, a single graph is unlikely to be able to tell all that there is to be told about a set of data. The purpose of a graph is to tell a story that emphasizes important relationships in the data. Although it should present the data fairly, by its very nature, it cannot be neutral. Figures 6.9 to 6.14 illustrate how several relationships may exist in the same data set and how the careful selection of a graphic form will emphasize certain data. Figure 6.9 shows the original graph. Figure 6.10 clearly indicates the marked impact that education has on both men's and women's wages, whereas Figure 6.9 does not emphasize this relationship. If one is interested in the relative difference in men's and women's wages, a percentage graph may be a better way to show the differences. Figure 6.11 shows that relationship.

Another way to look at the data is to ask, What do the differences in wages mean in the amount of money women earn over a certain period? A cumulative graph makes it easy to see the differences over time. Figure 6.12 shows that over 10 years, men, on average, earned almost $50,000 more than did women. The amount can be read directly on the graph.

One may also be interested in the rates of changes in men's and women's wages. Figures 6.13 and 6.14 make these relationships

127

FIGURE 6.9 Original income data and illustration of chart junk

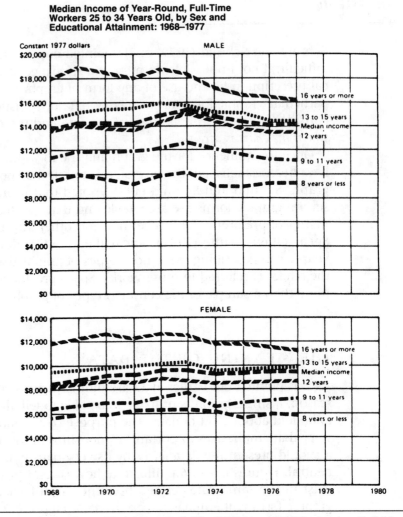

Median Income of Year-Round, Full-Time
Workers 25 to 34 Years Old, by Sex and
Educational Attainment: 1968–1977

clearer. Figure 6.13 is a log-linear graph of the yearly wages. It shows that the rates of change in women's and men's wages remained relatively constant for the 10-year period.

Figure 6.14 is a log-linear graph of cumulative wages. It not only shows that the rates of change in men's and women's wages paralleled each other, but that the rate of pay increase decreased over the 10-year period. A constant rate of increase would have shown up as a straight line. What apparently happened is that rather than both sexes receiving standard percentage increases each year, both sexes received nearly constant-dollar increases each

FIGURE 6.10 Illustration of how regraphing data emphasizes the impact of education on wages

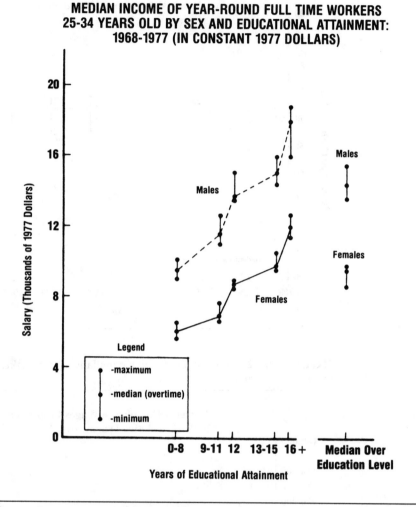

MEDIAN INCOME OF YEAR-ROUND FULL TIME WORKERS
25-34 YEARS OLD BY SEX AND EDUCATIONAL ATTAINMENT:
1968-1977 (IN CONSTANT 1977 DOLLARS)

SOURCE: From "How to Display Data Badly" by H. Wainer, 1984, *The American Statistician, 38,* Figure 16, p. 142. Copyright © 1984 by the American Statistical Association. Reprinted with permission. All rights reserved.

year. For more information on the interpretation of log-linear and linear graphs, see Schmid and Schmid (1979, p. 100).

Taken together, the five graphs (Figures 6.10 to 6.14) provide a wealth of data that are not apparent in the original graph. Some relationships may not be apparent until they are graphed. For example, the drop-off in the rate of increase was not clear until I graphed Figure 6.14, although a careful viewing of Figure 6.12 should have made the relationship apparent.

Figure 6.10 shows two important relationships that were obscured in the original graph: (1) the relationship of education to

FIGURE 6.11 Illustration of how a percentage graph shows differences

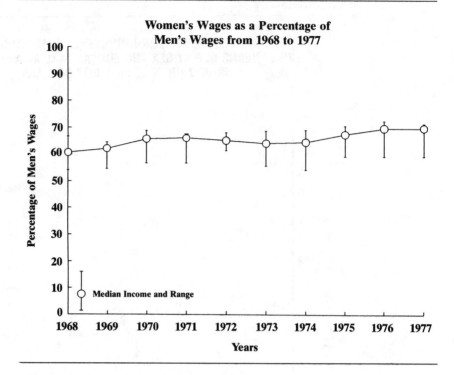

FIGURE 6.12 Illustration of how a cumulative graph makes it easy to see differences over time

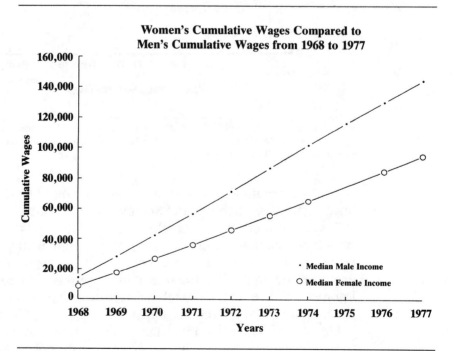

FIGURE 6.13 Illustration of a log-linear graph showing the rate of change in men's and women's wages

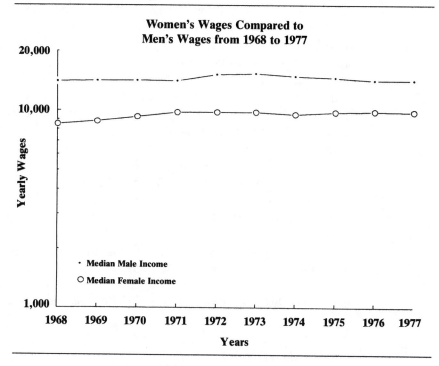

Women's Wages Compared to Men's Wages from 1968 to 1977

FIGURE 6.14 Illustration of a log-linear graph showing how rates of pay increases decreased over a 10-year period

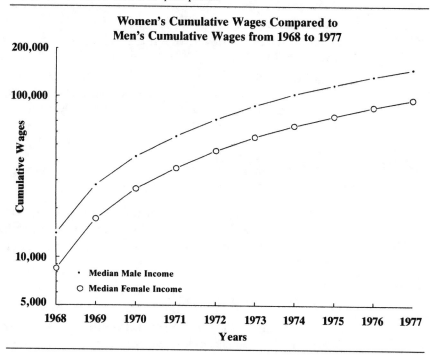

Women's Cumulative Wages Compared to Men's Cumulative Wages from 1968 to 1977

income and (2) the differences in income levels by gender (which were not emphasized in Figure 6.9). Figure 6.11, however, is better at showing the viewer the change in the income levels (in constant 1977 dollars) over a nine-year period. Figure 6.9 gives the viewer no information on this issue. The point is that different relationships will be important depending on the nature of the analysis, and the author should draw the graph to emphasize the important relationships. In the foregoing example, if the buying power of full-time workers is the issue, then Figure 6.14 gives a better picture of the data. If, on the other hand, the important issue is the impact of education and gender of the wage earner on income, then Figure 6.10 illustrates the relationships much more clearly.

Figure 6.15 shows how a graph can be used to communicate effectively meaning that may be lost in a table. The chart is not exemplary in other ways that will be discussed later. In spite of its shortcomings, it is an innovative way to depict a person's life experiences graphically. It certainly has much more visual impact than does a simple time line, which would give no indication of the magnitude of the person's negative and positive experiences. It is probably better than a bar graph in depicting the same information.

THE AUDIENCE

Audiences vary in their ability to understand graphs. Most professionals understand linear graphs, but many may not understand log-linear graphs. Therefore, one should use log-linear graphs carefully and provide an explanation of how to understand them. There are cases, however, when they are the best type of graph for showing relationships. Similar cautions should be observed in using area graphs. The major problem with area graphs is that the unsophisticated viewer may focus on the size of an area on the graph, rather than on the value attached to that area.

emphasizing data

Several factors contribute to a graph's ability to emphasize data. They include the density of the data, the data–ink ratio, shading and cross-hatching, clear graphic presentation, and complete captioning and labeling.

DENSITY OF THE DATA

Tufte (1983, p. 162) devised several methods for evaluating graphs. One is the data density index, whose formula is as follows (p. 134):

FIGURE 6.15 Illustration of a time line showing the magnitude and time relationships of life events and demonstrating lack of horizontal scale and labels

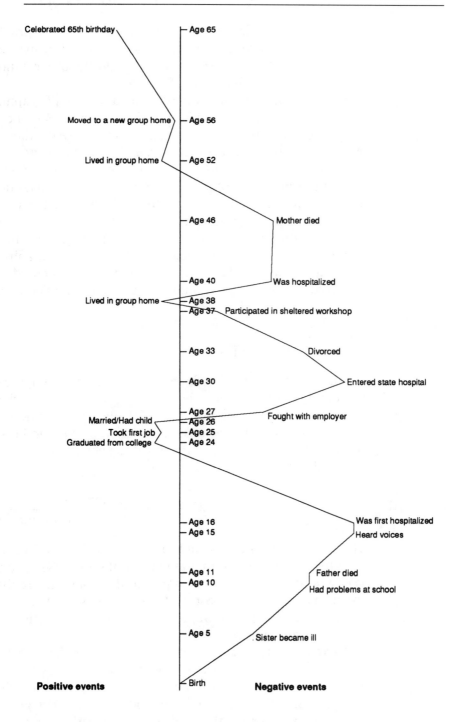

SOURCE: From "The Use of Time Lines and Life Lines in Work with Chronically Mentally Ill People" by J. Quam & N. Abramson, 1991, *Health and Social Work, 16,* Figure 4, p. 32.

$$\text{data density of a graphic} = \frac{\text{number of entries in data matrix}}{\text{total area of graphic}}$$

High data–ink densities do not guarantee that the graphics are excellent or even good (Wainer, 1984); indeed, they may sometimes make it difficult to interpret the data. On the other hand, low densities are rarely effective.

Tufte (1983, p. 74) measured the data density of graphics published in several scientific journals in 1979 and 1980. The median densities varied from 7.44 data points per square centimeter (in *Nature*) to about 1.08 (in the *Journal of the American Medical Association*) to 0.77 (in *Scientific American*). Nine graphs selected at random from several social work journals had low data densities; they had median data density values of approximately 0.28 data points per square centimeter and ranged from 0.82 data points per square centimeter to about 0.07 points per square centimeter. These low densities were due, in large part, to the graphs having large areas but few data points. Higher densities could have been achieved through using graphics that covered smaller areas.

DATA–INK RATIO

As Tufte (1983) noted, "A large share of ink on a graphic should present data information, the ink changing as the data change. Data ink is the non-erasable core of the graphic, the non-redundant ink arranged in response to variation in the numbers represented" (p. 93). Tufte used the following equation to compute the data–ink ratio:

$$\text{Data–ink ratio} = \frac{\text{data ink}}{\text{total ink used to print graphic}}$$

The formula may be difficult to use because it is difficult to measure the amount of ink in a graph, but the underlying concept is easy to understand and is important in designing graphs. If the data are hidden or obscured or deemphasized because of the amount of nondata ink, the graph does not effectively communicate information.

There are many ways to increase the ratio of data ink to nondata ink. Figure 6.16 is a typical segmented bar graph. A few modifications of the graph increase the data–ink ratio and make it more readable (see Figure 6.25 for the modifications). The graph was modified by removing the vertical bars and substituting simple lines with a dot at the top. Tufte (1983, pp. 123–137) gave several other suggestions for increasing the data–ink ratio of graphs.

FIGURE 6.16 Illustration of difficulty reading a stacked-column graph

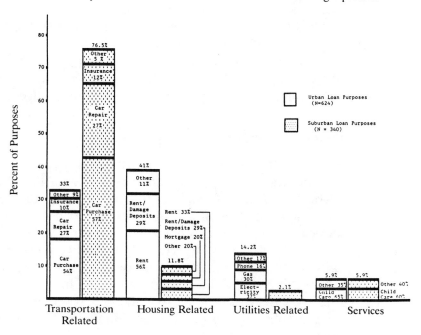

Purposes of interest-free loans to low-income single parents

SOURCE: From "Working, Still Poor: A Loan Program's Role in the Lives of Low-Income Single Parents" by L. Jones & E. Wattenberg, 1991, *Social Work, 36*, Figure 1, p. 149.

SHADING AND CROSS-HATCHING

Tufte (1983, pp. 108–122) also cautioned about using "chart junk," nondata ink that does not add to the viewer's understanding of the graph. Typical examples are over-busy grid lines; excessive ticks; redundant representation of the simplest data; and the excessive use of complicated forms, such as cross-hatching, to report different types of data. This problem and the problem of using multicolored inks have been exacerbated by the recent introduction of computerized graphics programs that often make extensive use of chart junk. Figure 6.9 contains examples of typical chart junk: an excessive grid structure and the use of complicated line forms that obscure the data points.

CLEAR GRAPHIC PRESENTATION

The clarity of a graph depends on several factors: clear and precise typefaces and symbols, readable typefaces, minimal use of color, and complete captioning and labeling.

Clear and Precise Typefaces and Symbols

Most graphs are reduced in size by journal publishers. Therefore, sharp, clear typefaces for the text and symbols are essential, so the text and symbols are readable when they are reduced in size. With the advent of copy machines that can reduce the size of images, there is little reason for graphics to contain problems of this nature because authors can readily determine if the text and symbols of their graphs will still be legible after they are reduced to size.

Readable Type

Publishers have known for years that certain typefaces are more readable and more appealing than are others. Tufte (1983) advocated the use of typefaces that include lowercase letters and serifs (short lines stemming from and at an angle to the upper and lower ends of the strokes of a letter (*Webster's Ninth New Collegiate Dictionary*, 1985, p. 1075). The graphs that were prepared specifically for this chapter follow the convention suggested by Tufte. When compared to the graphs reproduced from other sources, they are clearly more appealing and probably more readable (see, for example, Figures 6.11 through 6.14, which were specially prepared for this chapter).

Minimal Use of Color

Tufte (1983, p. 183) pointed out that 5 to 10 percent of the population are color blind. In addition, most professional journals and books are printed only in black and white, because color printing is expensive. For these reasons multicolored graphs should be avoided.

Complete Captioning and Labeling

Common problems in interpreting graphs also arise from the lack of attention to titles, labels for axes, legends, explanatory notes, and other labels on graphs. The title of a graph is an effective method of telling the reader the topic of the graph. Titles should answer "three basic questions: What? Where? When?" (Schmid & Schmid, 1979, p. 32). Titles are normally placed below the graph. Axes labels are used to label the horizontal and vertical axes of a graph. Legends are designed to help the reader discriminate between two or more data sets drawn on a common set of axes. They tell the reader what each plot of a data set represents and how to identify the data set. Explanatory notes, which are usually placed below the graph, describe the relationships shown in the graph. They are often used as substitutes for or included with proper titles, labels, and legends. This practice is unfortunate. Accurate titles and labels are essential. Inadequate titles and labels cannot be replaced by explanatory notes.

Problems involving captions and labeling are common in scientific journals and abounded in the graphs I reviewed. Many of the graphs displayed were not properly labeled or captioned. Representative examples are Figures 6.15, 6.17, and 6.18. Figure 6.15 lacks a horizontal scale and labels. Figure 6.17 (p. 138) has no vertical axis labels. Figure 6.18 (p. 139) uses textual abbreviations. The reader is left wondering what LOS (length of stay) and IHP (interim home care program) mean. The result is that each group is difficult to interpret.

accurate presentation of data

Thus far the discussion of graphic excellence has focused on issues that may best be described as matters of mechanical construction. Although these issues are important, graphs that meet all these criteria can still present data ineffectively. In the following sections, several issues that affect the interpretability of graphs are presented.

EMPHASIZING IMPORTANT RELATIONSHIPS AND NATURAL RELATIONSHIPS

A common problem with graphs is that the author's selection of which relationships to graph can significantly alter the reader's interpretation of the graph. Excellent examples are Figures 6.9 through 6.14.

Another common problem with graphs is that data are not presented in their natural sequence (or real time). As Johnston and Pennypacker (1980) pointed out,

> A "totally unjustified practice consists of putting discontinuance or inequality in the representation of time. . . ." Such dimensions as "sessions," "trials," and "blocks" must necessarily occur serially in real time, yet the tacit assumption is often encouraged that variations in real time intervals separating successive occurrences are of no importance in interpreting the nature of any observed variation. Though usually unintentional, presentation of such a display is tantamount to an act of almost unpardonable experimental grandiosity; for it implies that any time dependent influences that could have been operating were either of such negligible consequence or so well controlled that no loss in interpretation could result from distortion of

FIGURE 6.17   Illustration of truncated vertical axis

Client Satisfaction with Worker Helpfulness

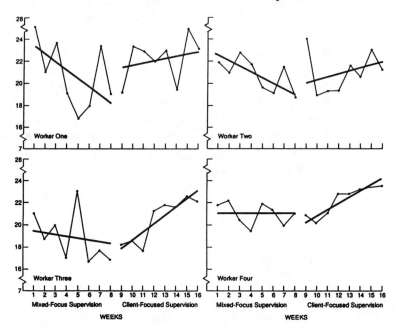

Generalized Contentment of Clients

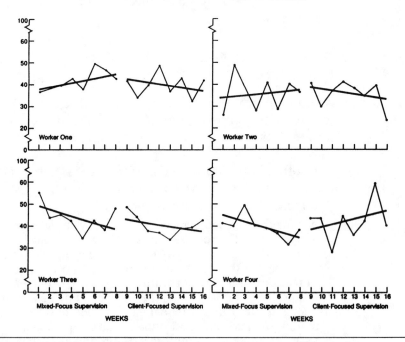

SOURCE: From "Changing the Focus of Social Work Supervision: Effects on Client Satisfaction and Generalized Contentment" by D. Harkness & H. Hensley, 1991, *Social Work*, *36*, Figure 1, p. 508, and Figure 2, p. 509.

FIGURE 6.18   Illustration of inadequate captioning

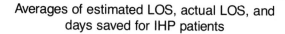

Averages of estimated LOS, actual LOS, and
days saved for IHP patients

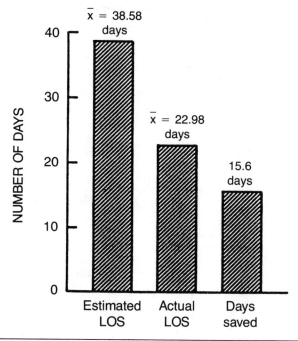

SOURCE: From "The Interim Homecare Program: An Innovative Discharge Planning Alternative" by P. Schwartz, S. Blumenfield, & E. Simon, 1990, *Health and Social Work*, 15, Figure 1, p. 157.

the represented time dimension. . . . In the event the viewer is a member of the scientific community who has no other access to the data, this practice may properly be viewed as highly misleading if not actually deceptive. (pp. 340–341)

An equally serious problem is altering the scaling of the axes at some point on the plot. The federal government produces many graphs that have this problem. Figure 6.19 (p. 140), for example, has four different scales on the horizontal axis. Participation rates for 16- and 17-year-olds and for 18- and 19-year-olds are in two-year increments. Those for 20- to 24-year-olds are in five-year increments, and those for 25- to 65-year-olds are in 10-year increments. The final increment, for those over 65, is left undefined, but presumably ranges from 65 to over 100 years. The graph cannot be redrawn because the data needed to redraw it are not presented, but it is clear that the shape of the distribution would be different if equal intervals were used on the horizontal axis.

Figure 6.20 is a dramatic example of the effect of changing the scale of a graph. In this case, the whole interpretation of the graph is completely altered by using the proper scaling on the *X* axis. A variation is to conserve space by truncating one of the axes, as was

FIGURE 6.19   Illustration of different scales on the horizontal axis

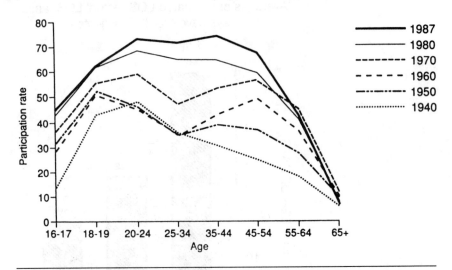

SOURCE: From "Women in the Labor Force: An Overview" by F. Blau & A. Winkler, 1989, in A. J. Freeman (Ed.), *Women* (4th ed., Figure 1, p. 271), Mountain View, CA: Mayfield. Copyright © 1989 by Mayfield. Reprinted by permission.

FIGURE 6.20   Illustration of the impact of using more than one scale on the horizontal axis

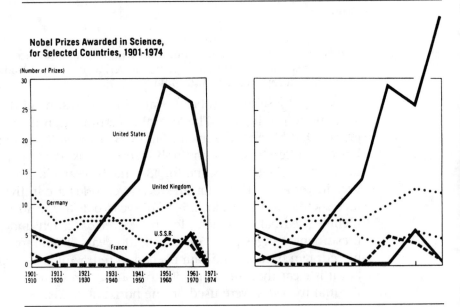

Nobel Prizes Awarded in Science, for Selected Countries, 1901-1974

SOURCE: From *The Visual Display of Quantitative Information* (p. 60) by E. Tufte, 1983, Cheshire, CT: Graphics Press. Copyright © 1983 by Graphics Press. Reprinted by permission.

done in Figure 6.17. The vertical axis on the first panel of graphs in Figure 6.17 starts at 7 and on the second panel, at 0. A casual reader may get the impression that clients' satisfaction with the workers' helpfulness and the clients' general contentment are similar when they are different. The reader may have noted that the vertical axes of Figures 6.13 and 6.14 do not start at 0. Logarithmic graphs have no zero point, so are usually started on a multiple of 10 (100, 1,000, and so on). Figure 6.14 violates this convention, but because the important comparison is between rates of change in the wages of men and women, starting the vertical axis at $5,000, instead of at $1,000, does not alter the graph's message.

Another common problem is the interruption of an axis with either two short parallel or wavy lines to show that the data presentation is not continuous. Cleveland (1984a, p. 270) referred to this practice as using "partial breaks" to indicate that there is a break in the continuity of the data presentation.

Partial breaks are generally used to show all data points on a single graph even though there were long periods between the initial data collection and the latter data points. Partial breaks tend to distort the data even when the same scale is used in both portions of the graph. "Visually the graph is still a single panel that invites the viewer to see, inappropriately, patterns between the two scales" (Cleveland, 1984a, p. 270). Figure 6.21 (p. 142) illustrates this problem.

The partial break invites viewers to connect points across the break even though no such connection is appropriate. Cleveland (1984a) stated that a better method of presentation is the "full scale break . . . [which] results in a graph with two juxtaposed panels . . . , each panel having a full frame and its own scales. . . . [This presentation of the data] shows the scale break about as forcefully as possible and discourages mental visual connections by viewers and actual connections by authors" (p. 270).

Figure 6.22 shows Figure 6.21 redrawn with full scale breaks. Figures 6.23 and 6.24 (pp. 143 and 144) illustrate how the use of political boundaries can distort the meaning of data. The use of areas in Figure 6.23 to represent federal expenditures implies that about half the total personal income in the country during 1963 went to cover federal expenditures, which is, of course, not true. Most western states cover huge areas and have low population densities, so the total personal income for these states is much smaller per unit of land area than is the income for the northeastern states, which have much smaller land areas and much higher population densities. Figure 6.24 shows the same data using those states. The visual impact is obviously different from that of Figure 6.23. The point is that land area is not the important relationship

FIGURE 6.21 Illustration of improper use of breaks in the horizontal axis and of lack of title

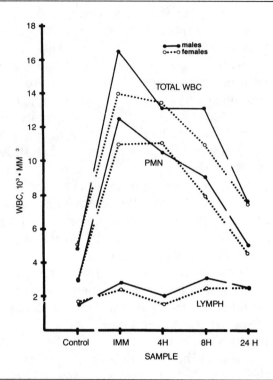

SOURCE: From "Hematological Changes Following a Marathon Race in Male and Female Runners" by C. Wells, J. Stern, & L. Hecht, 1982, *European Journal of Applied Physiology and Occupational Physiology, 48,* Figure 2, p. 45. Copyright © 1982 by Springer-Verlag. Reprinted by permission.

FIGURE 6.22 Illustration of proper plotting of discontinuous data.
NOTE: WBC = white blood cell count; PMN = polymorphonuclear cell count; Lymph = lymphocyte count.

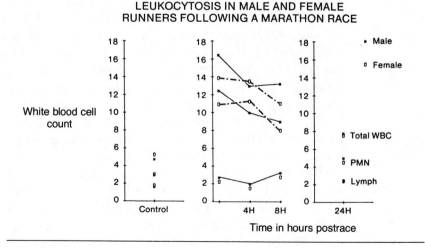

FIGURE 6.23 Illustration of problem of using area to represent magnitude. This figure overstates the amount of personal income needed to meet federal expenditures.

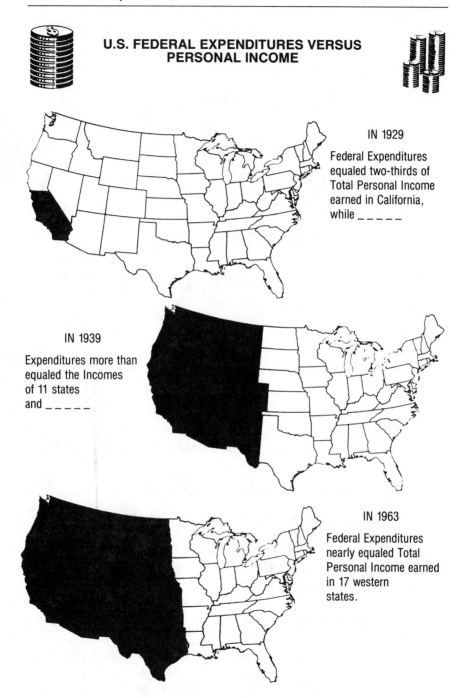

U.S. FEDERAL EXPENDITURES VERSUS
PERSONAL INCOME

IN 1929

Federal Expenditures equaled two-thirds of Total Personal Income earned in California, while _ _ _ _ _

IN 1939

Expenditures more than equaled the Incomes of 11 states and _ _ _ _ _

IN 1963

Federal Expenditures nearly equaled Total Personal Income earned in 17 western states.

SOURCE: U.S. Treasury Department and U.S. Department of Commerce.

FIGURE 6.24 Illustration of problem of using area to represent magnitude. This figure understates the amount of personal income needed to meet federal expenditures.

U.S. FEDERAL EXPENDITURES IN 1963
Equaled the Total Personal Income received by individuals
in these Northeastern States, plus the District of Columbia

SOURCE: U.S. Department of Commerce and U.S. Treasury Department.

in these data. A simple line graph would have presented a more accurate picture of the changes in federal expenditures over time.

SHOWING DATA IN CONTEXT

Another common problem of poor graphs arises from presenting the data out of context. Context refers to the data that precede or follow the research period. If the research data are presented in isolation, the viewer may make erroneous assumptions about trends in the pre- and postresearch periods. For valid comparisons to be made, the data before and after the experimental period must be shown. Figure 6.22 illustrates the proper procedure—both a preintervention period and a postintervention period are shown— although even longer periods would have been preferable.

The problem of showing data out of context is pervasive and serious. Tufte (1983) noted that the presentation of data out of context can lead to serious misinterpretations. He wrote, "To be truthful and revealing, data graphics must bear on the question at the heart of the quantitative thinking: 'Compared to what?'

The emaciated, data-thin design should always provoke suspicion, for graphics often lie by omission, leaving out data sufficient for comparisons'' (p. 74).

MINIMIZING PERCEPTUAL ERRORS

Technically correct graphs can sometimes be misinterpreted because of errors introduced by the viewer's perceptual system. Cleveland (1985) and Cleveland and McGill (1984) presented detailed discussions of these issues. Their major points were these:

1. The eye is responsive to area as well as shading. For example, the viewer's attention in Figure 6.2 is drawn not only to the black sections of the map, but to those sections that have larger cross-sectional areas. Thus, attention is much more likely to focus on the county in the north-central United States identified by the arrow labeled A than on the county identified with the arrow labeled B. Both counties, however, have cancer rates in the highest decile.

2. In addition to problems judging shading and area, humans also have difficulty judging volume, curvature, the length of lines, and the direction and angle of a line (Cleveland, 1985; Cleveland & McGill, 1984). Several of the graphs reviewed for this chapter contain perceptual problems. Typical examples are used in what follows to illustrate some of the more common problems encountered in various journals.

Figure 6.16 illustrates a common problem—the comparison of line lengths on a stacked column graph. Stacked column graphs are common in scientific journals. "This graphical method requires length judgment" (Cleveland & McGill, 1984, p. 545). The comparison of lengths is confounded by the fact that only the bottom segments in each column have a common baseline reference point on the Y axis. An alternative would be to present the data as a pie chart because, as Cleveland and McGill pointed out, a column chart can always be replaced by a pie chart. However, the estimation of angle and area required to interpret pie charts is as difficult as it is in the stacked column chart. Thus, Cleveland and McGill concluded that "neither form should be used since other methods are demonstratively better" (p. 545).

One possible way to improve this type of graph is to use a grouped-column chart. The advantage of the grouped-column chart is that the length of the bars can now be judged along a common scale. Cleveland (1984a) recommended still another alternative: the dot chart (see Figure 6.25 on p. 146). The dot chart requires less data ink and is easier to draw and to interpret than is the equivalent grouped-column chart.

FIGURE 6.25   Illustration of a dot chart

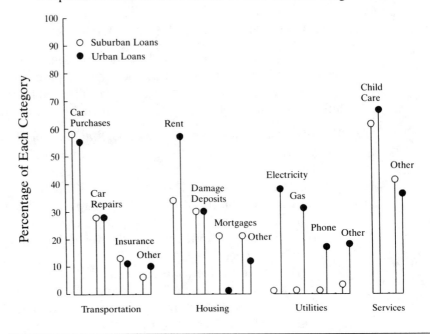

Figure 6.25 does not show the percentages of the total money loaned. A second graph with only the total would be best for presenting those relationships. Figure 6.16 included those totals, but the relationships shown in Figure 6.25 are not easily compared in Figure 6.16. So, two graphs are better for showing the multiple relationships in the data.

Other common problems involve judgments about the slope and the vertical differences between curves. Cleveland and McGill (1984) pointed out that humans tend to respond to the angle between lines rather than to the slopes of lines. Figure 6.26 clearly illustrates this problem. As Cleveland and McGill explained in relation to this figure,

> The elementary task in extracting curve differences is length. It turns out that making such length judgments is inaccurate and even more difficult than the divided bar chart. It is almost impossible to get even a rough idea of the behavior of the differences of the curves of the nine panels [on the left]. The problem is that the brain wants to judge minimum distance between the curves in different regions, and not vertical distance. Thus in each panel . . . , one tends to see the curves getting closer together going from left to right. The actual vertical differences are plotted [in the right panels of Figure 6.26]. . . . It is clear that [the left panels of Figure 6.26] have not conveyed even the grossest qualitative measure of the differences. (p. 548)

FIGURE 6.26 Illustration of difficulty in judging slopes

A: Curve difference charts

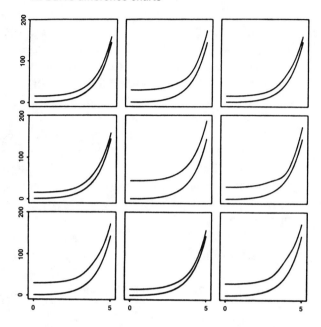

B: Actual curve differences in Figure 6.26A

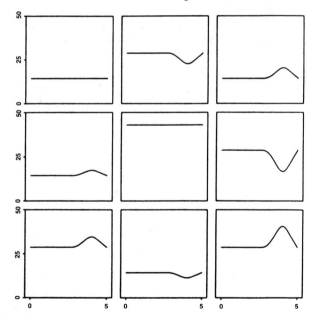

Vrancianu et al. (1982, p. 16) offered a different and innovative approach to the problem of evaluating slopes. They attempted to deal with the perception of differences in slopes by visually showing these differences at several points on the curves. This solution is certainly better than presenting the curves without data on slopes, but Cleveland and McGill's approach may still be preferable because it plots the differences directly, which eliminates the perceptual problems associated with interpreting differences in curves.

Humans are much better at comparing lengths of lines than they are at comparing areas or volumes. Figure 6.27 illustrates this problem. It is easy to tell that the length of one column is one-quarter the length of the other. But most people would not make the correct judgment in comparing the areas or the volumes in the figure. The smaller figures have one-quarter the area or one-quarter the volume of the larger figures, yet many people would guess that the smaller figures contain half the area or volume of the bigger objects.

FIGURE 6.27   Illustration of the difficulty judging area and volume

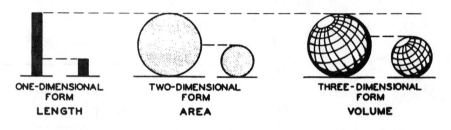

SOURCE: From *Handbook of Graphic Presentation* (2nd ed., Figure 4-1, p. 62) by C. Schmid & S. Schmid, 1979, New York: John Wiley & Sons. Copyright © 1979 by John Wiley & Sons. Reprinted by permission of John Wiley & Sons, Inc.

conclusion

The aim of this chapter has been to show the power of graphic presentations and to pinpoint a number of factors that contribute to graphic excellence. The rules and conventions discussed represent a brief overview of a complex subject. Nevertheless, if followed, the quality of published graphs in social work journals should noticeably improve.

references

American Society of Mechanical Engineers. (1960). *American standard time-series charts.* New York: Author.

Bashaw, W. (1969). *Mathematics for statistics.* New York: John Wiley & Sons.

Blau, F., & Winkler, A. (1989). Women in the labor force: An overview. In A. J. Freeman (Ed.), *Women* (4th ed., pp. 265–283). Mountain View, CA: Mayfield.

Brinton, W. (1914). *Graphic methods for presenting facts.* New York: Author.

Chambers, J., Cleveland, W., Kleiner, B., & Tukey, P. (1983). *Graphical methods for data analysis.* Belmont, CA: Wadsworth.

Cleveland, W. (1984a). Graphical methods for data presentation: Full scale breaks, dot charts, and multibased logging. *American Statistician, 38,* 270–280.

Cleveland, W. (1984b). Graphs in scientific publications. *American Statistician, 38,* 261–269.

Cleveland, W. (1985). *The elements of graphing data.* Belmont, CA: Wadsworth.

Cleveland, W., & McGill, R. (1984). Graphical perception: Theory, experimentation, and application to the development of graphical methods. *Journal of the American Statistical Association, 79,* 531–554.

Conant, J. (1951). *On understanding science: An historical approach.* New York: New American Library.

Council of Biology Editors. (1988). *Illustrating science.* Bethesda, MD: Author.

Harkness, D., & Hensley, H. (1991). Changing the focus of social work supervision: Effects on client satisfaction and generalized contentment. *Social Work, 36,* 506–512.

Johnston, J., & Pennypacker, H. (1980). *Strategies and tactics of human behavioral research.* Hillsdale, NJ: Lawrence Erlbaum Associates.

Jones, L., & Wattenberg, E. (1991). Working, still poor: A loan program's role in the lives of low-income single parents. *Social Work, 36,* 146–153.

Quam, J., & Abramson, N. (1991). The use of time lines and life lines in work with chronically mentally ill people. *Health and Social Work, 16,* 27–32.

Schmid, C., & Schmid, S. (1979). *Handbook of graphic presentation* (2nd ed.). New York: John Wiley & Sons.

Schwartz, P., Blumenfield, S., & Simon, E. (1990). The interim homecare program: An innovative discharge planning alternative. *Health and Social Work, 15,* 152–159.

Seltzer, J. (1991). Legal custody arrangements and children's economic welfare. *American Journal of Sociology, 96,* 895–929.

Spear, M. (1969). *Practical charting techniques.* New York: McGraw-Hill.

Tufte, E. (1983). *The visual display of quantitative information.* Cheshire, CT: Graphics Press.

Tukey, J. (1977). *Exploratory data analysis.* Reading, MA: Addison-Wesley.

U.S. Army. (1966). *Standards of statistical presentation.* Washington, DC: U.S. Government Printing Office.

Vrancianu, R., Filcescu, V., Ionescu, V., Groza, P., Persson, J., Kadefors, R., & Petersen, I. (1982). The influence of day and night work on the circadian variations of cardiovascular performance. *European Journal of Applied Physiology and Occupational Physiology, 48,* 399–405.

Wainer, H. (1984). How to display data badly. *American Statistician, 38,* 137–147.

Webster's ninth new collegiate dictionary. (1985). Springfield, MA: Merriam-Webster.

Wells, C., Stern, J., & Hecht, L. (1982). Hematological changes following a marathon race in male and female runners. *European Journal of Applied Physiology and Occupational Physiology, 48,* 41–49.

Zeisel, H. (1968). *Say it with figures.* New York: Harper & Row.

PART **II**

preparation

for publication

7 *peer review*

Linda Beebe

Scholarly and professional publications evolve as a result of discussion, review, and commentary from professionals in the same or related fields. The colleague who comments on the draft of a paper at an author's request and the journal reader who fires off an excoriating rejoinder to a published article are both participating in a form of peer review. Each is assisting in the development of knowledge. However, the term *peer review* generally is used to describe the formal review process that determines whether an article will be published in a professional journal. Although book publishers also use expert referees, the process differs substantially from the one used for journals. (See chapter 9, "Book Proposals," in this volume for more information on that process.) A similar process is used to evaluate grant proposals.

Around the middle of the 18th century, the societies that were publishing the major scientific journals, such as the Royal Society of London and the Academie Royale de Medecine, began to develop mechanisms for selecting what they would publish from the many submissions they received. Then, as now, organizations were most concerned that the journals published under their names would be seen as highly credible; consequently, they developed elaborate screening systems that are still recognizable in 20th-century practices.

Over the past 250 years or so, peer review has been assailed for bias, other breaches of ethics, delays in publishing important scientific information, and other crimes against society in general and against authors in particular. Nonetheless, peer review remains the route to publication for almost all scholarly writing; therefore, it behooves the author who wishes to be published to be aware of the philosophy, mechanics, and idiosyncrasies involved. This chapter provides a brief lesson in peer review practices.

purposes of peer review

Reduced to its barest definition, peer review is simply a gatekeeping function. The author's peers, called referees or reviewers, are asked to comment on the originality and significance of the author's work and to advise the editor whether the work should or should not be published. This gatekeeping function has stirred many authors to suggest that knowledge would be better served if there were no gatekeepers. Bishop (1984) offered one of the best responses to the "down with peer review" cry:

> The argument goes that new ideas and information could be published without delay and that science would therefore advance more quickly. Editors would accept anything that was readable, and the scientific community at large would sort out the wheat from the chaff after publication. The problem is that such a system would yield too much chaff. The proponents of unrestricted access to publication have failed to distinguish between the formal and informal systems of communication in science. They have the well-meant but misguided concept that the success of the free and easy exchanges in generating new ideas at meetings can be carried over into the literature. However, this concept overlooks the absolute necessity for scientific progress, that somehow, somewhere, there has to be a reliable record. Unrestricted publication would turn the scientific literature into a meaningless jumble in which nobody could find the significant papers. (p. 43)

From a practical as well as a scientific standpoint, it is not possible to publish all the manuscripts authors write. Much of what is written repeats, often exactly, what has been written before. Many papers are grievously flawed and could cause serious harm if practitioners were to use the information. If we were to publish every manuscript we receive, *Social Work* would be around 5,000 pages a year instead of about 600. Who could justify cutting down trees to publish enormous journals that people would not read?

Peer review, as it is practiced today, is intended not just to select those few manuscripts that will be published and to keep the seriously flawed conclusions out of the literature, but to help authors. One form of help—preventing seriously flawed work from being published—may not always be welcomed, but almost all journals also ask their reviewers to offer constructive critiques that will help authors improve their work. Although not all reviewers provide useful critiques, the majority try to write thorough and helpful comments. It is not unusual to see a full single-spaced page of comments and occasionally several pages. The value of reviewers' comments, however, should not be measured by their length.

One pithy paragraph can be as useful as a much longer review. Wise authors make good use of reviewers' comments no matter what length they are.

the peer reviewers

Although journals vary in the way they select reviewers, they generally have the same expectations. Reviewers or referees are unpaid volunteers and must be experts in the field and published authors. Generally, reviewers are distinguished from editors. The editor is the person who decides what will be published and what will not; his or her decisions are guided by the recommendations of the author's peers. Therefore, a journal usually is said to be peer reviewed only if reviewers in addition to the editor read and evaluate the manuscripts.

The rise of specialty journals in the 19th century changed the definition of a peer from a professional in the same field to one who is expert in a narrower segment of the field or even a specific approach or technique. Consequently, an administrative journal selects reviewers who are experts in management; a health journal, experts in health; and a research journal, experts in research. But they also segment further. For example, a health journal will look for specialists in aging, substance abuse, AIDS, and so forth. Editors generally try to have a mix of reviewers with knowledge of various methods, practice skills, and academic experience. Association publishers, like the NASW Press, often have policies that require a strong attempt to strive for balance in ethnicity, gender, and geographic location.

TYPES OF REVIEWERS

Most journals have editorial boards whose members generally serve as the first line of reviewers and participate in setting policy for the journals. A few journals have nonworking editorial boards that were selected for the prestige the members' names would bring to them, rather than for the impact their work would have on the quality of the journals, but authors generally can assume that the editorial board members listed on the masthead of a journal actually review manuscripts.

Some journals also use consulting editors or reviewers. These experts read and rate manuscripts but do not participate in setting policy. NASW Press journals generally have more consulting editors than editorial board members to maintain a pool of reviewers that is large enough to review manuscripts in a timely manner and to cover the areas of expertise that are required. These regular reviewers are also listed on the mastheads of the journals. In addition, editors occasionally receive manuscripts that are outside the expertise of all the reviewers in the regular pool of reviewers, and they will ask other experts to review and rate these manuscripts. Most journals follow the practice of acknowledging these experts once or twice a year.

SELECTION AND TERMS

How reviewers are selected and how long they serve varies significantly from journal to journal. Presidents of associations usually appoint their journal editors and editorial board members for set terms of office. For NASW Press journals, editors serve four-year terms, and members of editorial boards serve three-year terms. The editors, in turn, select consulting editors to fill the gaps in expertise. For journals that are not connected to associations, the editors generally appoint the reviewers, who may serve for a year or for upwards of 25 years. Neither system necessarily is better or worse. Either system is open to new reviewers, who, it is hoped, will bring a fresh perspective to the process of determining what will be published in the professional literature.

EXPECTATIONS OF REVIEWERS

The expectations set for reviewers are strenuous. The NASW Press tells reviewers that they should expect to receive two to five manuscripts a month and that they should return those manuscripts within three weeks, with clear, cogent, and constructive comments to the authors. As published authors, the reviewers are expected to understand the feelings of the authors who submitted the papers and to do everything they can to speed up the process. (See Figure 7.1 for NASW procedures for reviewing manuscripts.)

Reviewers are expected, to the best of their ability, to provide unbiased recommendations. If a reviewer recognizes an author, he or she is expected to withdraw from the evaluation of the manuscript. Whether a reviewer agrees with conclusions stated in the manuscript or the author's point of view should be immaterial. Most editors set forth the expectation that reviewers will offer constructive criticism. When reviewers do not provide usable comments, most editors feel compelled to write another critique so that the author will receive constructive comments.

Significant ethical issues accompany the invitation to serve as a reviewer for a scholarly journal. First, there is the issue of confidentiality. Most journals require that reviewers pledge to keep all reviews totally confidential. Reviewers are asked not to discuss the

FIGURE 7.1   Procedures for Reviewing Manuscripts for NASW Journals

1. Deadlines

Generally, the due date on your rating sheets will give you a three-week turnaround time. Occasionally—most often because another reviewer has not returned a review—you will receive a request for a "rush" review.

Please return your reviews as promptly as possible. We aim to notify authors of a decision within three months, and their manuscripts must go through many hands before the editor-in-chief makes a decision.

2. Changes in Your Schedule

Please notify the NASW Press if your schedule changes and you cannot return the manuscripts you have within a reasonable time. We can then reassign them so that the author does not have an inordinately long wait. If, for some reason, you will not be able to review manuscripts for a short period of time, let us know so we do not mail packages to you. Also, please let us know if your address changes.

We have a limited number of editors and consulting editors; therefore, we count on all of them to fulfill their obligations to review manuscripts. For a brief period, we can prevail on other hard-working reviewers to pick up the work. For the longer term, however, we expect each reviewer to complete a sufficient number of reviews in a timely manner.

3. Rating Manuscripts

See the sample rating sheet and reviewers' checklist for tips on completing the review.

4. Confidentiality

The NASW Press practices strict adherence to anonymous peer review. Neither the reviewer nor the editor-in-chief is told authors' identities, and authors are not told who (other than the editor-in-chief) reviewed their manuscripts.

▶ If you are familiar with the work or recognize the author, please call the editorial office, and we will assign the manuscript to another reviewer.

▶ All reviews are confidential, and they are to be used only for selecting articles for the journal to which they were submitted. They should not be used for selecting course materials, articles for another journal or a collected work, or references for a reviewer's work.

▶ Manuscripts should not be shared or discussed with anyone who is not a reviewer for the journal.

5. Returning Reviews/Manuscripts

You will receive a #10 business reply paid envelope to use in returning your reviews. Please **DESTROY** all manuscripts as soon as you have completed the review and send only the rating sheets back to the office. You may want to retain a copy of the rating sheet just in case the U.S. mail service fails us.

NASW PRESS 9/92

subject matter with colleagues or to reveal any knowledge of a manuscript before the announcement of its acceptance.

Second, reviewers are expected to maintain as objective a stance as possible. They are asked not to recommend rejecting an article on the basis of a personal or organizational bias. A particular point of view that is at odds with the reviewer's or the organization's principles should not be grounds for recommending rejection. Third, reviewers are expected to look at manuscripts only from the standpoint of recommending whether they should be published in that journal. Any other use of the manuscript is ethically considered to be the same as stealing. Incorporating portions into the reviewer's own writing, quoting from the work, or considering it for another publication is a serious breach of ethics.

different review processes

Journals vary widely in their review processes. On one end of the scale, the NASW Press journals maintain such strict anonymity that the editors never learn the identity of most authors and the authors never learn who besides the editors reviewed their papers. At the opposite end are journals that publish open reviews with the articles. In between there are various degrees of anonymity.

''DOUBLE-BLIND'' REVIEWS

In this process, neither the author nor the reviewer learns each other's identity. The author knows only that two or three of a pool of reviewers will rate the manuscript and make recommendations. Before the manuscript is sent to the reviewers, all information that would identify the author is removed. We carry the process even further at the NASW Press, where even the editor does not learn the author's identity during the process. When a manuscript appears on the accepted list, it is the first time the editor sees the author's name.

Many people have scoffed at the possibility of maintaining strict anonymity, and there have been protracted arguments against double-blind reviews in the biomedical fields, which generally do not practice them. Detractors argue that often an author is known to be an expert in the specialty, that knowing the author's expertise will provide greater confidence in the results, and that self-references will identify the author anyway. Authors frequently try to circumvent the process, bypassing the usual submission route or calling the editor directly about a manuscript. Hiding ''about the author'' blurbs and overt self-references in the middle of a manuscript are other favorite devices. In my experience, deliberate circumvention of the process annoys editors sufficiently that they are likely to be biased against, rather than for, an article; I highly recommend that authors honor the process.

The objective of this process is to eliminate as much bias as possible. How well it succeeds has never been conclusively proved. It can be said that reviewers identify authors much less frequently than one may assume. In one study, Rosenblatt and Kirk (1980) found that only 11 percent of 115 reviewers were able to identify the authors. Another study of a small general medicine journal found that 76 percent of the reviewers did not identify the authors (McNutt, Evans, Fletcher, & Fletcher, 1990). Although my experience is purely anecdotal, based on reading thousands of reviews and discussing dozens of papers with exceedingly knowledgeable editors, I think few authors are identified unless they simply tell who they are.

With the increased concern about fraud, it is likely that more journals will turn to double-blind reviews. The authors in the McNutt et al. (1990) study found that blind reviews increased the quality of the reviews significantly, and they suggested that the feasibility of continuing the process be studied further. At the First International Congress on Peer Review in Biomedical Publications, participants were nearly evenly split on the issue of whether reviews should be strictly anonymous: 46 percent said yes and 49 percent said no (Flanagin, Rennie, & Lundberg, 1991).

Double-blind reviews may not always guarantee strict anonymity; however, scrupulous attention to the effort reminds editors and reviewers of the need to guard against bias. Because diminishing bias protects the integrity of the literature and provides authors fair access to publication, I believe that the positive effects of double-blind reviews outweigh the inconveniences and occasional failures in the system.

ANONYMOUS REVIEWS

A quick scan of *An Author's Guide to Social Work Journals* (Mendelsohn, 1992) indicates that most of the 138 journals reviewed practice "anonymous" reviews. The term may mean that the author does not know the reviewers' identities, that the reviewers do not learn the author's identity, or that the editor does not learn the author's identity. Or it may mean that all three situations exist.

Nearly all journals, even those that disdain blind reviews, agree on the benefits of concealing the identity of the reviewers of a specific paper. With the specter of constant wrangling between reviewers and authors, editors fear that open reviews will lead to less critical reviews and a lack of reviewers who are willing to take on the job. Another dimension of anonymity is added when the reviewers do not learn the author's identity, and yet a third when the editor also does not know the author's name.

OPEN REVIEWS

By far the least common review process is an open one in which everyone involved knows who everyone else is. The open exchange between author and reviewer is intended to stimulate creative disagreement that will advance knowledge, and the process sometimes culminates in the publication of the original article and all the reviews. Some medical journals encourage their reviewers to sign the reviews that are sent to the author, and others use advisers whom the author has suggested be invited to review the work. Although open reviews have been used occasionally in the social sciences and frequently in the arts and literature, they are not the norm.

If you submit an article to a journal in the social sciences, you can expect not to learn who is reviewing it. Although I have no empirical data, my guess would be that more than half the journals will not tell the reviewers your name. Anonymity or the lack of it may not have any impact on how well your article is reviewed, but you should be aware of the potential anonymity so you do not unwittingly violate the protocols.

the mechanics

Before the manuscript reaches the reviewers or referees, it must go through some initial processing. Who does the processing varies from journal to journal. For many journals, the editor—sometimes with the assistance of an associate or administrative assistant—handles the work. For others that maintain complete anonymity—like the NASW Press—the staff handle all the initial processing, and the editor sees the manuscript only when the reviewers have made their recommendations. The basic process is the same, however.

PRELIMINARY REVIEW

This is intended not to be a substantive review of content, but a screening to identify obvious problems. The people who look at the manuscript ask several questions. Does the article fit the editorial scope of the journal? An article on the technical aspects of atomic waste management does not fit the scope of a journal that publishes articles for school social workers, for example. Second, does the submission meet the criteria for articles or columns in the journal? For example, NASW Press will return such submissions as a two-page rhetorical statement or a promotion of a specific product or service or a report of a meeting with a copy of our guidelines. Finally, we look at the manuscript itself. Did the author submit the appropriate number of copies? (We ask for five.) Is the manuscript double-spaced and legible with the pages in consecutive order? Is it the appropriate length? Editors have requested that we return all manuscripts that exceed 25 pages. Because the staff carry out this initial review, we screen out only those manuscripts that clearly do not meet our criteria, and two people must review the manuscript before it is sent back to the author. Very few manuscripts submitted are eliminated at this stage.

Some preliminary reviews are more extensive than are NASW's. The following statement from the guidelines of *Child Welfare* describes that journal's preliminary review: "CHILD WELFARE editors may prescreen manuscripts to eliminate extremely long or short articles, those where plagiarism or libel is suspected, those whose subject has been overdone, those that are overly similar to articles placed elsewhere by the author, and those otherwise unsuitable for CHILD WELFARE" (Child Welfare League of America, 1991).

RECORD KEEPING

The attention to detail that is required to produce high-quality professional books and journals starts when a manuscript arrives in the editor's or publisher's office. From that point, the person responsible must be able to tell exactly where the manuscript is in the process and what steps at what times it has gone through to get to that stage. Many publishers use some form of automated system to track the number of manuscripts in review, who is reviewing them, when the manuscripts arrived, what ratings have been received, and so forth. Each manuscript is assigned a control number and is logged into the system; then all the pertinent data are recorded in the automated system, as well as on a log sheet attached to the manuscript file.

ASSIGNING REVIEWERS

Most journals assign at least two reviewers to every manuscript. For all NASW Press journals except *Social Work*, three reviewers are assigned. Because we receive so many manuscripts for *Social Work*, only two reviewers read manuscripts submitted to that journal before the manuscripts go to the editor. We assign manuscripts on the basis of the reviewer reference profile that each reviewer completes before he or she begins work on a journal. In this profile, reviewers check off key words for areas in which they feel confident they can judge manuscripts. Their self-assessments, which occasionally are more encompassing than may be warranted, may be refined over time by the editor.

The second consideration in assigning manuscripts is how many manuscripts the prospective reviewer currently has. If the editor is attempting to maintain a fast turnaround time, it does no good to assign manuscripts to someone who already has five manuscripts waiting to be read. It is better to assign the new manuscript to someone who may be slightly less expert in the area, but more likely to be able to read the manuscript and provide constructive comments within an appropriate time frame.

what reviewers look for

Reviewers have three basic responsibilities: (1) to review a manuscript to determine if it should be published in that particular journal, (2) to explain their recommendations to the editor, and (3) to write constructive comments that will help the author understand the decision and improve his or her writing. Most professional journals provide reviewer guidelines. The reviewers use these guidelines to consider the merits of the manuscript, the quality of its presentation, and its suitability for the journal.

JOURNAL GUIDELINES

To make informed recommendations, reviewers need directions from the journal. First, they must know the purpose of the journal. The following mission statement sets forth the purpose of *Social Work:*

> *Social Work,* established in 1956, is a professional journal published by the NASW Press, a division of the National Association of Social Workers (NASW), and provided to all NASW members as a membership benefit. The journal is dedicated to improving practice and advancing knowledge in social work and social welfare. The editorial board welcomes manuscripts that yield new insights into established practices, evaluate new techniques and research, examine current social problems and social policies, or bring serious critical analysis to bear on problems in the profession. Literary articles that deal with issues of significance to social work also will be reviewed.

Many journals use a standard rating form that they expect their reviewers to complete as guidance to the editor. The rating sheet shown in Figure 7.2 is annotated for use in NASW's orientation

FIGURE 7.2   NASW Press Rating Sheet: Comments to the Editor

   Journal of the National Association of Social Workers
750 First Street, NE, Suite 700, Washington, DC 20002-4241
(202) 408-8600 • (800) 638-8799 • Fax: (202) 336-8312

Reviewer	Date Sent
Ms. No.	Due Date
Ms. Title	

HOW TO USE THIS FORM: This side is for recordkeeping in the editorial office and for the editor-in-chief's use. Please sign your name on this side only. The reverse side is for your comments to the author. Please type or print your comments legibly and do not suggest a final disposition in your comments to the author. (A photocopy of the comments will be mailed to the author with the editor-in-chief's decision.)

Please Rate:

_____ 1. *Accept.* Cite reasons for acceptance in Comments to the Editor below.

_____ 2. *Accept on condition of minor changes.* Use this rating when you require only minor changes and specify the changes in your comments to the author.

_____ 3. *Reject, but encourage resubmission.* Use this rating when you are asking the author for substantial changes. Be specific in your comments to the author.

_____ 4. *Reject.* Please try to supply constructive suggestions for the author.

If rated 1 or 2, please recommend placement: ·

_____ Article _____ Comments on Currents _____ Points and Viewpoints

If rated 3 or 4, please indicate principal reasons for rejection:

_____ Lacks clarity _____ Lacks documentation
_____ Poorly written _____ Not relevant to this journal
_____ Not sufficiently important _____ Not original
_____ Faulty methodology _____ Lacks currency

Other _____

COMMENTS TO THE EDITOR

1. Use this space for any comments you wish to make to the editor-in-chief. Comments might include rationales for acceptance or rejection or any reservations you have about the rating.
2. The journal seeks quality articles that advance social work knowledge. If you realize that the work is not new, that it has been published elsewhere in some form, please note it here.
3. The journal also seeks constructive controversy and professional dialogue about current issues that the profession must resolve. Reviewers should not recommend rejection on the basis of disagreement with the author's point of view.

Date	Reviewer's Signature

package for reviewers. When a rating sheet is mailed to a reviewer with a manuscript, the Comments to the Editor section is blank.

In addition to a rating sheet, many journals provide a checklist that is intended to help reviewers rate manuscripts objectively. NASW currently mails the checklist shown in Figure 7.3 with each manuscript.

Second in importance to the actual decision are the comments the author receives on each manuscript. The savvy editor, moved by public relations motives as well as compassion for the author, coaches the reviewers in writing these comments. "The Tone of the Review" (Figure 7.4), written for the *Journal of Applied Behavior Analysis,* has been widely used in instructions to reviewers throughout the social sciences. Figure 7.5 shows the second side of the *Social Work* rating sheet, another approach to encouraging constructive comments. As in Figure 7.2, the annotations are used only in orientation packages.

Overall, editors try to encourage reviewers to work promptly, consider manuscripts objectively, and write kind and constructive

FIGURE 7.3 NASW Press Reviewers' Checklist

General

1. Is the content likely to be of interest and utility to the readers of this journal?
2. Has the author clearly defined the purpose of the article?
3. Have the authors accomplished what they said they would?
4. Is the material well organized in a logical manner?
5. Is the content new? interesting? significant?
6. Is the writing jargon-free and readable?
7. Are the conclusions supported?
8. Are the implications for social work clearly drawn?
9. Is the article of an appropriate length for the journal and the subject matter?

Documentation

1. Does the author build on and acknowledge the work of others?
2. Are the references generally current?
3. Are the references complete—or has the author overlooked other important work on the topic?
4. Are the references central to the article—or do they appear to be the result of a general literature search on the topic?

Figures and Tables

1. Are they necessary? understandable? self-explanatory?
2. Does the information relate logically to the text?
3. Could unwieldy sections of the text be presented more clearly in a table?
4. Could some of the tables be combined?

FIGURE 7.4   The Tone of the Review

The purpose of the peer review system is to encourage authors to continue their work as well as to select manuscripts for publication. Therefore, it is important that reviewers' comments not only give detailed reasons for suggested revisions or recommended rejection, but that they convey a respect for the author's efforts and include suggestions for improving the research. The *tone* of the review is as important as the quality of the suggestions. The following suggestions for format and wording may help assure that the tone of the review is helpful, not harsh.

> Pay careful attention to the first sentence or paragraph of a review. The beginning should refer to the manuscript in such a way that the author will know that the reviewer read it, and it should express appreciation for some aspect of the work—the research, the difficulties of working in that area, or some particularly fine point. Then, additional sentences can address problems and recommended changes.
>
> Try to minimize the use of words that convey a negative impression, such as "irrelevant," "inadequate," "poor," or "sloppy."
>
> Avoid sarcastic or accusatory comments such as "Is this finding even worth mentioning?"
>
> Use conditionals to help soften the tone. For example, "could," "would," "might" are all words that suggest, rather than command.

The following examples demonstrate how a reviewer can convey problems without introducing a harsh tone. In each case, the sentences contain essentially the same information, but are delivered in a different tone.

1a. Most of the introduction is irrelevant to the rest of the manuscript.
1b. The introduction could have been more directly related to the aims of the study.

2a. It would be impossible for anyone to replicate the procedures.
2b. A more adequate description of the procedures would be required for replication.

3a. The use of the term "co-operative teachers" is very deceiving.
3b. A more accurate definition of the term "co-operative teachers" is necessary to avoid confusion.

4a. Why didn't you assess the reliability of your measures?
4b. It is necessary to report the reliability of your measures so that the reader can judge the impact of your findings.

SOURCE: From the guidelines of the *Journal of Applied Behavior Analysis,* Society for the Experimental Analysis of Behavior, University of Kansas, Department of Human Development, Lawrence. Adapted by permission.

FIGURE 7.5 NASW Press Rating Sheet: Comments to the Author

Ms. No. _____ Ms. Title _____

NOTE: Manuscripts are rated on the following criteria:

• Contribution to knowledge	• Currency
• Readability	• Conceptual level
• Editorial policies	• Clarity
• Writing style	• Methodology
• Importance of subject matter	• Originality
• Documentation	

COMMENTS TO AUTHOR

1. Please type or print neatly. Because we do not have resources to retype comments, the author will see what you send to NASW.

2. Do not tell the author who you are or what decision you are recommending to the editor-in-chief.

3. Be as constructive and sensitive as you can. NASW adopted the practice of providing feedback to authors to help them improve their writing and refine potentially publishable articles.

4. Be as specific as you can about the changes you think are needed to make the article publishable. Authors who receive a "reject, but encourage resubmission" will be asked to respond to reviewers' comments and to detail how they have done so.

5. The maximum length for articles is 18 pages, typed double spaced. Often articles will benefit from condensation. Your recommendations about what is extraneous are very helpful.

6. Conversely, there may be pieces missing. Do note any major gaps.

7. You are concerned primarily with substance and merit, rather than editorial details. However, you also may want to comment on editorial concerns, such as the consistent misuse of language. For some papers with good content and serious editorial problems, you may want to suggest that the author seek professional editorial help.

8. Remember that other reviewers are reading the same paper, and they may reach different conclusions.

9. Authors derive considerable benefit from your thoughtful work! You can have a significant impact on the social work literature.

THANK YOU!

Recommend that the author consider submitting the manuscript to another journal: _____

critiques. "NASW Press Gentle Reminders" (Figure 7.6), which we periodically include in reviewers' packets, summarizes some of the concerns we have about approaches to reviews.

SCIENTIFIC MERIT

With guidelines from the journal in hand, the reviewers must evaluate the merits of the manuscript. The first consideration is whether the article presents new information that will advance the field. Reviewers look for a clear statement of the problem or research question that prompted the author to write the article and want to see evidence that the author accomplished what he or she set out to do.

Next, the reviewer considers whether the author has provided solid documentation that supports the stated conclusions. In their role as gatekeepers, reviewers must guard the literature from

FIGURE 7.6 NASW Press Gentle Reminders to Reviewers

1. Please be prompt. Think how you feel when you are waiting for a decision on the fate of your own work.

2. Please type or clearly print your comments to the author. NASW does not have adequate staff to type comments. When staff have to type messy handwritten comments, the decisions are delayed.

3. Please mark the decision you are recommending. Sometimes the editor-in-chief can determine your recommendation from your comments, but that is not always the case.

4. Please be kind. Your constructive comments are extraordinarily helpful to authors. We often get phone calls, especially on "reject, recommend resubmission" decisions, from authors who want to say "thank you" for the helpful comments they received. Sometimes, however, the comments regrettably are more disparaging than helpful.

5. Please be realistic. Could the author be expected to make the changes you are recommending—or are you asking for a different paper? Do not recommend a "reject, recommend resubmission" decision unless you are interested in reading a second or third iteration. (Revisions are returned to the original reviewer with the original comments and the author's cover sheet that describes the changes.)

6. Please tell us if we have assigned a manuscript that you are not comfortable reviewing. Although we try to follow reviewer reference sheets in making assignments, we don't have a foolproof system. Don't agonize over something you don't feel good about—call the editorial office, and we will reassign the manuscript right away. Then you can destroy the one we sent to you.

untrue or unproved conclusions, whether the author submits them out of naïveté or chicanery. The reviewers' job is to test the scholarly rigor of every manuscript and to point out any problems. Therefore, they will scrutinize the hypothesis, the methodology, the references to the work of others, and any other evidence the author brings to bear on the issue.

Outdated references or overlooked contributions are two of the most frequent complaints, and they can be a dead giveaway of an old paper that has been dusted off for recirculation. If you are submitting a paper that came out of your dissertation, be sure it is current. Reviewers look for current knowledge as documented in primary sources, that is, scholarly refereed journals and original books, as opposed to secondary sources, such as newspapers and textbooks. Excessive reliance on one source, usually presumed to be the author, not only offends reviewers in a double-blind process, but signals that the author may not be as rigorous as scholarly writing requires.

Judging the originality and the significance of a paper is the most difficult task for the reviewer; the problem it presents is the reason that refereed journals insist on having strong scholars as reviewers. Carter (1987) noted that the task "requires that the reviewer be sufficiently imaginative to recognize the worth of an unconventional contribution and sufficiently skeptical to recognize a subtly defective one" (p. 6)

In addition to originality and significance, reviewers look for generalizability so that others can apply the knowledge. For research papers, reviewers ask, "Could other researchers replicate these findings?" Finally, reviewers are seeking a level of difficulty, not in the paper—no one deliberately selects a paper that is difficult to read—but in the work the paper reports.

QUALITY OF PRESENTATION

In addition to presenting new and important information, the author of a journal article must also make it accessible to the reader. Therefore, reviewers consider whether the article is logically organized, clearly written, and concisely presented. In evaluating the quality of the presentation, they look critically at tables and figures. Are the tables and figures useful in clarifying the content? Or do they repeat what is stated clearly in the text, adding weight, not value? Conversely, could awkward prose be stated succinctly in a table?

Although reviewers are not expected to perform as copy editors, they often comment on poor writing style. A lack of precision and improper use of language elicit the most frequent comments. Robinson (1988) used the question "Would George Orwell approve?" as one of her criteria for accepting a manuscript. Orwell, whose 1946 essay "Politics and the English Language" is considered a classic on writing, viewed bad writing as an indication of sloppy thinking. Thus, Robinson decided that if she could say yes to the question "would Orwell approve?" the manuscript must demonstrate clear thinking and writing.

SUITABILITY FOR THE JOURNAL

Subject matter, level of writing, and type of discourse are all components of this criterion. Whereas a clinical journal would welcome an article on various treatment approaches for anorexia, an education journal probably would not. Generic journals define appropriate subject matter more broadly than do specialty journals, but all of them are looking for material that will meet the needs of their readers.

Reviewers for scholarly journals reject speeches and other informal communications; instead, they look for the level of writing that the journal customarily publishes. Likewise, reviewers reject opinion pieces unless they are submitted to an opinion column, and they expect articles to conform to the published criteria for the journal.

Journal editors try to maintain as much consistency in their review process as possible. In addition to rating sheets and other checklists for reviewers, authors can look at mastheads and published guidelines for submissions to the journals. All these guidelines provide clues to how a submission will be considered.

possible decisions

The editor uses the recommendations and the comments of the reviewers to decide whether the manuscript should be published in that journal. If the reviewers agree, the editor's decision may be easy, and more often than may be expected, there is agreement. When reviewers offer conflicting recommendations, the editor generally takes one of two courses of action: He or she serves as a supplementary reviewer or requests yet another review. Few editors like to delay the process, but when they are not expert in a subject, they generally choose delay as a lesser evil than making an uninformed decision.

There are basically four possible decisions. Although journals may label them differently, any decision is likely to be a variation of one of the following.

ACCEPT

This decision, although it is the one all authors eagerly anticipate, is rare—certainly fewer than 10 percent of all submissions to journals in the social sciences are accepted outright, and for many journals the figure is 1 to 5 percent. If an editor accepts a manuscript on the first round, it is likely that there was total agreement among reviewers with virtually no caveats. The author receives a letter of acceptance and generally some form of contract, and the manuscript joins others waiting to be published in the journal. Lag times from acceptance to publication vary among journals from a few weeks to more than two years.

MINOR CHANGES REQUESTED

The language for this decision varies from journal to journal. Some letters say that the manuscript has been accepted on condition of minor changes. For NASW Press journals, the letter states that we are interested in publishing the manuscript if the changes detailed in reviewers' comments are made. We never guarantee publication because occasionally an author will revise a manuscript so drastically and with such disastrous results that the revision is ultimately rejected. This decision is used when the changes requested are basically cosmetic: There may be minor problems with references, a confusing point that needs clarifying, or a quibble over language. For NASW Press journals, revisions in this category are returned only to the editor unless he or she specifically requested that another reviewer see them again. Although this decision is rarely used, the author who receives this kind of letter can feel comfortable that the manuscript most likely will be accepted. At the NASW Press, probably 99 percent of the manuscripts in this category are published.

MAJOR REVISIONS REQUIRED

Some journals label this decision "reject, suggest resubmission." If a manuscript elicits this response, reviewers detected major flaws, and they should have provided detailed descriptions of the problems and suggestions for improving the manuscript. At the NASW Press, we recommend that reviewers use this rating only if they think the author can salvage the manuscript and if they want to see it again. NASW editors have varied in their use of this decision. Some see it as a primary tool for encouraging authors and stimulating submissions; they often are willing to work with authors through several revisions. Others use it sparingly because they think that to do otherwise offers false expectations of possible publication. The manuscripts in this category that ultimately are published generally go through at least two revisions.

Many journals, including the NASW Press journals, now request that authors submit an anonymous cover sheet with revisions that details precisely where and how they responded to the reviewers' comments. Used judiciously, this cover sheet is also an opportunity for an author to disagree with the recommendations and to describe why they could not be followed. Day (1988) noted that an author must offer a point-by-point rebuttal that is dispassionate and not antagonistic. He pointed out that editors are attempting to make scientific decisions. Saying that a reviewer's comments are "stupid" is not likely to elicit a positive second review; on the other hand, every editor knows that every reviewer, even the most expert, is wrong at some point. Gently setting the record straight, with no tone of reproach, can help the editor reach a favorable decision.

REJECT

The majority of manuscripts (depending on the journal, from 50 percent to well over 75 percent) that are submitted to scholarly journals receive outright rejections. The letter is likely to say that the editor found the manuscript "unacceptable" or "unacceptable at this time" or that the editor has determined the journal is unable to publish it.

Authors who receive reject letters should not be overly dismayed—they are in good company and almost every published author has a string of reject letters—but they should consider the comments carefully before they invest time and effort in revising a particular manuscript. Some journals will not re-review manuscripts they have rejected. The NASW Press treats formerly rejected manuscripts like new submissions except that we stamp them "unsolicited revision" to tell reviewers that the journal has reviewed the manuscript previously. No author should resubmit a rejected manuscript without making major changes to it if it was rejected on its merits. If the journal to which it was originally submitted was not an appropriate one, revisions might not be necessary. Also, authors should be aware that sometimes a journal rejects a good article, simply because the backlog is too great or the journal already has articles on the topic. You should be able to ascertain the reason for rejection from the comments you receive.

issues and problems in peer review

Since the peer review system was established nearly 250 years ago, authors and editors alike have wrestled with its problems. Lloyd (1985) lumped peer review with publication, promotion, priority, profit, prestige, progress, and perniciousness—and he found the whole lot "big trouble in River City" (p. 64). Others have been less tongue-in-cheek, but equally concerned about problems related to perceptions of bias, lack of consistency and reliability, and the time lags that occur in professional journals.

BIAS

Bias—against authors, points of view, and subjects—is the most common charge levied against peer review. You can't get published, authors say, unless you are an insider, know the editor, or are a household word in your specialty. Although most journals publish a mix of newcomers and established authors, usually by happenstance, the potential for bias obviously exists if decision makers know who the authors are. That potential is the impetus for the strict application of anonymous reviews, as well as for clear guidelines and criteria.

Another common perception is that rejected articles are not accepted because they reflect an unpopular view or concern a subject matter that is not in vogue. How much of the lag time in getting new issues into the literature is related to how long it takes the authors to develop publishable materials and how much it is related to bias is an unknown. Guarding against bias is an ongoing effort for the editors, and one way that journals do so is by using a large, diverse pool of reviewers.

Most good journals look for controversy to stir up the dialogue that is the very heart of the professional journal. Most editors differentiate semantics from new provocative ideas and findings that will stimulate the development of knowledge. Although all editors make mistakes at one time or another, it is important to remember that mistakes are not necessarily bias.

RELIABILITY AND CONSISTENCY

The author whose article is rejected by one journal after a round of reviews and revisions and accepted immediately by a second journal understandably raises issues of consistency. The editor, faced with conflicting reviews from three respected reviewers, also worries about reliability. Because reviewing is not an exact science, absolute reliability probably is unattainable. Miller and Serzan (1984) suggested that the lack of consistency is directly related to the lack of agreed-upon, published criteria for refereed journals. The extent to which journals publish information guides for authors, rating sheets, guidelines for reviewers, and other evaluation standards has a direct impact on the reliability of the reviewers' recommendations. In addition, some lack of consistency among journals can be explained by the differences in the journals' needs to fill pages.

TIME LAGS

Professional journals rarely publish fast-breaking news. First, the research and writing for a single article can take weeks, months, or years. Then the peer review system takes over. Most journals listed in Mendelsohn (1992) report review times of four to six months; some complete reviews within a few weeks, and some take a year. Most articles go through that process two or more times. Then there is a lag time from acceptance to print.

Without levying page charges, journals have only two real options to reduce the lag time from acceptance to print: They can accept fewer manuscripts, or they can reduce the length of articles they accept. Efficient systems and high expectations of reviewers can reduce review times. Nonetheless, like all intellectual endeavors, peer review cannot be accomplished instantly. It is unlikely that time lags in professional publishing will be significantly decreased soon.

conclusion

Peer review is the system used to determine what will be published in professional journals. In their essential gatekeeping role, referees are asked to identify flawed or fraudulent materials that should not be published, as well as important new knowledge that should enter the professional dialogue. In their equally important role as mentors and coaches, reviewers are asked to encourage creativity, good writing, and rigorous scholarship.

Despite the flaws that reflect human frailty, peer review continues to be the means by which professional journals select their contents. Sharp (1990) noted that "author, editor, and reviewer form a triangle. The angles may come under strain, but all three parties share a common purpose and should seek that courteously, even affably, and certainly efficiently." Authors who seek to be published in journals that are considered prestigious by virtue of the quality of their articles and the reputations of their reviewers should understand the process and help editors to select their materials by responding to editorial suggestions in a collegial manner.

Peer review is an evolving process. Twenty years ago, authors who submitted manuscripts to *Social Work* received form reject cards with no comments. The habit of asking authors to detail changes in revisions, as well as the reasons they declined to make changes, which many journals practice and which provides a level of dialogue never seen before in anonymous reviews, has become common only within the past five or six years. Authors who participate actively and affably in the process that has such an impact on their professional lives can help peer review become more effective and efficient.

references

Bishop, C. T. (1984). *How to edit a scientific journal.* Philadelphia: ISI Press.

Carter, S. P. (1987). *Writing for your peers: The primary journal paper.* New York: Praeger.

Child Welfare League of America. (1991). *Author's guide to publication policies.* Washington, DC: Author.

Day, R. A. (1988). *How to write and publish a scientific paper* (3rd ed.). Phoenix: Oryx Press.

Flanagin, A., Rennie, D., & Lundberg, G. D. (1991). Attitudes of peer review congress attendees. In *Peer review in scientific publishing: Papers from the First International Congress on Peer Review in Biomedical Publication,* pp. 261–263 (sponsored by the American Medical Association). Chicago: Council of Biology Editors.

Lloyd, J. E. (1985, June 26). Selling scholarship down the river: The pernicious aspects of peer review. *Chronicle of Higher Education,* p. 64.

McNutt, R. A., Evans, A. T., Fletcher, R. H., & Fletcher, S. W. (1990). The effects of blinding on the quality of peer review: A randomized trial. *Journal of the American Medical Association, 263,* 1371–1376.

Mendelsohn, H. N. (1992). *An author's guide to social work journals* (3rd ed.). Washington, DC: NASW Press.

Miller, A., & Serzan, S. (1984). Criteria for identifying a refereed journal. *Journal of Higher Education, 55,* 673–699.

Robinson, A. (1988). Thinking straight and writing that way. *Gifted Child Quarterly, 32,* 367–369.

Rosenblatt, A., & Kirk, S. (1980). Recognition of authors in blind review of manuscripts. *Journal of Social Service Research, 3,* 383–394.

Sharp, D. (1990). What can and should be done to reduce publication bias: The perspective of an editor. *Journal of the American Medical Association, 263,* 1390–1391.

8 *journal submissions*

Linda Beebe

Scholarly journals are the primary outlet that educators and practitioners have to communicate and test out their work. Yet many authors, even well-published ones, do not fully understand the conventions and procedures for submitting articles to a scholarly journal. This chapter describes these conventions and tells you how to select a journal and how to present the article.

Since 1665, when the first scientific journals were published in France and England, scholarly journals have served as the primary form of communication among professionals. As Bishop (1984) noted, "Collectively, the journals, reviews, abstracts, indexes, and retrieval systems constitute the literature of science. . . . The heart of this literature is the primary research journal upon which all the other parts depend and from which they are derived" (p. 4). Journal articles, in general, reach their audiences more quickly than do other forms of professional communication and, most important, provide a forum for the open exchange of information that is not possible with other means of publication.

Books and personal correspondence were the primary forms of scholarly communication until Denis de Sallor first published *Journal des scavans* in January 1665. Two months later, the first issue of *Philosophical Transactions of the Royal Society* was released in England. Tracing the evolution of the scholarly journal, Osborn (1984) emphasized the importance of the journal as a means of dialogue among professionals. Before the publication of scholarly journals, scholars had shared discoveries, inventions, or new theories by circulating correspondence among their colleagues. The limitations of communicating by letter were particularly frustrating in an age of great experimentation in science, when universities were gaining in importance and scholars were working in communities rather than in isolation. In that increasingly competitive environment, the importance of speed—for getting credit for one's work, for engaging in public debate, and for gaining access to information—stimulated the dominance of journals over books as the primary means of communication.

Journals have continued to dominate professional communication. In the 18th and 19th centuries, journals proliferated as specialties emerged in the natural and applied sciences. That trend increased exponentially in the 20th century. Today, writers in any discipline can choose to submit to one of a vast array of journals.

characteristics of scholarly journals

Although journals vary widely in their audience, their purpose, and their content, all scholarly journals share some basic characteristics and conventions. The author who knows the conventions and follows them carefully will always have an edge over the author who does not. There is no single formula for producing a good article in the human services literature, but there are some common expectations.

ORIGINALITY

Articles in scholarly journals are expected to report original results that will advance the current knowledge base and that have not been reported elsewhere. Bishop (1984) noted with some asperity that "to advance knowledge means that the paper must describe something new, and newness implies that it has not been published before" (p. 6). The requirement of originality has several implications for authors:

▶ Take care not to duplicate someone else's work. Although you should build on the work of others, you should not repeat it.
▶ Take your topic beyond what is currently known. Editors generally welcome substantive review articles that capture and analyze what is known about a specific topic. Authors who simply rehash old material generally find their work rejected.
▶ Avoid self-plagiarism. Never submit an article that has appeared in any other medium.

If publication in a professional journal is your objective, always think "journal article first." Every journal editor has heard comments like the following: "My article in *X* newsletter got such a good response; I'm sure your readers would find it useful." "But it wasn't published in the professional literature. How can you turn this down because it was published in *The New York Times*?" "It's never been published in English before." "I had a chapter in *X* book that I'd like to see get wider distribution in the literature." Not one of these previously published pieces is acceptable for a primary journal.

A scholarly or primary journal, by definition, publishes only original work. You may use a journal article to develop a book chapter. In fact, book chapters sometimes are reprinted from journal articles with permission from the publishers. But you cannot do the reverse.

It is important to differentiate between informal and formal communications. Professionals communicate works in progress in many informal ways that would not preclude formal publication in a journal. Correspondence, conference presentations, journal columns designed to showcase preliminary findings, and even some conference proceedings are examples. If your presentation is compiled in a conference proceedings just as you gave it, with every other presentation given at that conference, and distributed only to conference participants, you probably can safely submit the polished and refined version to a journal. If the presentation is selected from many in a peer review process to be one of a few published in a book, then you probably have lost the opportunity to submit that particular work to a primary journal.

SCHOLARLY RIGOR

Journal articles are expected to demonstrate serious scholarship, if not pure scientific rigor. As a writer, you need to show the reader not only what you know, but how you found it out. Professional knowledge is a continually evolving phenomenon that grows little by little with the contributions of each new insight. You need to substantiate and corroborate your work sufficiently, so readers will have confidence in your findings and use them as a building block for future work.

The *Random House Dictionary of the English Language* (1987) defines scholarship as "learning; knowledge acquired by study" (p. 1751). *Webster's Ninth New Collegiate Dictionary* (1987) defines a scholar as "one who has done advanced studies in a special field; a learned person" (p. 1051) The natural sciences have prescribed a scientific method that requires controlled experiments and significant analyses of data. Scholars in the social sciences have more options. They will be challenged, however, to demonstrate that they have approached their task in a systematic way, that they have built on previous work, and that they are expanding knowledge in the field.

EFFICIENCY

In an age of information overload, the requirement for efficient communication is even more important. One aspect of efficiency is brevity. Journal articles are not books or monographs; journals generally require that a manuscript be no longer than 20 pages, typed double spaced. Many journals consider 16 pages, including references and tables, the outside limit for manuscript length. Do not try to cheat by creating narrow margins, using small type, or setting the spacing at a space and a half. You will simply make the article more difficult for the reviewers to read, and they then will be less likely to find it acceptable.

Clear, lucid prose contributes to the efficiency of the article. Do not confuse turgid, ponderous language with scholarship or the complexity of a subject. The more complex the subject, the more important it is to simplify the language to ensure that the reader will understand the article. Carter (1987) noted that authors often include information that is clearly written, but superfluous. Excise any text that is not essential to the purpose of your article, and you will improve the chances that the article will be accepted for publication. A corollary of this rule is to be certain to include enough information that readers can understand the article. Judicious repetition and transitional phrases improve comprehension and therefore add to the efficiency of the article.

The degree to which articles are efficient has a direct impact on how many articles can be published and how quickly articles get into print. Most journals in the human services, unlike those in the natural sciences, do not impose page charges, which are per-page fees for publication; therefore, they cannot simply expand their size to match the number of articles that are ready for publication. Some journals have even reduced pages as the costs of postage and printing have increased. Rather than printing fewer, longer articles, most prefer to deliver information more efficiently. If all other factors are equal, a 16-page article will always be preferable to a 26-page article.

components of a journal submission

The way you package your article will influence the outcome of the review process. In general, journals request that each submission include the following components: a cover sheet; title page; abstract; text; references; and tables or artwork for figures, if pertinent.

COVER SHEET

The cover sheet should contain the following:

- ▶ the full title of the article
- ▶ information on all authors: name, degrees, and titles; full addresses; telephone numbers
- ▶ the date of submission.

If there is more than one author, the authors should be listed in the order they would prefer for the byline of a published article, and one author should be designated as the corresponding author.

If the journal practices anonymous review, the staff or editor will remove the cover sheet before the manuscript is circulated for review and keep it with the manuscript file, rather than circulate it to the reviewers. The cover sheet is the only component of the manuscript that should identify the author.

TITLE PAGE

The title page will be circulated to reviewers with the manuscript. Remember that a title is a label for your article. Be as specific and

---

protocols

The professional literature in any discipline will be richer and more diverse if authors do not follow a rigid formula to write their work. There are, however, a few basic protocols that all authors should observe.

1. Submit only original materials, that is, materials that have not been published elsewhere in any form.
2. Submit to only one journal at a time.
3. Document and credit the work of others.
4. Respect the time of reviewers. Do not submit first drafts or speeches.
5. Respect your own work. Be sure your manuscripts are clean and legible, free of typographical and grammatical errors.
6. Follow the guidelines of the journal to which you are submitting your article for length, format, reference style, and number of copies.
7. Maintain the highest standards of professional ethics.

descriptive as possible, but do not try to tell the reader everything about the article in the title. Verbose, pedantic titles endanger acceptance and can even delay the decision because reviewers turn first to more inviting manuscripts.

ABSTRACT

An abstract is a summary of the article that will help readers determine whether they need or want to read the full article. The abstract should distill the key concepts in the manuscript. Day (1988) noted the differences between an informative abstract and an indicative one. An *informative abstract* briefly states the problem, the method used to study the problem, and the principal conclusions. A good informative abstract can enable the busy reader to keep up with the literature without reading the full article. An *indicative abstract,* on the other hand, is descriptive rather than substantive; therefore, it is less useful as a resource.

Reviewers often use abstracts to evaluate the importance of the work and the author's ability to provide a succinct summary. Primary journals publish abstracts at the beginning of articles as a service to readers. Abstracts are also placed, usually without change, in the secondary abstracting and indexing services. If an abstract cannot convince readers that an article makes a valuable contribution to the literature, the article is not likely to be cited, and it may not be as widely read as the author hoped.

Write the abstract as a single paragraph of about 150 words. Because an abstract should be self-contained, do not include any references or tables. You do not want to waste these few words on background or marginally useful information. Instead, focus on the contribution of the article; the conclusions you, the author, reached; and the facts that support those conclusions.

TEXT

How the text is presented depends on the type of article, the subject matter, the audience, and the requirements of the individual journal. You must introduce the subject matter so the reader knows your purpose and how you plan to achieve it. You need to talk about implications: What are the most important aspects? What do they mean? How can others use this information? In between you need to communicate how and why you reached the conclusions you did.

REFERENCES

Reference lists follow the text in the manuscript package. They, like all elements in the package, should be typed double spaced. The style of reference you use will depend on the journal to which you are submitting your article. Essentially, there are three reference styles.

Author–Date Citations

In this style, references are cited in the text using the author's last name and the date of publication. In the natural sciences, this style often is called the Harvard system, and in the social sciences, the APA (American Psychological Association) system. The advantage to the reader is that one knows the source without referring to the reference list. The disadvantage is that citations of a large number of references sometimes interfere with the flow of the article. This system occupies slightly more space than does a numbered system.

Numbered Reference System

Until the 1980s, this was perhaps the most common reference style. Citations are listed by number in the order in which they appear in the text. The advantage to readers is that they can find the references easily in the order in which they appear. The disadvantage is that one cannot ascertain the source without turning to the reference list. Also, the system separates multiple references to the same source. For authors and publishers, this system can present logistical problems in revisions because the addition or deletion of a reference results in a total renumbering of the references.

Alphabetized Number System

A hybrid of the author–date and numbered reference systems, this style uses numbers in the text, but lists the numbered references in alphabetic order. The references are numbered, not in the order in which they appear in the text, but in the order they appear on the list. The system appears to have been designed to combine the efficient use of space in the numbered system with the advantages of alphabetizing.

TABLES AND ARTWORK

Tables and artwork for figures should *not* be incorporated into the text. Instead, each should be placed on a separate page and added to the manuscript package at the end. Text, references, and tables or artwork for figures should be numbered sequentially from page 1 to the end.

Data that cannot be presented easily and understandably in text should be placed in tables. Tables should be self-explanatory and should supplement, not duplicate, the text. Remember that your objective is to make your data as accessible as possible to your reader. Whereas you can communicate complex data more readily in a table, it is better to incorporate data from short tables into the text. The table title should describe the table completely, so it can remain independent of the text. Do not duplicate the tables in words; instead, interpret or highlight the findings presented in the tables. Be consistent in terminology and formats when you present a series of tables. Number tables in Arabic numerals in the order in which they appear in the text.

Before the advent of computer graphics, many people considered artwork an expensive extra. In general, journals require that authors provide figures in a form that is camera ready, that is, ready to be photographed for printing. Computer graphics now enable authors to fulfill the requirement to supply camera-ready artwork for figures and graphs with ease. Some precautions are still in order. Review the journal to determine appropriate sizes. Be aware that the reproduction of any figure is likely to reduce its legibility, particularly if the artwork must be scaled to fit the length and width of the page; therefore, keep all elements large enough to be legible even if the overall figure is reduced in size. Reproduction quality of less than the laser printer 300 dpi (dots per inch) will not be acceptable to any journal. If you do not have the capacity to produce publication-quality artwork, some journals will produce the artwork and bill you for the cost.

basic logistics

Knowledge of basic logistics can prevent some long delays and agonies in moving an article from conception to print. Peer review is a time-consuming task, and it can be extremely frustrating to lose time because you did not meet some basic requirements.

NUMBER OF COPIES

Do not send one copy of an article and expect it to be reviewed. Peer review is expensive in itself; journals are not able to absorb the cost of reproducing copies of the submissions they receive. Before you send in your article, check to see how many copies are required. In general, journals request four or five copies. The NASW Press requires five copies: three for reviewers, one for the editor-in-chief, and one for the file, so the journal always has a central file of all manuscripts in circulation.

NO SPEECHES

Authors often test their work in presentations before they submit it to a professional journal. In general, this is a sound idea because it enables them to take their original work and modify it in accord with the response they receive in the presentation. In practice, many authors submit the unexpurgated version of their speech and are greatly disappointed when the reviewers' comments relate more to the format than to the content. You cannot expect reviewers to help you convert a speech to a scholarly article; therefore, you must make the changes in format if you expect a serious review of the content. (See the chapter "Basic Writing Techniques" in this book for information on how to convert a speech to an article.)

CLEANLINESS AND LEGIBILITY

All journal editors can tell you stories about the manuscripts they have received. Some manuscripts look like an elephant has been stomping on them. Some are stained with jelly or spaghetti sauce. Some are printed in typefaces so faint that it is nearly impossible to read them. Some are so dirty and dog-eared that it appears as if they have been recycled through four or five journals. Many authors do not number pages, and pages are often out of order. All these characteristics are recipes for rejection.

If you are serious about publishing, you need to take serious care of the appearance of your submissions. Number the pages. Always send clean copies. If you think you can send out copies that another journal returned, review each copy page by page. You may be surprised to learn that a previous reviewer annotated the text. Never send out copies printed on a dot matrix printer. If you do not have access to a laser printer, take your disk to a copy house and pay the minimal fee it charges to print letter-quality copies.

HARD COPIES AND DISKS

In general, the number of copies that journals request applies to hard copies. Authors should always retain one copy of the article in hard copy. In addition, journals may also request or require a copy of the article on a disk. Even when journals do not review or edit manuscripts on a computer, they often request copies on a disk to simplify typesetting. A journal's instructions for authors will describe the specifications for submitting disks if disks are required or desired.

appropriate submissions

Sometimes articles are rejected not because they are poorly written or poorly organized or because the content is not useful, but because they are not submitted to the right journal. You need to study journals to understand the requirements of each journal and how being published in a specific journal will have an impact on you as an author.

KNOW THE OPTIONS

All successful authors read the literature. The best writers are voracious readers, and those who are the most successful in getting their articles accepted are the writers who understand the requirements of the various journals. Presumably, you already read the literature in your specialty, but if you want to expand your possibilities, start by reviewing abstracting and indexing services, such as *Social Work Abstracts*. The list of journals reviewed for abstracting in your field is an excellent starting point. Go to the library and browse through *Current Contents*. Some disciplines publish a guide to journals like the NASW Press's *An Author's Guide to Social Work Journals* (3rd ed.), which presents such publishing details as editorial focus, length of time for review, and all the logistical information you need to submit an article to any of more than 130 journals.

STUDY YOUR CHOICES

Once you have selected some potential journals, first read their mastheads to see what kinds of articles they seek. This may sound simplistic, but the NASW Press often receives submissions to *Social Work in Education, a Journal for School Social Workers* that address education for social work, not social work in schools. Clearly, the authors have never read the journal.

You need to read the journals you select to see what types of articles they publish. What audience does a journal address? What style of writing does a journal favor? If a journal features concise reports that are explicitly directed to informing practice, an editor is not likely to accept lengthy, heavily methodological articles. Many journals publish articles in a variety of styles, but others do not. Request an information guide or instructions for authors sheet, so you can learn such practical information as how many copies are needed, where to submit, whether an abstract is required, and what reference style is acceptable. Although you can glean most of this information from reading a journal, the information guide generally offers additional help.

MAKE AN INFORMED DECISION

Authors sometimes are so concerned about whether a journal will accept their work that they overlook the importance of their choice of which journal to approach. If you have done your homework, you will have selected the journal that is most appropriate for the article in terms of content and style, but there are other factors as well. Time is an issue. How long is the review process? The review process for journals varies from two to six or more months, with four months being about the average time between the receipt of the submission and the decision. How long is the lag time from acceptance to print? Lag times range from a month or two to two years. That lag time can be tested, in part, by looking at the frequency of publication and the number of articles per issue. Some journals also publish dates of acceptance with each article.

You also will want to consider what Day (1988) called the Prestige Factor. Although determining exactly which journals are prestigious is subjective, some measurements are available to you. Where are the most important papers in the field being published? Is the journal refereed? Are the referees who review manuscripts well published and knowledgeable in their fields? Nonrefereed journals or those whose reviewers are not leaders in the field are considered less prestigious. Where is the journal abstracted and indexed? The more prestigious journals are abstracted in several major abstracting and indexing services, which are used by writers in many disciplines.

Finally, there is the circulation factor. After all, you want not just to be published, but to have people read and respond to your work; therefore, you want to know how many people subscribe to the journal and who they are. Generic journals tend to have a broad focus and a wide audience. Specialty journals tend to have a narrower focus and a smaller number of subscribers. One is not automatically better than the other. The readers of a specialty journal can be presumed to have a particular interest in that specialty, whereas many readers of the generic journal probably do not. Another consideration is that the competition is likely to be keener for the larger, generic journal. If you are choosing between specialty journals, you will find that they often vary greatly in their readership. Look for a statement of ownership in the late fall or early winter issues to learn the total circulation. Whereas large prestigious journals often have low acceptance rates because they receive so many submissions, some good smaller journals receive so few submissions that they accept the majority of the manuscripts they receive.

All these factors may influence your decision about where to submit your manuscript. Making the right choice can ease the trauma of submitting your work for review and ultimately enhance your professional reputation. Lest this sound too daunting, you should know that there probably is a group of "right" choices, from which you can safely choose any one, rather than a single "right" choice. Remember, too, that you must submit to only one journal at a time. Most journals' acknowledgment letters remind authors of this fact, and nearly all journal editors consider submissions to more than one journal at a time to be a serious breach of professional ethics. Because peer review requires such a large investment of time, journal editors need to be assured that any manuscripts they review could be published in their journal. Furthermore, multiple submissions of the same manuscript expose authors and publishers to the risks of legal liability for copyright violations.

great expectations

Once you have dropped your manuscript in the mail, what can you expect? First, within a month, you should receive an acknowledgment thanking you for your submission and telling you that it is under review. The acknowledgment generally also gives you a rough idea of how long the standard review takes. If you do not receive a postcard or letter, by all means call the journal office or the editor.

The length of time required for a review depends on a variety of factors. (See chapter 7, "Peer Review," for more details on the process.) Journals rarely can be assured that all reviews will be conducted within exactly the same time when they are as dependent on volunteers and the U.S. mail as they currently are. However, you should not sit silently and wait. If you have not received a decision letter within the time the acknowledgment specified, do not be shy about inquiring when you may hear. Sometimes, a manuscript goes astray for months while a patient author sits at home and wonders when the letter will arrive.

When the letter does arrive, you probably will not be happy with the message. Only a small percentage of journal manuscripts are accepted on the first submission. Acceptance rates for NASW Press journals, for example, range from 20 percent to about 30 percent; many of the manuscripts finally accepted have gone through two or more revisions. Although none of us likes the reality, there is hardly an author alive who has not been rejected. Do not be crushed by the rejection. On the other hand, do not assume that the editor is biased and ignorant. Use the reviewers' comments to help polish and sharpen your material, so you can build on the work you have done. You may also want to think about submitting your manuscript to another journal or considering such outlets as columns in a scholarly journal or a less formal newsletter.

Whatever you do, do not stop writing. The knowledge base of your profession cannot exist only in the minds of its practitioners. That knowledge must be recorded and built by rigorous review and dialogue in the professional journals.

references

Bishop, C. T. (1984). *How to edit a scientific journal.* Philadelphia: ISIS Press.

Carter, S. P. (1987). *Writing for your peers: The primary journal paper.* New York: Praeger.

Day, R. A. (1988). *How to write and publish a scientific paper* (3rd ed.). Phoenix: Oryx Press.

Osborn, C. (1984). The place of the journal in the scholarly communications system. *Library Resources & Technical Services, 28,* 314–324.

Random House dictionary of the English language (2nd ed., unabridged). (1987). New York: Random House.

Webster's ninth new collegiate dictionary. (1987). Springfield, MA: Merriam-Webster.

9 *book proposals*

Linda Beebe

There is a mystique about a book that appeals to most writers. Part of the attraction may be that a book appears to be weightier, more tangible, and more visible than some other forms of professional writing. A journal article is buried within an issue; to see it, the reader must find the correct issue, search the table of contents, and turn to the appropriate page. In contrast, a book's cover and spine announce the author's name to everyone who sees the book on a table or in a bookcase. The book is longer and heftier. Authors often assume that a book will have a wider circulation than will a journal article, although this supposition is not always true. And, because a book requires more labor than most other forms of professional writing, authors assume that the rewards also are greater.

For a variety of reasons, professionals who write would like to publish books. If you are among those who seek to capture their knowledge and their experience in a book, I hope that this chapter will help you produce a salable book proposal.

characteristics of scholarly books

The scholarly book is intended to advance professional knowledge. Although scholarly presses increasingly publish academic books that may be of interest to the intelligent layperson, the primary audience is professionals in the author's discipline and in related disciplines. Scholarly books are measured, not by their weight or the length of their reference lists, but by the degree to which they communicate knowledge and ideas that will inform the reader. All the processes that lead up to the publication of a professional book—evaluation of a proposal, revisions of first drafts, copyediting, design, production, and so forth—are intended to enhance that communication.

At one time, the presses of professional organizations, the university presses, and the divisions of commercial presses that publish professional books could be expected to exclude poetry, short stories, and other types of fiction. That no longer is always the case. Those publishers will, however, reject material that is more suited to journals or proposals for what they consider "nonbooks."

DIFFERENCES BETWEEN JOURNALS AND BOOKS

Journal articles and books vary in a number of ways. For example, the level of originality mandated for journals is not required for books. Book authors frequently include substantive portions of material that they or others have published earlier in journals. In fact, they may have used the critical discussion and dialogue, which journals provide and books do not, to refine their materials for their books.

Books, in contrast to the intent of most journals, often present established ideas or basic information, such as that found in textbooks or manuals. Practitioners read journals to keep up with state-of-the-art developments and to learn about new research or innovative programs. They may read books to master skills or to reinforce information they gained earlier.

Whereas the results of research may be published in stages in the journal literature, a book is expected to be complete within its covers; consequently, an author must have sufficient comprehensive, valid material to justify the length of a book. One of the most frequent criticisms of book proposals is that the author has presented material that more appropriately could be condensed into a journal article.

Book and journal publishing differ from an operational viewpoint as well. Instead of being constrained by postal regulations, subscription obligations, and firmly set issue dates, book publishers may release as many or as few books a year as the pool of accepted manuscripts and their budgets permit. Producing a single book is considerably less expensive than starting a new journal and carries fewer long-term liabilities; however, producing a book generally is considerably more expensive than producing a single issue of a journal. Furthermore, a book will succeed or fail on the basis of one author's work, but one article will not have a major impact on the market for a journal. Whereas journal articles are complete when they are accepted, books rarely are, and the publisher is dependent on the author to produce a readable, salable manuscript within the time limits proposed. The impact of these differences is that publishers scrutinize book proposals carefully.

CHARACTERISTICS OF A NONBOOK

Many of the proposals that publishers receive are for what has been described as nonbooks. Armstrong (1972) included dissertations (the prime example), coffee-table books, anthologies, readers, *festschriften*, and symposia in his list of nonbooks. Ascribing the existence of these phenomena to market and vanity, Armstrong noted,

> Like the coffee-table book, some symposia and festschriften are dedicated to vanity; like the anthology, their parts are often disparate; like both, they are in general mundane and without interest to any save the specialist with a marked tolerance for the dull, the inane, and the inconsequential. . . . There are more profound traits than vanity and market, however, which the genres of nonbooks have in common, and these are the features which perhaps distinguish them most significantly from the book. The coffee-table book is likely to be deficient in thoughtfulness and in coming to grips with a problem, though it may be both synthetic and programmatic. The anthology often rates somewhat higher in thoughtfulness but again fails to grapple with the issue. The symposium and the festschrift at their best can exhibit thoughtfulness and thoroughness, but common emphases, perspectives, and values are absent. (pp. 102–103)

Twenty years later, publishers continue to be besieged with proposals for a variety of nonbooks. If your proposed book includes one of the following, you should think seriously about revising it before sending it to a publisher.

Reader or Anthology

Readers, collections of articles published in a single journal or selected from several journals, were common texts 20 years ago, often produced by professors who had searched arduously for materials that were appropriate for specific courses. Online and CD-ROM databases have made the published reader obsolete in an age when a college copy center can provide a coursepack on any given subject in a few days. Document-delivery services and customized books on demand in quantities as few as 10 further erode the potential success of any reader. You may indeed bring a totally new perspective to your collection of materials, but the book publisher is unlikely to find a market for the reader. But collections of original articles—that is, articles that were not previously published, may be successful if they are cohesive and well written.

Conference Proceedings

At some point in the development of every major conference, a professional-organization publisher is likely to hear from the planners, who are eager to see that the state-of-the-art knowledge presented at the conference is captured in proceedings. The publisher who declines this opportunity is generally seen as a tyrant who is blocking the progress of the profession. But most publishers will reject conference proceedings, and with good reason. In general, conference proceedings turn out to be bad books, collections of poorly written articles with no cohesive linkages. The exceptions are the proceedings of specialized conferences in which good writers have been invited to speak on a narrow subject.

Festschriften

These tributes to a leading member of a profession take many forms. A festschrift may be a collection of the person's writings with comments from the collector. Or it may be a collection of original articles that address the person's theories or body of work. One author may take on the task, or several may join the effort. If you are considering a festschrift, keep Armstrong's words in mind. Most festschriften, unfortunately, add nothing to a profession's knowledge base and consequently have virtually no audience.

Dissertations

By far the most common nonbook is the unretouched dissertation. Authors, who have spent years toiling on documents that have such an impact on their future, can be forgiven for assuming that others will find their dissertations equally fascinating and important. The truth is, however, that almost no dissertation is published until the author revises it substantially.

Dissertations are designed to demonstrate that doctoral candidates can conduct research and document all their findings, not to produce books. Armstrong (1972) suggested that education and knowledge would be better served if doctoral students were required to write a book, not a dissertation, but graduate schools do not appear to have made any progress in that direction. The tyranny of the dissertation tradition often results in the documentation of minutiae, elimination of the author's point of view, and strangled prose full of jargon.

In "The Thesis and the Book," Halpenny (1972) noted that the dissertation in most disciplines resembles the book structurally in that it, too, has a table of contents, generally a preface or introduction, chapters, a bibliography, and so forth. The book and dissertation differ significantly in their presentation and tone, in their intended audience, and in their level of documentation. Halpenny recommended that authors first take some time away from their dissertations to consider how books derived from them may meet the needs and interests of a much broader audience.

If you want to pursue a book, see how you can broaden the scope of what is likely to be narrowly focused research to address a current need in your discipline. Use the knowledge you have gained to come to conclusions and to make judgments on the subject. Do not think that you need to document every statement. And most of all, write in a tone that will connect you to your audience. Many dissertations have evolved into fine books, and yours can too, if you devote the energy and time required.

components of the book proposal

Some authors box up their 700-page manuscripts and send them off into the world. Others mail a one-page letter expecting to receive a contract by return mail. Neither method generally succeeds because neither one gives the publisher sufficient information and each creates work that appears to have a small potential for return.

The 700-page manuscript might be accompanied only by a hand-scrawled note from the author. Who is the audience? What is the purpose of the book? Why did the author choose this publisher? Publishers rarely read a manuscript until the author provides appropriate information to help them evaluate its prospects. In the meantime, the manuscript takes up space in an office already overburdened with paper.

The single-page letter is almost as troublesome to the publisher. Although it does not take up as much space as a manuscript, the letter adds an unnecessary step to the process and indicates that the author may just be fishing, instead of having a clear plan for a book. Publishers handle these letters in one of three ways: (1) They conscientiously write a personalized letter, sometimes weeks later; (2) they send out a form letter; or (3) they toss the letter in the trash.

It is not that publishers are not looking for proposals. On the contrary, most are actively seeking good manuscripts; after all, they need new books to stay in business. A sound proposal for a professional book actually stands a good chance of being accepted if you supply a prospectus with enough detail that the publisher can determine whether the book may be viable. The following describes the components of a book proposal.

THE PROSPECTUS

The prospectus should demonstrate that the author has a clear plan for the book. If the prospectus is compelling and thorough, the publisher's confidence that the author can write a useful and salable book will be enhanced. The author needs to cover several items in the prospectus: the book's purpose, subject/contents, type and length, markets and competition, and the work plan and timetable for completing it.

Purpose of the Book

What is your aim in writing the book? To whom is the book directed? How will the audience use it? What will the book accomplish? What needs will it meet? Why is it important? Do not make extravagant claims, but do not undersell your book either.

Subject/Contents

Summarize the content of the book briefly. Describe the key issues, research, or other detailed information that will be included. Because you will be attaching a detailed outline or an annotated table of contents, you need only summarize here.

Type of and Length of Book

Is it a textbook? A professional book? A manual related to professional licensure or credentialing? Is it a collected work? Would you describe it as a how-to book? How long do you estimate the final manuscript will be? Although these are estimates, you should give careful thought to the proposed length. Publishers incorporate this information into their analysis of your competence to complete a book. If you propose an in-depth study of a complicated topic in 100 manuscript pages (approximately 60 typeset pages), you have told the publisher you do not have a clear idea of what the book entails.

Will the book contain a significant number of figures and tables? Are there other factors that may enhance the quality of the book—and add to the cost of production? Describe any features that make the book unique.

The Market

Who constitutes the market? How big is the potential market? What evidence leads you to believe that potential readers will buy the book? Where can the publisher reach them? Is it a growing or diminishing market? How will your professional activities—speaking, teaching, practice—help publicize the book? Try to quantify as much as you can and strike any grandiose claims, such as "All 50,000 members of the _____ society will buy this book." If you expect that the book will be used in classrooms, name the courses and estimate the number of students who are enrolled in them. If the book is aimed at practitioners, estimate how many practitioners work in the specialty the book addresses and explain how they will find the book useful. If the book will appeal to professionals in more than one discipline, describe the disciplines and explain why the book will appeal to them.

The Competition

Identify and assess the competing books. What are the current books in this subject area? What are their strengths and weaknesses?

How is the proposed book superior or different or complementary? The fact that other books exist in the field is not a serious problem as long as you can make a good case that yours will also be useful to readers. Include all the information you can about competing books: their authors, titles, publishers, publication dates, length, price, any other useful data. This section is particularly important because it demonstrates your knowledge of the literature. Expert reviewers will dismiss the author who ignores competing books or who provides distorted assessments of them.

Work Plan—Timetable

Is this a brand new idea, or have you completed several chapters? How do you plan to proceed? When can you provide sample chapters? When do you expect to complete the manuscript? Include your history of meeting deadlines if it is to your advantage. Be as specific as you can, but consider the dates you propose carefully because you may be expected to live up to them.

DETAILED OUTLINE OR TABLE OF CONTENTS

Most publishers want to see at least a detailed outline or table of contents before they make a decision on a book. Even a tentative outline gives the publisher a sense not only of your framework, but of how you will organize the work. Be as specific as possible and be certain that your outline and prospectus agree. If you have proposed to write a 500-page manuscript on developing a rational health care policy for the United States, the publisher will expect more than a one-page outline that lists an introduction and five chapters.

If you are proposing to produce an edited book—that is, a collection of articles written by different authors—include the names of the prospective authors of the respective chapters. Publishers recognize that an editor probably will have to make some changes in authors, but your original choices will give the publisher good information to use in evaluating your proposal. Although edited books are common in the human services, publishers scrutinize them carefully because they tend to be extremely uneven. It is wise to indicate how you expect to achieve an even balance of high-quality authors and how you will deal with authors who delay or who produce unpublishable material. The more attention you pay to quality assurance in the beginning, the more comfortable the publisher will feel about accepting your proposal.

AUTHOR'S VITA

Unlike journal articles, which often are reviewed anonymously, a book manuscript always includes not only the author's name, but enough description of the author's experience to help the publisher determine the author's qualifications to write the book. Each book requires a substantial investment, and publishers, who are interested in remaining solvent, look for evidence that the author is capable of writing a book that will recoup its investment and make a profit. On the other hand, publishers are not interested in wading through reams of unrelated paper. Include a vita that shows your education and work experience and that details your previous publications that are relevant to the book. By all means, include all your published books and full articles, as well as related presentations, but summarize such tangential materials as unrelated presentations, book reviews, and letters to the editor.

SAMPLE CHAPTERS

Often book proposals undergo a two-step review process. First, the publisher will review the proposal, then ask for representative chapters. Interest in receiving sample chapters with the proposal varies from one press to another. The NASW Press, for example, welcomes one, two, or three representative chapters as examples of the author's writing style and ability to develop the subject. We are happy to have the chapters because they often speed up the process for us, but not all publishers agree. If you do not include chapters, but have completed them, be sure to indicate that fact in your work plan and always offer to send completed chapters on request.

successful submissions

Because book proposals, unlike journal articles, may be submitted to more than one publisher at a time, you have considerably more freedom in selecting publishers. You could send a copy of your proposal to every publisher listed in *Books in Print* if you were willing to spend the time and the money required for photocopying and postage. Doing your own market survey on potential publishers, so you can limit your submissions to those who are most likely to have an interest in your proposal, is apt to be a much more successful route.

STUDY THE CHOICES

In any discipline, you can choose from a variety of organizational and commercial presses. Vanity presses, those enterprises that charge authors to publish their work, and self-publishing are other options; however, they are likely to be both expensive and unsatisfactory in terms of the number of people who read the book. Finding publishers to consider should be relatively easy. As a professional, you probably are exposed to a barrage of advertising for the professional literature. Read the ads in the professional journals. Save the direct-mail solicitations you may have been tossing in the trash. Look at references as a resource for publishers, not just as citations for the literature. You can also request full catalogs and subject catalogs directly from publishers. For an even broader selection, read the annual *Subject Guide to Books in Print* to identify publishers you may have missed in your review of advertising and citations. Another good source for publishers is *Literary Marketplace*; your local or university library should carry both publications.

As you study the materials you collect, you should consider the publishers' offerings in two respects. First, look to see who the publishers' audience is and what type of books they are publishing. The publisher of professional books—like the NASW Press—who produces only books directed to human services professionals in practice or education, is much less likely to be interested in a trade book directed to consumers of professional services. On the other hand, the trade publisher—that is, the publisher of fiction or popular nonfiction—is less likely to be excited by a textbook or a book on a professional practice. The two kinds of publishers have different marketing and distribution patterns, designed to reach their particular niche easily and profitably; consequently, a book outside their normal product line will be less appealing unless there are unusual circumstances.

Second, you should look at the subject matter and slant of the publishers' current offerings. The publisher who is known for reference books in your discipline, for example, is likely to consider your proposal for a unique new reference work. Publishers who primarily do how-to books, on the other hand, will be less interested in a scholarly reference. The publisher who produces advocacy books may be excited about a book on community organizing, whereas a publisher of strictly clinical books may not. As you read advertisements over time, you will get a better sense of who is publishing what. However, there are no hard and fast rules. Although publishers generally look for manuscripts that fit their overall publishing strategy, as exhibited in what they have produced, they may also be looking for books to fill what they see as gaps in their program. For example, some publishers may not have published any books on child welfare, not because they choose not to, but because they have received no viable proposals.

Once you have identified several potential publishers, request their guidelines for submitting a book proposal and study the guidelines carefully. You are looking not just to see if the publisher would be interested in your proposal, but to determine if you would want that publisher to publish your book. You should consider the following elements.

Editorial and Production Quality

What is your judgment of other books the publisher has produced? Have you found them useful? Are they well edited, or do you wince at grammatical errors and get frustrated over their poor organization? Are they well designed, so you find the covers appealing and the text comfortable to read?

Marketing

What level of marketing is done? And how do you react to the promotions you see? Are the advertisements and flyers or brochures attractive and appropriate to the book? Does the publisher appear to have access to the best market for your book?

Services to the Author

Will the publisher handle such tasks as proofreading, indexing, and preparing figures, or will these tasks be your responsibility? What royalties does the publisher pay? When are the royalties paid? Are advances available?

Another consideration is whether a large or a small publisher is best for your book. As a small publisher, my bias is to tell you that small publishers can provide more personalized attention and may produce a book in a shorter time. On the other hand, a large publisher may employ editorial staff with special expertise in your area and may be able to add your book to a specialized list that gets more overall marketing exposure. There is no clear-cut better-or-worse choice; the experience you have will depend on the particular publisher and perhaps the particular editor you acquire.

Perhaps the best option is to talk to your colleagues who have published. Ask what their experiences have been and if they would recommend their publishers or if they have other suggestions.

MEET WITH AN EDITOR OR PUBLISHER

Most publishers or editors are happy to meet with prospective authors, whether they have submitted a proposal or are considering doing so. Keep in mind that they must continue to find and produce successful new books if they are to stay solvent. In addition, most publishing professionals came to this business because they care about advancing knowledge, and they are generally friendly people who are eager to share what they know about publishing. If you plan to be in a publisher's area or live near a publisher, write a brief letter asking to set up an appointment and then follow it up with a phone call.

You may also be able to arrange a meeting at a professional conference. Publishers attend conferences, not just to sell their current books, but to learn more about the current state of knowledge and to meet prospective authors. Arranging a meeting before you get to the conference is best if you can manage it (often advance programs carry a list of the exhibitors who will be attending). If you do not reach a publisher in advance, however, go to the exhibit hall early in the conference and try to make arrangements to meet. Publishers expect these requests and most likely will still have time available if you get there early enough.

Regardless of the stage you are in, whether the publisher already has your proposal in review or you are just thinking about submitting one, you are not likely to be offered a contract in a meeting. The meeting, however, is an excellent opportunity for an exchange of information that can have a major impact on the outcome of your proposal. You have a chance to discuss the book in more depth than a proposal permits, and the publisher can ask you questions about it. You also can learn more about how the publisher works, what services the publisher can provide, how work is scheduled, and so forth. Jot down your questions in advance and try not to take more than an hour for the meeting.

Don't worry that your questions may appear naive or stupid. Book publishing is complex overall, and services and practices vary from publisher to publisher. Fischel (1984) classified publishing services in seven areas: (1) editorial, (2) production, (3) informational, (4) distribution, (5) marketing, (6) financial, and (7) legal. Figure 9.1 lists the services the NASW Press provides in each of these areas. You may find fewer services in smaller companies and more in larger ones, but the classification and examples may be useful to help formulate your questions.

SUBMIT AN ATTRACTIVE PROPOSAL

Once you have determined where you want to submit proposals and learned what the publishers require to review a proposal, you are ready to package yours. The overall package should be neat, clean, and legible. Print the proposal on a laser printer and label all the components clearly. Pay careful attention to grammar and spelling and make certain that any references are properly styled and accurate.

You may need to change the package for different publishers. Publisher A may require three copies, whereas Publisher B may want only one. (The NASW Press requires four copies.) Although the components described earlier are fairly standard, some publishers may want less information; others may require more. Although the body of your cover letter may be the same for every package, take the time to personalize the letters so the publisher thinks you have some direct interest in that press.

what to expect

Patience may well be the most useful virtue an author can possess because few aspects of publishing move quickly. The outcomes can be so satisfying, however, that most authors find the waiting worthwhile.

THE REVIEW PROCESS

In most publishing houses, your proposal will be sent to expert readers or advisers for comments and ratings. Some presses, like the NASW Press, use peers who are volunteers; others, primarily commercial houses, pay reviewers a small fee for each proposal they read. The number of readers varies from one publishing house

FIGURE 9.1 NASW Press Services

1. **Editorial Services**
   Expert peer review
   Advice on improving the manuscript
   Expert copyediting and styling
   Proofreading
   Indexing

2. **Production**
   Professional design—text and covers
   Selection of appropriate suppliers
   Selection of appropriate equipment and materials
   Supervision of work by editors; typesetters; and the printer,
       binder, and shipper
   Quality control
   Scheduling

3. **Informational**
   News releases to the press
   Announcements to the book trade
   Promotion of book reviews
   Other publicity as feasible
   Library of Congress cataloging information

4. **Distribution**
   Response to inquiries
   Inventory management and warehousing
   Order fulfillment
   Tested sales policies (credit, discounts, returns)
   Returns and claims
   Mailing lists of potential book buyers
   Possible international sales

5. **Marketing**
   Direct-mail campaigns using in-house and rented mailing lists
   Access to a large market for human services books
   Schools and library coverage
   Effective copywriting and production of materials
   Advertising
   Some exhibits and displays at conventions
   Catalogs and other brochures
   Promotion of educational use and adoption
   Promotion of use in special training courses
   Linkages to other products in the same field
   Reputation and prestige of the NASW Press imprint

6. **Financial**
   Investment of prepublishing costs, including the cost of indexing
   Ongoing investment of maintaining the cost of the inventory
   Credit to customers who qualify for credit
   Stable, ongoing operations that are the result of the NASW Press
       handling payrolls and other bills
   Collection of permissions fees and other payments

7. **Legal**
   Application for copyright
   Advice on permissions, copyright, libel, and other matters as necessary
   Willingness to defend the copyright against its infringement

SOURCE: From *A Practical Guide to Writing and Publishing Professional Books* (pp. 26–27), by D. N. Fischel, 1984, New York: Van Nostrand Reinhold. Copyright 1984 by Van Nostrand Reinhold. Adapted with permission.

to another. The criteria used to evaluate proposals submitted to the NASW Press, which generally are read by at least three reviewers, are as follows:

1. quality of writing
2. completeness of coverage
3. timeliness and importance of subject matter
4. potential market
5. salability
6. effective relationship to NASW's program priorities
7. knowledge of the competition.

Timing varies significantly from one publisher to another and even from one proposal to another. Your proposal may arrive at the optimum time, when reviewers are available and return a review quickly. Or the staff member who assigns reviewers may be away when your proposal arrives, and when it is assigned, it may need to be reassigned several times before the publisher obtains a satisfactory expert review. Thus, there is no set time within which you may expect to receive a response. At the NASW Press, reviews often require three to four months; other publishers advertise eight weeks. You should receive an acknowledgment quickly. If a review seems to be taking longer than you expect, do not hesitate to inquire about when you may hear. Your inquiry may stimulate an investigation into why a reviewer has been remiss in returning your proposal.

When you receive a response, it is not likely to be an offer of a contract. Most proposals go through some revisions or further explanations before they are accepted. Even if the publisher rejects the proposal outright, the comments you receive may help you place the manuscript with another publisher. Try not to look at the comments defensively, but to use them to strengthen your proposal, to be resubmitted to the publisher who made the comments or sent to another one. On the other hand, do not be afraid to disagree with the comments. If the reviewer simply did not understand some aspect, you may be able to clarify it so that the publisher will find the proposal acceptable without major revisions.

THE CONTRACT

When the proposal is accepted, you will be offered a contract that will spell out the details of the materials you will provide to the publisher and the services the publisher will provide to you. Publishers generally have a stock contract, which they will offer you, but you may wish to have other provisions inserted. With some exceptions, at least some provisions of most contracts can be negotiated if you feel strongly about them. Although you are unlikely to engage in a protracted discussion between attorneys (most contracts for professional books are settled easily), you should take time to read the contract carefully and ask an attorney or a knowledgeable colleague to review it if you have had no experience with author contracts.

The following are just a few of the provisions you can expect to see in a contract.

Copyright

The contract will specify who holds the copyright. In some houses, the author retains the copyright; others, like the NASW Press, require a copyright transfer as part of the contract to ensure that they can protect the copyright and sales of the work that they are investing so much capital in. (These presses generally agree to return the copyright to the author if they permit the book to go out of print at some point in the future.)

Manuscript Delivery Date

All contracts specify a date that the publisher expects to receive the completed manuscript, and publishers generally also specify a grace period, at the end of which they can refuse to accept the manuscript with no penalties. This delivery date often frightens authors who are uncomfortable committing to a date. As long as you set a rational date and sign the contract in good faith, you can expect the publisher to be somewhat flexible if unexpected problems prevent you from delivering the manuscript on time. But do not expect a publisher to agree to a delivery date three or four years from the contract date because the topic may not be salable that far in the future. Twelve months is about average, although some call for 18 months.

Royalties

Most book authors receive payment in the form of royalties, which are defined as a percentage of sales revenues. The NASW Press royalty schedule is 10 percent of the net receipts for zero to 3,000 copies sold; 12.5 percent for 3,001 to 6,000 copies; and 15 percent for over 6,000 copies. These are fairly typical rates. New authors, who have read about the Tom Clanceys of fiction who receive millions of dollars for a book, are often dismayed by royalty clauses. Royalties are a protection for both the publisher, who must invest a large sum of money in a book that may not sell, and for the author, whose book may sell more copies than originally planned. Fischel

(1984) described royalty arrangements as contracts between authors who risk their labor and publishers who risk their labor and their capital. Even if sales are high for a particular title, profit margins are slim in the publishing world because of the complexities outlined in Figure 9.1.

Most professional books also are sold at substantial discounts. For that reason, many publishers (including the NASW Press) specify that royalties will be paid on the net receipts, rather than on the list price of the book. The difference can be considerable. For example, 1,000 copies of a $20 book would yield $20,000 in sales and $2,000 in royalties if the press received the list price for all copies. If the average discount is 20 percent, however, sales of 1,000 copies would yield only $16,000, or $1,600 in royalties.

Some publishers still offer royalties on list, rather than on net, but their numbers are declining, and the author should be aware of the potential hazards. For the publisher, royalties represent a cost of sales. If the costs of production and sales are high, then the publisher must price the book high. Unfortunately, if the book is priced too high, the likelihood of high sales is poor, and the book may be put out of print rapidly.

If the publisher offers advances on royalties, the amount of the advance and the method of accounting for it against royalties also will be included in the contract. In trade publishing, substantial advances are common, both because the potential exists for substantial sales and because trade authors often earn all their income by writing. Publishers of professional books, on the other hand, rarely provide advances; those who do usually will pay only a few hundred dollars to cover some of the costs of obtaining permissions or illustrations.

Among the other provisions in an author contract are agreements related to legal liability for both parties; other royalty issues, such as payment schedules and reductions for various reasons; subsequent editions; who pays for tasks, such as indexing, getting permissions to reprint material published elsewhere, or preparing camera-ready art; and so forth. (See appendix A for a sample contract.) In addition, the contract will stipulate the publisher's agreement to produce the finished book.

MANUSCRIPT DELIVERY AND PRODUCTION

You will no doubt be in contact with your publisher once or twice while you are writing, if just to provide reassurance that you are working. At some point, you will want to verify the details for delivering your manuscript. The NASW Press requests two paper copies (all double-spaced) of the manuscript plus a disk containing the complete manuscript. Although we do not edit online, having the disk helps reduce the costs of typesetting a book even though the typesetter must enter all the editorial changes. We also need completed copies of all necessary permissions. If you are editing a collected work, we need copyright transfers on the forms we provided you from every author whose work is included in the book.

Once you receive the acknowledgment that your manuscript was received, you may not hear from the publisher for what seems like a long time. First, someone in the press must review the completed manuscript, then the book's editor must develop a production schedule, and then the book must be copyedited before it is returned for your review. If you know that you will not be available to work on clearing the manuscript at certain times, tell your publisher. You should not underestimate the time you may require to clear the edited copy. Almost every author must complete references, search for other information, and rewrite portions when the manuscript has been edited. In many cases, the copy editor also will recommend that some portions should be reorganized. For more information on clearing the edited manuscript, see chapter 10, "Production Procedures," in this book.

REWARDS

Although we may be too reticent to say it out loud, most of us fantasize about fame and riches. Alas, authors of professional books are unlikely to receive six-figure royalty checks, see their book reviewed in *The New York Times* Book Review section, or appear on the "Tonight Show."

First, the royalties: Don't quit your job when the book comes off press. Even successful authors who have published several books rely on their teaching or practice for most of their income. A high percentage of professional books never sell more than 1,000 copies while they are in print, and some sell fewer than 750. If you have low expectations, you may then be pleasantly surprised.

What kind of publicity can you expect? The publisher probably will announce the book to the trade press and offer review copies to all potential reviewers. You can expect to see the book advertised in the publisher's next catalog and in flyers or brochures that may include related books. The book may be advertised in professional journals, either by itself or more likely with other related books. Other promotional outlets include card decks (packages of cards, each advertising a different product or service, that appear in your mail) and trade shows.

Some publishers are equipped to arrange appearances on talk shows and at seminars; others will provide support in the form of book flyers and sample copies. Although you may be self-conscious about it at first, it behooves you to promote your own book vigorously. It is the norm for authors to carry around flyers advertising their books. Arrangers of seminars will find you an even more welcome speaker if you have a book on the subject, and they may wish to arrange sales and autograph sessions in conjunction with your presentation. Book yourself into author forums at professional conferences. Ask colleagues whom you respect in your topic area to read the book and provide testimonials. Pursue avenues for book reviews. Even though not all book reviews will be favorable (and some may be downright nasty), they are essential to getting your book into libraries and may stimulate professors to adopt the book for their courses. All these activities will increase the sales of your book, and the increased sales will make you and your publisher happy.

So, you won't get rich. You may—no, probably will—receive negative reviews. There can be countless annoyances—typographical errors in the book and misperceptions in the advertising copy; the 50 copies you order for your fall classes do not appear in the bookstore until Thanksgiving; the most important journal in your field assigns your archenemy to review the book. Why would anyone want all this grief? Well, there is the indescribable thrill of holding the tangible expression of your knowledge and work in your hands. You will learn an enormous amount from writing a book, not just about the publishing process, but about your topic and yourself. You will have the satisfaction of having contributed to the knowledge in your field. And, a good book is likely to help advance your career.

Good luck. If the first proposal is not accepted, do not give up. Use the readers' comments and keep working. The rewards really do outweigh the pain.

references

Armstrong, R. A. (1972). The qualities of a book, the wants of a dissertation. *Scholarly Publishing, 3*, 99–109.

Fischel, D. N. (1984). *A practical guide to writing and publishing professional books: Business, technical, scientific, scholarly.* New York: Van Nostrand Reinhold.

Halpenny, F. G. (1972). The thesis and the book. *Scholarly Publishing, 3*, 111–116.

10 *production procedures*

Nancy Winchester and Linda Beebe

Congratulations! Your manuscript has been accepted for publication. It is now ready to be edited, typeset, and printed. Before long the final product will be in your hands. What can you expect between now and then? What are your responsibilities? This article gives a brief introduction to the production work that is required to put your work into print and offers some pointers on what you should do to help the publisher present it in the best possible way. Although we focus on journal articles, the editing and production processes are similar for books and other published materials.

what happens first?

When you received notice that your article was accepted, you also received a contract. Sign it and return it as soon as possible. Your article will not go to press until the publisher has a signed contract in hand, and you do not want to take any chances on delaying the publication date. (See appendix A for a sample journal contract.)

Meanwhile, the publisher has moved your manuscript folder from the circulation file, where it resided during the time the manuscript was in review, to the file of accepted manuscripts, from which tables of contents for future journal issues are developed. At the NASW Press, once your article is slated for publication, the file will be handed over to the editorial department. The production process begins.

how long will it take?

You are understandably eager to see your article in print after you have spent so much time writing and revising it. Perhaps the topic is particularly timely, or the data can fast become outdated. Perhaps you are in line for a promotion or tenure decision, and having an article published would be helpful. Although the editor will no doubt sympathize with you, the speed with which your article appears in print will relate more to how many other authors, who have concerns similar to yours, are waiting in front of you.

Just how long might the author of a journal article reasonably expect to wait before his or her article appears in print? Publishers vary greatly—from one to another and even from one journal to another within the same publishing house. The waiting time depends on the size of the publication; its frequency; the number of submissions; the backlog of articles accepted for publication; the work load of the staff; the complexity of the manuscript itself (a lot of tables or graphics, for instance); and any special typesetting, printing, or binding constraints.

Reported lag times from acceptance to print for journals in social work and social welfare range from around three or four months to a year or considerably more, with the nine- to 12-month range most typical (Mendelsohn, 1992). A book may take more time or less, depending on the publisher. At the NASW Press it will probably be off press in six to nine months, but up to 18 months is not uncommon in the industry.

what does the copy editor do?

Finally, your article is scheduled for an upcoming issue. Now it goes to a copy editor. New authors often are bemused (not to mention anxious) to find that someone is going to edit their material. After all, the work has gone through substantial review and revision. It has been accepted by a prestigious journal. Why would it need more work? Well, the reviewers and editor have worked with you on substantive changes in content. Although they may have pointed out some problems with language and consistency, they generally do not go through the manuscript line by line, word by word, the way a copy editor does. Who needs editing? Virtually everyone. Even the work of seasoned writers benefits from a second pair of eyes.

Copy editors help with clarity, brevity, and logic, and they ensure that an article does indeed have a beginning, a middle, and an end. The ultimate goal of the editorial effort is a printed product that is as easy as possible to read, understand, and remember. The copy editor is your behind-the-scenes partner, helping to make sure readers will understand the work in the way you intended it to be understood.

UNDERSTAND THE AUTHOR'S WORK

What must happen to get an article ready for publication? The copy editor first reads every piece of correspondence in your manuscript file. He or she must become familiar with you and with your concerns, ideas, revisions, and corrections. The copy editor checks that the signed contract is in house and reviews memos from the editor, reviewers, publisher, and managing editor—no slip of paper in the file goes unturned. At the end of this review, he or she will have gained a strong sense of all that has gone into the article's evolution.

Second, copy editors become familiar with the manuscript itself. At a minimum, they skim the abstract, if one is included; introductory paragraphs; and conclusion. They need to gain a sense of the subject and the way the author has organized it.

EDIT FOR CONSISTENCY AND LANGUAGE

Once the copy editor is familiar with your work, he or she begins the actual editing. Some articles require substantial work; others do not. Generally, copy editors do the following:

- ▶ correct spelling and grammar
- ▶ check consistency of usage of words, abbreviations, and numbers
- ▶ improve readability by varying sentence length and structure and by correcting punctuation
- ▶ ensure that the work is logically organized
- ▶ make the writing concise by eliminating unnecessary words and redundant statements
- ▶ compare columns of numbers in tables and figures against numbers in the text
- ▶ check the totals in tables
- ▶ check the documentation and call to the author's attention any discrepancies between references cited in the text and those cited in the reference list.

Copy editors work not only to correct wording, but to ensure that appropriate language is used. Colloquialisms, for example, are expressions used in conversation and are not suitable for formal publications. Clichés are trite expressions, and rhetorical flourishes pompous language. Overuse of jargon sounds pretentious, and mixed metaphors are confusing. None enhance an article's effectiveness or readability. In fact, inappropriate words and phrases impair readability, and the copy editor who deletes casual, trite, or pompous language is sparing you the embarrassment of having these less-than-professional expressions appear in print under your name.

Throughout their work, copy editors attempt to correct language and consistency without introducing errors or altering the substance of the author's work. Occasionally, the editors of NASW Press journals will ask the copy editors to work with the authors in reducing excessive length (this has become a more common request as we see more and more bloated articles); in those cases, the copy editor may suggest eliminating whole paragraphs and sections. Good editors try to maintain the author's voice or tone while they improve the language. Occasionally, copy editors may query the author on context—for instance, on undocumented statements presented as fact, on inconsistent statements, or about relevant issues that are not included in the manuscript. Figure 10.1 is an example of the type of checklist used by copy editors.

CHECK REFERENCES AND DOCUMENTATION

Probably no copy editor in the world would argue that the biggest, most persistent problem copy editors face in their work is references and documentation. The completeness and accuracy of the references are the author's responsibility. But a skilled copy editor is invaluable in making sure that things really are in order.

During the course of editing a manuscript, the copy editor checks every citation in the text against the reference list. If the text citation appears in the reference list, it is checked off in both the text and in the reference list. With the exception of personal communications (see part III of this volume, "NASW Quick Guide to Mechanics"), all documentation in the text must be included in the reference list. Conversely, all entries in the reference list must be cited in the text. The author is alerted to any discrepancies.

Probably the most common problem is variations between the reference list entries and the author–date citations in the text. Maybe an author's name is spelled two different ways. Maybe the publication dates do not agree. Perhaps page numbers do not mesh. Once again, the copy editor will call the problem to the author's attention.

The reference list itself is a gold mine of possible pitfalls: suspicious volume or page numbers for journal titles, missing publishers for books, incomplete information for newspaper articles (give the exact section and page number). The seasoned copy editor is stranger to none of these and will be sure that for every item in the

FIGURE 10.1   Example of a copy editor's checklist

COPYEDITING CHECKLIST

Preliminary Tasks
- ☐ Print neatly and legibly using a dark black pencil.
- ☐ Place illustrations and tables at the end of the manuscript.
- ☐ Number all pages sequentially; page 1 is the title page.
- ☐ Style title, byline, and author blurb according to style guide.
- ☐ Create a style sheet indicating treatment of acronyms and any judgments.

Editing
- ☐ Review and correct spelling, grammar, and punctuation.
- ☐ Correct capitalization, number style, abbreviations, use of italics or quotation marks, and sequence of anything alphabetic or numerical.
- ☐ Check parallelism throughout text; rewrite when necessary to make elements in a series parallel.
- ☐ Be sure all pronouns have clear antecedents.
- ☐ Mark subheads A, B, or C (rarely D) in the margin. Follow outline style; that is, if using a secondary subheading, then provide at least one other secondary subheading under the same principal heading. However, in a few cases, use of outline style may seem contrived. In those cases, it may be necessary to make an exception to this rule.
- ☐ Mark end-of-line hyphens to be retained as necessary.
- ☐ Spell out acronyms and abbreviations at first mention, without periods. Query author if meaning is unknown.
- ☐ Eliminate sexist language.
- ☐ Style lists and code "list" (for numbered lists) or "bullet list" in margin.

Illustrations and Tables
- ☐ Note in the margin the placement of tables or figures at the first mention of each table or figure (for example, "Table 1 about here"). Data in tables and figures must match data in text.
- ☐ Check simple mathematical computations for accuracy—for example, percentages should equal 100 (plus or minus one percentage point), addition should be correct, and so forth.
- ☐ Ask author to confirm that illustrations are original with the article. If not, author must provide written permission from the copyright holder to adapt or reprint the illustration.

Queries
- ☐ Type author queries on a separate sheet of paper. Be sure that queries are tactfully and unambiguously worded.
- ☐ Query the author for missing page numbers of quotes of more than three words and, if the quote is more than 300 words, query author for permission to reprint the material.

References
- ☐ Check references in text against the reference list. Query author for missing items and inconsistencies. Check alphabetic order of references.

reference list the following information appears: all authors'
names; publication date; article title, journal title, volume number,
and inclusive pages for a journal article; and chapter title, book
title, book editor, location of publisher and publisher's name, and
inclusive pages for a book chapter. If any of these items is missing,
expect to hear from the copy editor. For further details on the
reference list, see part III of this book, "NASW Quick Guide to
Mechanics."

Once the copy editor is comfortable with the edited manuscript,
he or she will make a file copy and return the edited manuscript
to the author for review. How the process just outlined works
depends on the size and resources of the publishing office. The
staff—the director of publications, the managing editor, or a project
manager—may assign the manuscript to a copy editor, or the
editor may make the assignment. The copy editor may be a full-
time staff person or a free-lance editor. Or, on small journals, the
editor or managing editor may act as the copy editor in preparing
the article for publication.

what does the author do?

Nearly all publishers give the author an opportunity to review the
copy editor's changes and suggestions before the article is printed.
What exactly will you receive from the copy editor? If you receive
an edited manuscript, it may appear in one of two forms. Many
scholarly publishers still prefer to edit pencil on paper so that authors see all editorial changes. If your publisher uses pencil on
paper, you will get your original manuscript with handwritten
editorial changes penciled in. (You were asked to provide double-
spaced copy to allow room for the copy editor to insert changes
that will be legible to you and to the typesetter.) An example of a
copyedited page is shown in Figure 10.2. Figure 10.3 explains the
editor's marks.

Other publishers use one of the numerous software packages
that allow editing to be done online. Most of these packages offer a
redlining feature that highlights changes and, depending on the
sophistication of the package, may also show the original text. You
will most likely see the article typed as the copy editor intends it to
appear in print with all the changes he or she has inserted
underlined.

A number of scholarly presses send only typeset proof to authors, with queries written in the margins. The advantage to the
author is that a typeset proof is far easier to read than a marked-
up manuscript. The disadvantage is that editorial changes are not
readily apparent.

FIGURE 10.2   Example of a copyedited page of a manuscript

Ⓐ ~~Legal and ethical~~ confidentiality guidelines ~~applying to~~ *in* specific situations‚

Ⓑ ~~1)~~ **Informed Consent**‡Informed consent means/involving the student and/or family   Ⓠ *(Query 3)*
that the school social worker must
in the decision to disclose confidential information. ~~During the initial phase of~~ working
When the school social worker begins
with a client, ~~negotiations should take place to establish~~ ground rules regarding the
the two should negotiate
sharing of information within the family, within the school‚ and with other agencies.
the worker should inform   *about*   *and*
~~The client should be informed of~~ the limits of confidentiality‚ When information is
requested by
~~shared with~~ outside agencies, the following guidelines apply: ⌐a⌐•The request for

(bullet list)

information must be in writing. ⌐b⌐•The request must state specifically what data are
being sought and for what purpose. ⌐c⌐•The client must be informed of the request, and
his or her permission must be obtained for disclosure. ⌐d⌐•The agency releasing the
must
information must include a statement of rules for the receiving party to follow ~~in order~~
to maintain the confidentiality of the material.
that professionals
Ⓑ ~~2)~~ **Child Abuse and/or Neglect**‡All fifty states have statutes mandating ~~the~~
identification and reporting of suspected child abuse and/or neglect ~~by professionals.~~
Each school district must establish
Clear policies and procedures ~~need to be established within each school district. These~~
~~guidelines should be worked out~~ in consultation with school administrators, teachers,
support staff, parents, child protective service workers, police representatives‚ and
representatives of community organizations. The guidelines should include
for the reporting professional   *process*
confidentiality safeguards‚ in relation to‚ reporting‚ and appropriate follow-up.
the
Ⓑ ~~3)~~ **Substance Abuse**‡Several federal laws guarantee strict confidentiality to youths
receiving alcohol and drug abuse services. School-based substance abuse programs‚
must conform to these federal guidelines‚ with the exception of classroom education
programs‚ State laws vary considerably in relation to ~~the~~ age and parental involvement
is   *is should establish*
requirements when youth‚ receive substance abuse services. School district‚ guidelines
~~should be established~~ to clarify the parameters of confidentiality guaranteed to the
regarding the   *ment of*
student and the responsibility of the school social worker/‚ involve‚ appropriate
resources, including the family‚ and/or law enforcement officials.

FIGURE 10.3 Editorial and proofreader's marks

Mark	Description	Mark	Description
	Delete		Insert colon
#	Insert space		Insert hyphen
eq #	Make space equal	set	Insert question mark
	Close up space		Insert apostrophe or single quotation mark
	Delete and close up space		Insert quotation marks
	New paragraph	eq	Insert equals sign
tr	Transpose elements; change order the	( )	Insert parentheses
sp	Spell out	I/M	Insert em dash
ital	Set in _italic_ type	I/N	Insert en dash
rom	Set in roman type		Move type one em to left or right
bf	Set in _boldface_ type		Move right
wf	Wrong font		Move left
lc	Set in LOWERCASE letters		Center
cap	Set in capital letters		Move up
sc	Set in _small capital_ letters		Move down
V	Insert here _or_ make superscript	fr	Flush right
∧	Insert here _or_ make subscript	fl	Flush left
	Insert comma		Straighten type; align type horizontally
⊙	Insert period	‖	Align type vertically
;	Insert semicolon		

REVIEW THE EDITED MANUSCRIPT

In whatever form you receive your edited manuscript, your job is to read it carefully word for word and to review all the changes the copy editor has made. Do not be alarmed by what may seem to be extensive changes. Some of the handwritten changes are simply instructions to the typesetter. For example, the subheads will be marked according to their level (for example, A, B, or C), and any type that is to be set in boldface or italics will be identified. Page numbers and other extraneous text that will not appear in the printed version will be deleted.

Read the copy editor's work carefully to ensure that no errors have been introduced and no meanings misconstrued during editing. A query sheet will usually accompany an edited manuscript. Although you may be tempted just to delete the editor's changes, try to read the queries as you go through the edited manuscript and understand why the changes were made. Good copy editors will explain why they have suggested a major change. Take the time to review the edited manuscript thoroughly, keeping in mind that this may be the last time you see it before it is in print and therefore unchangeable.

ANSWER ALL THE QUERIES

As the author, you are responsible for answering the copy editor's queries as completely as possible. Please do not answer yes when an editor asks, "Do you mean A or do you mean B?" Sometimes the answer is not easy, but ignoring the question will not resolve the problem because the copy editor will telephone you and repeat the question. If you cannot answer A or B, perhaps you need to rewrite the sentence or paragraph that triggered the question. Be sure that you answer every query on the sheet. If the copy editor has asked, "OK as edited?" you need to respond yes or "no, change to . . . ."

The types of queries you may encounter vary widely. By far the largest source of editorial questions involves reference information. Although copy editors help authors by identifying problems, they rarely have the time or the resources to complete the citations; instead, the author must do that. Authors always are responsible for the accuracy and completeness of references. The importance of accurate references can hardly be stressed enough. Imagine the frustration of the reader trying to follow up on a book or article for which the wrong information is given. Your objective is to inform readers, not frustrate them, so when a copy editor presses you to complete references, consider it help, not harassment.

Completing references that you included originally is not the only request you may encounter. In addition, the copy editor may ask you to document facts for which no reference was given. Do not respond, as more than one author has, "That's common knowledge!" or "I'm the expert—my saying so is good enough!" You are indeed the expert; therefore, facts that need documentation for others may seem self-explanatory to you. In general, if the copy editor requests documentation, the statement probably should be documented.

RESPOND QUICKLY, BUT CAREFULLY

When you receive the edited manuscript, you will be asked to return it within a specified time, usually within a few days or sometimes within 48 hours. Your timely response is essential. Publishing and deadlines go hand in hand, and every step of the production process has a deadline. When a deadline is missed early on, other deadlines further down the line are jeopardized—including that bottom-line off-press date. One of the most frustrating aspects of a production editor's job is having an issue ready to go to press, except for clearance from one author who is holding up the entire journal by not returning a manuscript or completing a reference.

Most publishers request that authors refrain from writing on the edited manuscript itself and respond instead on the query sheet or a separate piece of paper. But you may find it necessary to write on the edited copy if you are asking the copy editor to restore text or are correcting wording. If you do need to write directly on the copy, and when marking proofs, use a bright color different from the one used by the editor. Before you return the manuscript, be sure to read it carefully one last time to double-check that it reads as you want it to.

REMEMBER WHOSE WORK IT IS

As you review the copy editor's work, you should remember that the article is your work and that it will appear in print under your name. A talented copy editor will no doubt improve your manuscript, but that does not mean you should ignore any changes that trouble you. If the copy editor has changed the meaning of what you said, say so and suggest another way to fix the problem the copy editor identified. If new wording offends you, say so. "Stet" (which means "let it stand") is an appropriate term to use when you strongly believe that the original language should be retained. As long as you respect the work of the copy editor and do not arbitrarily demand that all the original language be restored, you should feel comfortable voicing your disagreement. But be sure you express that disagreement immediately, while changes can still be made. Sometimes an author calls after an article is published to complain about how an article was edited. At that point, nothing can be done. Remember that publishers send edited manuscripts to authors so that they can correct problems. Occasionally, you and the copy editor will need to negotiate changes because you dislike something he or she has done, but your preferred wording violates the house style. The copy editor can tell you why he or she made the changes, and you should be prepared to explain why you find them unacceptable. Then you will be able to reach a conclusion that is acceptable to both you and the publisher.

FULFILL ANY OTHER RESPONSIBILITIES

You may have been asked to supply a disk as well as a paper copy of your manuscript. Some journal publishers require authors to incorporate editorial changes onto the disk and submit the corrected disk to the copy editor. This is by no means a universal practice; however, it does occur. Many publishers, including the NASW Press, employ professional typesetters to incorporate all editorial changes.

Some journal presses and most book publishers send both manuscripts and proofs to authors. However, authors may have to pay for the alterations they make in proofs. Regardless of the stage at which an article or book is reviewed, authors should be satisfied when they are finished their review that the material is indeed ready for publication.

If your article includes figures or graphs, you will be asked to provide camera-ready copy, that is, material that can be used with no alterations for printing. To be camera ready, the figures must be produced on a 300 dpi (dots per inch) laser printer (or one with even better resolution) or hand drafted with black ink by a technical artist. They also must be sized so that they can be used as is or reduced legibly. (See chapter 6, "Graphics," for more information.) Often, authors submit figures that will not be legible once they go through the printing process. If yours is one of these, you will be asked to submit a corrected figure. Some publishers, like the NASW Press, will produce figures for you and bill you for the cost.

For some journals, you may have one other responsibility, and that relates to page charges. A fair number of scholarly journals require or request that authors pay page charges—perhaps $50 per final typeset page of an article—to help defray the cost of publication. Others now levy a processing fee for accepted articles. The journal's guidelines should reflect any fees.

how is the article produced?

When you return your manuscript, the copy editor incorporates all your responses to questions into the master edited copy and addresses any concerns you have raised. If you have not been thorough in responding to queries, he or she will telephone you. At this point the copy editor also marks the manuscript for type— and off it goes to the typesetter.

TYPESETTING

Procedures for typesetting, like those for editing and review, vary from publisher to publisher. The typesetter, who is a professional trained in graphics and the nuances of type, will either enter all your manuscript or, using your disk, incorporate only the edited changes. Traditionally, typesetters first generate galleys—unformatted, unpaginated sheets of type—that are proofread.

The proofreader's task is formidable. He or she must

► check the type word for word against the edited manuscript to ensure that the editor's and author's changes have all been incorporated
► check all entries in the reference list against the text (again!)
► check that the figures and tables are reproduced accurately and (at a later stage) positioned correctly in the text
► check all other components of the page against the type specifications to be sure that the layout and format are correct.

Figure 10.4 is an example of the type of checklist used in proofreading galleys. The typesetter then incorporates all the corrections and formats the pages according to the journal's specifications.

DESKTOP PUBLISHING

A few words should be added here about desktop publishing, a technology that has been widely and rapidly embraced since the mid-1980s. Publishers are often asked, "But can't anyone produce a book or journal with desktop publishing?" Desktop publishing offers tremendous flexibility and capability. It is ideal for internal documents and newsletters, for example. But unless the user has some training in type and design, beware of the results. Professional designers and typesetters understand type and the elements of the page in a way that allows them to produce more attractive, readable, and accessible products than would otherwise be possible. All too often someone without the necessary training tries to use

FIGURE 10.4   Example of a checklist used for proofreading galleys

---

PROOFING GALLEYS

Proofing

☐ Proof word for word against the original manuscript.

☐ Proof medical terms, dosages, and unusual text (that is, math symbols, formulas, and foreign words) character for character.

☐ Ensure that author names in the byline exactly match those in the author blurb.

☐ Proof reference lists carefully and check consistency of style. Check the alphabetic order of the reference list.

☐ Cross-check reference citations in text and in reference list for consistency. Put a check mark in text above the citation and in the reference list to the left of the citation if they match. If they do not match, query the author.

☐ Mark editorial changes for obvious errors. Query editor if making judgment calls.

☐ Check simple mathematical computations for accuracy and query editor if they are incorrect.

Format

☐ Are heads correctly styled?

☐ Are heads parallel? Heads generally should follow outline style.

Figures and Tables

☐ Are figures and table callouts highlighted? Are placements indicated in margin next to first callout of each table or figure?

☐ Are titles and captions set in proper type?

☐ Is copy positioned per style or per manuscript instructions?

☐ Do figures and tables correspond with their captions?

Final Step

☐ Read through proof, being especially alert for typos.

---

all the desktop publishing capabilities in one document. We often see one-page flyers produced with desktop publishing that feature four or five different typefaces—with italics and boldface of each. Imagine how that would work in a book or journal! Better to let a professional handle the job.

INDEXES

Most professional books are indexed. Entire journal volumes are too, at the end of a volume year, but individual journal articles are not. A good index includes more than key words. It is conceptual as well. A good indexer attempts to understand the material being indexed well enough to anticipate the ways in which readers who are not thoroughly familiar with the content may look up an idea, term, or topic in the index.

Word-processing capacity for basic indexing has convinced many authors that professional indexing is no longer required. That belief is reinforced by the fact that many publishers require that authors index their own books or pay for a professional indexer. Other publishers, including the NASW Press, view professional indexing as an investment in the book and absorb the cost of indexing themselves. Although many journals now ask that authors identify key words for their articles, they generally do not use them to create the annual index. Instead, the key words are published with the abstract at the beginning of the article as an aid to abstracting services. The index cannot be completed until all other copy is absolutely firm because the page numbers must be picked up for the index.

PRINTING

When all the pages are formatted, the journal or book is proofread once more and corrections are made. For books and journal issues that contain an index, the index is proofed and at least some random page numbers are checked for accuracy against the text. At last, it is time to print.

In the 25 years or so since phototypesetting replaced "hot type" (individual metal characters), technology has phenomenally speeded up the process of printing and provided the publisher with many options. Today, a publisher may send camera-ready pages to the printer on resin-coated paper that the printer then photographs for printing. Alternatively, the publisher may generate film from typesetting and save a step in the printing. Or, some publishers are providing disks or telecommunicating type via modems and telephone lines.

Before the book or journal is actually printed, the printer usually provides the publisher with a proof. The most common proof, the blueline, seems to hold great mystique for people who are not publishing professionals. Book authors often ask, "Will I get to see a blueline?" No, only the publisher looks at a blueline, and then only for specific checks. According to the *Chicago Manual of Style* (1982), bluelines "provide the editor with his or her only chance to check on the placement of halftone illustrations, and are useful for checking the positioning of typed material on the page and for making sure that everything intended for inclusion in the book is actually there" (p. 631). A blueline is not meant to be read. It gives the editor one last chance to check

► the sequence of pages
► the alignment of pages
► margins

- ▶ the correct placement of tables and figures
- ▶ any dirt or scratches on the negative.

Because changes at this stage are very expensive, most publishers require that editors make only essential changes, that is, changes to correct errors that would cause the publisher extreme embarrassment if they were not corrected.

The journal is printed and bound as soon as the bluelines are returned to the printer. Advance copies are delivered to the publisher, and the rest of the print order is sent to a fulfillment house or mailed to subscribers.

what will the author receive?

Most journals provide a certain number of free copies to authors who are published in an issue. Some journals provide a quantity of free reprints, and others provide reprints for a fee, usually in minimum quantities of 50 or 100. The NASW Press sends five issues of a journal to all authors and offers reprints of individual articles for a fee. For book authors, the NASW Press, like most publishers, stipulates in the contract the number of complimentary copies the author will receive. Books are sent to the author as soon as the book is off press; additional copies may be offered at an author discount.

Often authors, especially those who are teachers, wish to use their published articles in other ways. You should be aware that if you transfer your copyright to the publisher, as the NASW Press and many other publishers require that you do, you are not free to reprint your article at will. Most publishers will grant you permission to use your material, but if the article is to be used in a course pack, they will most likely require that the copy house pay a royalty on the article. To be safe, always consult the publisher's permissions department before you photocopy any article for broad distribution.

conclusion

In this chapter, we have reviewed briefly the processes an article goes through to get from the manuscript stage to publication in a scholarly journal. Because publishers vary widely in their resources and their customs, your experience may differ slightly from the one outlined here. It is likely, however, that your article will be edited, you will be asked to answer queries and approve edited copy, the manuscript will be typeset and incorporated into a journal issue, and the final product will be printed and delivered to subscribers. All these activities probably will take place within a short period, even though that period may occur several months or more after your article is accepted. Therefore, it is important to respond as quickly and efficiently as you can. Perhaps the most important message in this chapter is that the copy editor is your ally, not your enemy. If you work cooperatively with him or her, you can be sure that your work will be presented in as professional a manner as possible.

references

University of Chicago Press. (1982). *The Chicago manual of style* (13th ed., rev. and exp.). Chicago: Author.

Mendelsohn, H. N. (1992). *An author's guide to social work journals* (3rd ed.). Washington, DC: NASW Press.

PART III

NASW quick

guide to mechanics

Editorial Staff: Lisa Ann Braxton, Christina A. Davis, K. Hyde Loomis,
Stephen D. Pazdan, Nancy A. Winchester

abstract

An abstract enables a reader to review the contents of an article quickly. In addition, researchers can easily access abstracts through databases. Therefore, it is important to describe the contents of an article as clearly and as thoroughly as space permits. An abstract generally should be about 150 words and should indicate the purpose of the study or discussion in the article and conclusions reached.

A report of an empirical study should have an *informative abstract*. This type of abstract presents the conceptual content and summarizes the essential ideas of the article. It answers the following questions:

▶ What is the author's thesis? What hypotheses or theories does the author present?

▶ How does the author develop the main hypotheses? What data did the author use? On what methods did the author draw to isolate the data? Did the author use novel methodology? Are the data qualitatively or quantitatively manipulated? What tests, scales, indexes, or other instruments did the author use?

▶ Do the findings support the hypotheses?

▶ What conclusions did the author draw? Are the proposed hypotheses, ideas, concepts, or theories accepted or rejected? What new relationships are found? What old ones are reaffirmed or rejected?

An article that reviews theory or the literature cannot be quickly summarized. Therefore, it is described in an *indicative abstract*. This type of abstract briefly describes the topic of the article; the thesis or organizing construct and scope of the article; the sources used; and conclusions, implications, or applications.

Write the abstract in a positive tone whenever possible, using specific, concrete language. Delete jargon, clichés, slang, and needless words. Avoid using "this paper" or "this manuscript." Instead, "this article" or "the present article" is preferred.

author information

In the journals of the National Association of Social Workers (NASW), the author information is written in prose style. It contains information about the author, including the full name as it appears on the title page of the article; his or her highest degree and any certifications; job title; employing organization; and full mailing address for primary author and city and state for secondary authors.

The author information also includes any acknowledgments an author wishes to make for grants or substantive contributions to the content of the article, as well as information about the previous presentation of the article at a conference.

Examples

> Sanford Schwartz, PhD, is assistant professor, School of Social Work, Virginia Commonwealth University, 1001 West Franklin, Richmond, VA 23284-2027. Herman V. Wood, MSW, is director, Interstate Court Service, St. Louis, MO. An earlier version of this article was presented at Social Work '89: NASW's Meeting of the Profession, San Francisco, October 1989.

> Linda E. Jones, PhD, is assistant professor, School of Social Work, University of Minnesota, 400 Ford Hall, 224 Church St., SE, Minneapolis, MN 55455. Esther Wattenberg, MA, ACSW, is professor, School of Social Work, and is with the Center for Urban and Regional Affairs, Hubert H. Humphrey Center, University of Minnesota. The research for this article was supported in part by The McKnight Foundation and the Center for Urban and Regional Affairs and the School of Social Work at the University of Minnesota. The authors thank Mary Ann Reitmeir for assistance with data collection and Carol Skay for assistance with data analysis.

capitalization

Avoid unnecessary capitalization. In general, follow the usage set out in *The Chicago Manual of Style* (13th ed., rev. and exp.), unless otherwise instructed in this section.

AMENDMENTS

Capitalize all amendments to the U.S. Constitution.

> *Examples:* First Amendment, Fifteenth Amendment, *but* the amendment, the Smith amendment

DEGREES

Capitalize abbreviations of degrees without periods. Lowercase degrees when written out.

> *Examples:* MSW, PhD, master of social work, master's degree

FIGURES AND TABLES

For figure and table titles, follow the rules given under "Titles and Headings" in this section.

Capitalize main words in table column headings; capitalize only the first word in table stubs. See a sample table under the section "Tables."

Capitalize in-text references to figures and tables, but do not capitalize in-text references to equations.

Examples: Figure 3, Table 1, *but* equation 1

FOLLOWING A COLON

A complete sentence following a colon begins with a capital letter. A vertical list following a colon begins with a lowercase letter. The exception is if items in the list are complete sentences. In that case, capitalize the first word of each item.

Examples: He asserted the following: Most states will opt for administrative review panels.

The following three events appear to push an individual in stage 2 of homelessness into stage 3: (1) The economic circumstances of an individual's life are reduced; (2) the social support network crumbles; and (3) a long-term inadequate diet, ill health, and social decompensation begin to take their toll.

The following symptoms must be present in the sufferer:
► mild fever or chills
► sore throat
► painful lymph nodes.

This weighting procedure involves several assumptions:
► On average, respondents were contacted halfway through their current spell.
► The length of the current spells indicates the likely future lengths of spells.
► The overall risk of homelessness will remain constant at 1988 levels.

ORGANIZATIONS

NASW Press style is to lowercase all shortened or substitute names of agencies, councils, committees, commissions, chapters, and the like. Specific names of councils, committees, and so on remain capitalized when referred to in full.

Example: The National Association of Social Workers, *but* the association

PARTS OF A BOOK

Do not capitalize in-text references to chapters, parts, or appendixes of a book.

PREPOSITIONS

Capitalize prepositions in the name of an organization if that is how the group designates itself.

> *Example:* Philadelphia Women Against Rape

Otherwise, lowercase all prepositions.

TESTS, SCALES, AND FORMS

Capitalize the name of any form, checklist, or testing index used for research and cited in an article if it has been developed by someone and published previously. There should be an author–date citation after its first mention.

> *Example:* Initial screening consisted of administering items from the Structured Clinical Interview for DSM-III–R, or SCID (Spitzer, Williams, & Gibbon, 1986) and the Hamilton Rating Scale for Depression (Hamilton, 1960, 1967).

TITLES AND HEADINGS

Capitalize all words in article titles except for prepositions, conjunctions, articles, and the "to" in infinitives. When a capitalized word is hyphenated, follow the rules in *The Chicago Manual of Style*, section 7.124. Also, capitalize the first word after a colon or a dash. In section headings within an article, follow these same rules.

TITLES AND OFFICES

Lowercase all job titles, civic titles and offices, military titles and offices, religious titles and offices, and titles of nobility when they follow a name or are used in place of a personal name. Capitalize titles only when they precede the name.

> *Examples:* John Roberts, professor of social work, and the mayor met to discuss educational concerns.
>
> Professor Jane Taylor, DSW, spoke at the conference.

case studies

Case studies can effectively exemplify a technique an author is advocating. Case studies should be brief and should present only the information essential to the point being made. To protect the confidentiality of the client in the case study, use fictitious names and give a first name only or an initial without a period. Use subheadings to set case studies apart from the rest of the text.

Example

Case Study

Gail, a pregnant 18-year-old woman, was brought to the hospital by her maternal grandmother. The grandmother sought medical help for Gail out of her concern about Gail's pregnancy and problems with drug and alcohol abuse. . . .

figures

Illustrations can effectively enhance the reader's understanding of the text. They should supplement, rather than duplicate, the text. Figures include graphic material such as photographs, line drawings, graphs, or a combination of these. Figures are often used to present patterns or trends, whereas tables present a large amount of information (usually numbers) in an organized and concise way.

▶ Position each figure on a separate sheet of paper and place after the reference list at the end of the manuscript. Number these pages sequentially, following the last text page number.
▶ Number all figures consecutively, beginning with Figure 1. Be sure all illustrations are mentioned in the text.
▶ Figure captions should be as short as possible while giving an accurate idea of the information included in the illustration. Titles should enable illustrations to stand apart from the text and still be understood.
▶ Provide camera-ready artwork for figures. An original laser printout or professionally prepared artwork is required.

italics

Use italics sparingly in text.

ITALICIZE

In Equations

▶ All letters in equations (except Greek letters) as appropriate.

In References

▶ Databases (see examples under "In Text," below). Also, secondary publications.

Example: Index Medicus

▶ Titles of books, plays, motion pictures, essays, symphonies, operas, poems long enough to appear as a book, pamphlets, published documents, newspapers, periodicals, and journals.
▶ Volume numbers that are part of a title.

In Tables

▶ Letters used as statistical abbreviations in table column headings and stubs, but not percent signs (%) or dollar signs ($).

In Text

▶ Databases.

Examples: Family Resources Database, SWAB Database

▶ Introduction of a new term; ideally, the definition should immediately precede or follow the term. Italicize the word the first time only.

Example: During the 1860s, the psychiatric disorder *neurasthenia*—a neurosis characterized by weakness and fatigue—existed. In the 20th century, neurasthenia symptoms. . . .

▶ Titles of books, plays, motion pictures, essays, symphonies, operas, poems long enough to appear as a book, pamphlets, published documents, newspapers, periodicals, and journals. Italicize the name of a city in a newspaper title only when it is a specific part of a title.

Example: The New York Times, but *The Sun*, not *The Baltimore Sun*

DO NOT ITALICIZE

▶ Foreign words and abbreviations appearing in *Webster's Ninth New Collegiate Dictionary*, except *sic*.
▶ Slang words. Use quotes rather than italics for slang words, if it is necessary to use slang at all.
▶ In text, titles of unpublished matter; parts of published works (including chapters); book series; radio and television programs; and short musical compositions. Instead, place these elements within quotes.
▶ In text and in the reference list, abstracting and indexing services.

Example: DIALOG

numbers

In general, spell out numbers one through nine and use figures for numbers 10 and above. However, always use numbers with quantities that comprise both whole numbers and fractions, as well as with million, billion, percent, section, chapter, and page numbers.

> *Examples:* three years; 10 years old; nine-year-old child; age 17; two weeks; one hour; a seven-point scale; a 10-point scale; 2½ (*not* two and one-half), *but* one-half; 3 million; 11 billion; 1 percent; section 5; part 2; chapter 3; pp. 8–15

Use numbers when referring to specific points on a scale.

> *Example:* rank subjects from 1 to 5

Use numbers when referring to centuries or decades.

> *Examples:* the 1960s, *not* the sixties
> 20th century

Spell out ordinals up to, but not including, 10.

> *Examples:* fifth grade, *but* grade 5
> third week, 21st century, 10th conference

Spell out fractions that are used without a number and hyphenate whether a fraction is a noun or an adjective.

> *Examples:* two-thirds consensus, one-half, *but* 4½

Spell out numbers that begin a sentence (or rework the sentence).

> *Example:* Forty-five students responded. (A total of 45 students responded.)

With number ranges, use "to" in text. Use a dash in tables and in the reference list.

> *Example:* The mortality rate of babies weighing 1,000 to 1,500 grams dropped from 50 percent in the late 1960s to 20 percent in the mid-1980s.

Mixing categories within a sentence is acceptable.

> *Example:* Three boys, ages four, five, and 11 years old, and 14 teachers participated in the study.

Spell out ages if referring to them generally.

> *Example:* Most of the respondents were in their forties.

Refer also to the section entitled "Statistics and Math."

231

pronouns and first-person rule

PRONOUNS

Use pronouns carefully so that their antecedents (that is, the nouns to which they refer) are clearly understood. The following pronouns are most frequently used without a clear antecedent: it, they, we, this, these. These words should nearly always be accompanied or replaced by a specific noun.

Pronouns must agree in gender (that is, masculine, feminine, or neutral) and in number (that is, singular or plural) with their antecedents.

> ORIGINAL: Each client must decide for themselves.
> BETTER: Each client must decide for himself or herself.
> *or, even better:* Clients must decide for themselves.

Take care that the same pronoun does not refer to two different antecedents.

> ORIGINAL: The reform movement is a successful outcome of the legislation. Opponents, however, continue to criticize it.
> BETTER: The reform movement is a successful outcome of the legislation. Opponents of the legislation, however, continue to criticize it. [the legislation]
> *or*
> The reform movement is a successful outcome of the legislation. Opponents of the movement, however, continue to criticize it. [the movement]

FIRST-PERSON RULE

For years, the standard convention has been that scholarly works require the use of third, not first, person. The NASW Press considers the use of the first person appropriate for scholarly work depending on the context and the way in which it is used. Language that has been forced into the third person to conform to a rigid house style comes across as pompous and contrived. Further, the use of the third person often results in excessive use of the passive voice, which takes the life out of an article. It is important, however, that the focus be on the information the article imparts instead of on the author. Excessive use of "we feel," "I think," "I did," and so forth emphasizes the author, not the information, whereas language such as "we studied" or "in the study we found" simply imparts information.

ORIGINAL: It was found that attendance in the group was improved by providing child care.

BETTER: We found that providing child care improved attendance in the group.

The first person should not be used globally. For example, it is not accurate to say "we" when you mean the entire social work profession.

ORIGINAL: We seek to treat both the individual and the environment.

BETTER: Social workers seek to treat both the individual and the environment.

It is difficult to set an absolute rule for the use of the first person. Although it is always preferable to say who did what instead of putting an action in the abstract (say "we determined" rather than "it was determined"), the use of the first person will be less frequent in a quantitative research report. On the other hand, an ethnographic report, which requires that the researcher/author be personally connected to the research, demands the use of the first person.

punctuation

AMPERSAND

Use an ampersand or "and" in publisher names, according to publisher preference.

For parenthetical author references, use an ampersand. If the reference is not enclosed in parentheses, then use "and." In the reference list, use the ampersand to separate authors.

Examples: (Mayers & Spiegel, 1992)

Rosenblatt and Mayer (1975) described an analogous blurring of boundaries. . . .

APOSTROPHE

Possessives of singular nouns take 's.

Examples: Marx's theory, Haynes's study

Possessives of plural nouns take only an apostrophe.

Examples: social workers' practices, *but* women's group

Do not use an apostrophe to form plurals of acronyms or numerals.

Examples: MSWs, 1920s

BRACKETS

Use brackets within parentheses to enclose additional parenthetical material.

Example: (National Association of Social Workers [NASW], 1991).

COLON

Use a colon after a word, phrase, or sentence to introduce something that follows, such as a formal question or quotation or an example. A colon may replace "that is" or "for example," but should not be used after these words or after "such as," "namely," or "for instance" unless a complete sentence follows.

Following a colon, begin a complete sentence with a capital letter.

Examples: To form an alliance with a client is to collaborate with those regenerative possibilities: There is a plasticity of the self that is always seeking to transcend impairment and to mobilize resources.

Weil (1990) suggested that case managers perform any combination of the following roles: problem solver, advocate, broker, planner, community organizer, and expediter.

In reference lists, use a colon to separate subtitles of publications from titles. Capitalize the first letter of the subtitle.

Example: Bass, D. S. (1990). *Caring families: Supports and interventions.* Silver Spring, MD: NASW Press.

Refer also to "Lists" in this section.

COMMA

Use commas to separate items in a series.

Example: Negative conflict was evident in marriages, families, and communities.

Use commas to set off the elements in addresses and names of geographic places or political divisions.

Example: Schools in Prairie Village, Kansas, have experienced a sudden growth in Soviet refugee students.

Use a comma before and after the year when the exact day is included in the date. However, when only the month and year are included in the date, do not use commas to set off the elements.

Examples: November 3, 1993, is the date of the next conference.
The journal was launched in May 1967.

Use a comma to set off a nonessential or nonrestrictive clause, that is, a clause that the sentence can do without.

Example: These characteristics, which may vary, were common among high-income dropout youths.

Do not use a comma before an essential or restrictive clause, that is, a clause that identifies, limits, or defines the word it modifies.

Example: This article presents information about the epidemiology of depression that can help clinicians in their everyday work.

Use a comma to separate two independent clauses joined by a conjunction.

Example: The social work profession addresses the "bodiliness" of human behavior, but a cursory review of social work texts and journals reveals little discussion about the body.

Do not use a comma to separate compound predicates (two or more verbs having the same subject).

Example: The results contradicted Brown's hypothesis and indicated that the recidivism rate among the prisoners was much higher.

DASH

Use a dash to set off an abrupt thought or a change in the construction of the sentence.

Example: The alleviation of the miscommunication caused by diverse languages will not resolve all misunderstandings--obviously, tangible happenings also cause problems--but "slippage" in communication almost guarantees misunderstanding.

HYPHEN

Refer to *Webster's Ninth New Collegiate Dictionary* for guidance on use of hyphens. Also refer to the section in this guide entitled "Usage."

Use a hyphen to attach a prefix to a proper noun or numeral.

Examples: pre-Bush, anti-Hispanic, pre-1989

Hyphenate words in which the meaning would be changed if the hyphen were not included.

Examples: re-cover (to cover again)
re-formation (rather than reformation)

Spell as one word compound adjectives with -fold or -score unless formed with figures.

Examples: twofold, 10-fold, fourscore, 10-score

Place a hyphen between words combined to form a unit modifier immediately before the word modified, except in special cases.

Examples: family-focused strategies, neighborhood-based approach, open-ended care

In cases in which the meaning is clear and readability is not improved, it is unnecessary to use a hyphen to form a temporary compound.

Examples: civil rights legislation, durable goods drive, high school student

Compounds with well-, ill-, better-, best-, little-, and lesser- are hyphenated when used *before* the noun.

Examples: lesser-known clients, well-known client, *but* the client is well known

Hyphenate cardinal numbers plus unit measurements.

Examples: 15-minute meeting, three-month study

Hyphenate adjectival and noun compounds with fractions and with "half."

Examples: one-half as much, two-thirds, 7½-month delay

Hyphenate when two or more compound words have a common base.

Examples: fourth- and sixth-graders
two-, three-, and four-year studies

Hyphenate "self" compounds.

Examples: self-image, self-discipline, self-knowledge, *but* selfless

Do not hyphenate compounds with the suffix "-like," unless they are formed from proper nouns or words ending with two l's.

Examples: childlike, Chicago-like, bull-like

Do not hyphenate words denoting social divisions, or geographic or political areas that end with the suffix "-wide," unless the compound would be long and awkward.

Examples: statewide, countywide, worldwide, township-wide

Do not hyphenate adjectives formed of two proper nouns that each has its own meaning.

Example: Roman Catholic doctrines

Do not hyphenate adverbs or combined adjective elements used *after* the word modified.

Examples: He is not well known in the community, *but* he is a well-known man.

Do not hyphenate adverbs ending in "ly."

Examples: highly developed strategy, poorly conceived plan, highly complex issue

Use a hyphen when adding prefixes to words of more than five syllables; otherwise, close up the word.

Examples: post-experimentation, posttest

Hyphenate if a prefix added to a word results in a string of three identical letters.

Example: pro-oolong

LISTS

Punctuate only after the last item in a vertical list when the items are all phrases. Do not capitalize the first letter in each item.

Examples

The following topics are described in the article:
- role of health care in prevention and early detection
- dual diagnosis, such as mental illness and substance abuse
- treatment issues.

In the session, group members
- dealt with their feelings related to having AIDS
- discussed safer sex practices
- evaluated the group experience.

These families receive
- instruction in empowerment
- printed material on the child's disorder or, if requested, an audiotape on the disorder
- a clear explanation of the treatment plan.

In vertical lists, if any item in the list is a complete sentence, then capitalize the first word of each item. Terminate each item with a period.

Example

Employers must act within the following three guidelines:
1. An employer cannot fail to hire or cannot fire an employee whose safe job performance is unaffected by his or her impairment.
2. An employer must make reasonable accommodation to facilitate the employment of an otherwise qualified individual with a disability.
3. People considered disabled under federal and most state statutes include those with visible physical impairment, mental impairment, infectious diseases, and chronic and congenital conditions and those perceived to have such conditions.

PARENTHESES

Use parentheses when an enumeration is incorporated into a sentence.

Example: Four themes affected the women's assimilation into the dominant social structure: (1) family needs, (2) English-speaking ability, (3) the women's roles, and (4) the schools' roles.

Do not use parentheses in a vertical enumeration.

Example

The group's three goals are to
1. educate group members about common problems
2. enhance group members' understanding of their feelings
3. improve communication.

PERIOD

Do not use a period with acronyms or with academic degrees.

Examples: ACSW; CSWE; NASW; UNICEF; BSW; DSW; MS; MSW; PhD, *not* Ph.D., *but* U.S. (use abbreviation only as an adjective; spell out United States when used as a noun)

Do not use a period with initials of clients represented in case histories.

Example: Ms. A, *not* Ms. A.

As an alternative, use a first name only.

Example: Adele

QUOTATION MARKS

Use quotation marks to enclose the first occurrence of a term to indicate special meaning, slang, or irony. Do not use quotation marks for subsequent occurrences.

Use single quotation marks to enclose a quote within a quote.

Example: Weick and Pope (1988) . . . remind that "only one person can truly 'know best,' and he or she is the person whose life is being lived" (p. 16).

Refer also to the section entitled "Quotations."

SEMICOLON

Generally, use a semicolon to separate items within a series that are subdivided by a comma.

Example: The most common needs for data are to satisfy the requirements of the agency, state, or funding source; to document the outcome of services to clients (as well as client systems); and to aid in determining the need for program changes.

However, when parentheses enclose numbers in an enumerated list or enclose author–date citations, and no other punctuation subdivides the series, then use commas.

Examples: Three programs exist: (1) classroom training, (2) family workshops, and (3) staff enrichment.
. . . as cited in Jones (1990), Levine (1988), and Franklin (1992).

quotations

Attribute each quotation to its original source and, for quotations of more than three words, specify the page number in the original source. In addition, obtain written permission from the copyright holder to use quotations of more than 300 words. Ensure that quotations correspond exactly to the original wording, spelling (athough typos can be fixed), and punctuation.

SHORT QUOTES

Place all quotes from other sources that are shorter than six manuscript lines long within quotation marks. Quotes within quotes should be enclosed within single quotation marks. Cite the specific page number of the quote from the original source in parentheses after the close quotes but before the period, as follows: ". . . with learning problems in the regular classroom" (p. 23). You do not need to cite a page number for quotes of three or fewer words.

Proverbial, biblical, and well-known literary expressions need not be quoted.

Do not quote the words *yes* and *no*, except in direct discourse.

Quotation marks should enclose the first occurrence of a term to indicate special meaning, slang, or irony. Do not use quotation marks for subsequent occurrences.

LONG QUOTES

When a quotation is longer than six manuscript lines, set it off from text as an indented extract with no quotation marks. Cite the page number of the quote from the original source in parentheses after the final period in the extract. Quotes within extracts should be enclosed within double quotation marks.

Example

> There is no such thing as absolute and untrammelled "discretion" . . . No legislative act can without express language, be taken to contemplate an unlimited arbitrary power exercisable for any purpose, however capricious or irrelevant, regardless of the nature or the purpose of the statute. (p. 140)

A simple rule can be used to determine what punctuation precedes a long quote: A colon should be used only if the sentence preceding the quote is complete. If the sentence is incomplete, punctuate as would be grammatically correct if the quote were straight text. The following examples are not longer than six lines but illustrate punctuation preceding a quote.

Examples

> However, these changes became the norm:
> > After Virginia Robinson in 1936 defined supervision as an educational process, the concept of therapy . . .

> The Fourth Circuit Court of Appeals wrote,
> > A prison inmate is entitled to psychological treatment if a physician . . .

CHANGES IN QUOTED MATERIAL

Use three dots (ellipses) to indicate that words have been left out of the middle of a sentence in a quote and four dots to indicate that words were omitted between sentences or following a sentence. If an entire paragraph (or line of poetry) had been left out, center five dots on a separate line.

The first letter or the first word of a quote may be changed to upper or lowercase without enclosing the letter within brackets. Delete ellipses at the beginning of an incomplete sentence.

If interpolating a word or phrase into a quotation, enclose that word or phrase within brackets, not parentheses.

When words not italicized in the original are italicized for emphasis, the notation [italics added] follows the quote and precedes the page number.

Example

Ketcham (1988) emphasized that
although Mill *condemned* selfish individualism and
acknowledged the validity of social obligations,
he saw *social purpose* and programs as no more than
the sum. . . . [italics added] (p. 383)

references

Authors are responsible for the completeness and accuracy of the references in their manuscripts. Generally, take basic reference data for published material from the title page of a book or pamphlet, the first page of an article, or the title page of a periodical. Take dates from the copyright page.

In general, a citation in the reference list comprises the following components in the order listed: author surname(s); author initial(s); publication date; title of article or book; for periodicals, journal name, volume number, and inclusive page numbers for the article; for books, location of publisher (city and state) and publisher name. See the subsection "Citation Forms" for examples.

GENERAL STYLE POINTS

Arrange entries in the reference list alphabetically (by surname of the first author), then chronologically (by earliest publication date first).

In a reference that appears in parenthetical text, use commas (not brackets) to set off the date.

Example: (see Table 2 of Philips & Ross, 1983, for complete data)

Within a paragraph, do not include the year in subsequent references to a study as long as the study cannot be confused with other studies cited in the article.

Example: In a recent study, Jones (1987) compared. . . . Jones also found. . . .

Use the past tense for in-text reference citations.

Example: Hartman (1981) discussed. . . .

Capitalize the first word after colons and em dashes.

Delete commas in large page numbers.

Example: Federal Register, 42(163), 42474–42518.

Delete *The* in the title of magazines and periodicals in the reference list, unless doing so would make the title sound awkward.

Examples: Atlantic, New Republic, New York Times, The Sun

IN-TEXT AUTHOR–DATE CITATIONS

Reference citations in text primarily acknowledge original specific contributions or opinions of other writers. Indicate the source of quotations in text and, for any quotes more than three words long, provide page numbers. Arrange author–date citations alphabetically in text (by surname of the first author), then chronologically (by earliest publication date first). Use a semicolon to separate reference citations in text.

Examples: (Abramovitz, 1988a; Miller, 1989; Ozawa, 1982, 1986, 1990)

(Duncan & Morgan, 1979; Lindquist, Telch, & Taylor, 1983; J. Smith, 1992; P. Smith, 1992)

Citations of Same Surname
If two authors with the same surname and year of publication are cited in text and their first initials are different, include both authors' initials in all text citations to avoid confusion.

Example: (M. Henderson, 1990; P. Henderson, 1990)

Citations of Secondary Sources
In reference citations in text, generally avoid citing a secondary source as in "Jones (as cited in Roberts, 1990)." Instead, cite the primary source (Jones) and include that source in the references.

Personal Communications
Personal communications consist of letters, telephone conversations, interviews, and the like. Because they do not provide recoverable information, personal communications are not included in the reference list. Cite personal communications in text only. Use the following style: (personal communication with [first initials and last name], [title], [affiliation], [month, day, year of communication]).

Example: (personal communication with R. Fischer, professor of social work, University of California, Los Angeles, May 20, 1992)

If the entire reference citation is not parenthetical, then incorporate the name, title, and affiliation outside of the parentheses, and put the words "personal communication" and the date inside the parentheses.

> *Example:* J. T. Jones, professor of sociology at the University of Maryland (personal communication, June 11, 1992), suggested. . . .

REFERENCE LIST

Citation Forms

Following are examples of citations found in reference lists.

Article in an edited book

> Griss, B. (1988–1989). Strategies for adapting the private and public health insurance systems to the health-related needs of persons with disabilities or chronic illness. In B. Griss (Ed.), *Access to health care* (Vol. 1, pp. 1–38). Washington, DC: World Institute on Disability.
>
> Hayden, W., Jr. (1988). A curriculum model for social work management. In P. R. Keys & L. Ginsberg (Eds.), *New management in human services* (pp. 58–69). Silver Spring, MD: National Association of Social Workers.

Article in a journal

> Holland, T. P., & Kilpatrick, A. C. (1991). Ethical issues in social work: Toward a grounded theory of professional ethics. *Social Work, 36,* 138–144.

Book

> Bartlett, H. M. (1988). *Analyzing social work practice by fields* (rev. ed.). Silver Spring, MD: National Association of Social Workers.
>
> Feldman, D. A., & Johnson, T. M. (Eds.). (1986). *The social dimensions of AIDS: Method and theory.* New York: Praeger.
>
> James, F. J. (in press). *Factors which shape the risks of homelessness: Preliminary observation from Colorado.* Denver: University of Colorado Graduate School of Public Affairs.
>
> McReynolds, P., & Chelune, G. J. (Eds.). (1990). *Advances in psychological assessment* (Vol. 6). San Francisco: Jossey-Bass.

Encyclopedia of Social Work and encyclopedia supplement

When citing the NASW *Encyclopedia of Social Work,* do not cite all the editors. Instead, cite only A. Minahan (Ed.-in-Chief). Also, do not cite all the editors for the supplement; cite only L. Ginsberg et al. Be sure to cite the correct volume number (Vol. 1 or Vol. 2) for the *Encyclopedia.*

> Sze, W. M., & Ivker, B. (1987). Adulthood. In A. Minahan (Ed.-in-Chief), *Encyclopedia of social work* (18th ed., Vol. 1, pp. 75–89). Silver Spring, MD: National Association of Social Workers.

Rauch, J. B. (1990). Genetic services. In L. Ginsberg et al. (Eds.), *Encyclopedia of social work* (18th ed., 1990 suppl., pp. 113–134). Silver Spring, MD: NASW Press.

Legal references

Follow *A Uniform System of Citation* (14th ed., pp. 55–56, and inside front cover) for citation forms of legal references.

Cite the name and year of an act in the text. If possible, cite statutes to the current official code or supplement; otherwise, cite the official session laws (see *A Uniform System of Citation*, p. 55, for examples).

For citations of the *Federal Register*, attempt to cite the original source. If the *Federal Register* is the original or only source the author can provide, then use the following format:

Education for All Handicapped Children Act (P.L. No. 94-142). (1977). *Federal Register, 42*(163), 42474–42518. [Note: This act does have an original source and is used as an example only.]

The following are examples of legal references that appear frequently in NASW Press journals and books:

Adoption Assistance and Child Welfare Act of 1980, P.L. No. 96-272, 42 U.S.C. §671

Bilingual Education Act of 1968, §§880B et seq., 20 U.S.C. (1970)

Brown v. Board of Education of Topeka, 347 U.S. 483 (1954)

Education for All Handicapped Children Act, P.L. No. 94-142; 89 Stat. 773, 776, 794; 20 U.S.C.A. 1411 (Nov. 29, 1975)

Education for All Handicapped Children Act Amendment of 1986, P.L. No. 99-457, 100 Stat. 1195

Education of Exceptional Children Act No. 754, Part I: Educational Opportunities for Exceptional Children; Chapter VIII, Title 17, La. Rev. Stat. of 1950 (1977)

Family Support Act of 1988, 42 U.S.C. §1305

Protection and Advocacy for Mentally Ill Individuals Act of 1986, 42 U.S.C. §10801

Social Security Act of 1935, IV A U.S.C. §401

Limited circulation publication

Kelley, E. (1988, March). *Newsletter of the NASW Committee of Social Workers for Peace and Social Welfare.* (Available from the National Association of Social Workers, 750 First Street, NE, Washington, DC 20002-4241.)

Newspaper

Raymond, C. (1990, September 12). Global migration will have widespread impact on society, scholars say. *New York Times,* pp. A1, A6.

Nonprint media

When citing a review of nonprint media, include (if available) length (number of minutes) and format (such as videocassette, audiocassette).

> *Breaking silence.* Produced and directed by Theresa Tollini. Berkeley, CA: Future Educational Film, 1986. 132 minutes. VHS videocassette.

Paper presented at a conference

> DiCacco, J. (1990, November). *Using interpreters: Issues and guidelines for the practitioner in a multilingual environment.* Paper presented at Social Work '90: NASW's Meeting of the Profession, Boston.
> Romero, J. (1990, May). *Culturally appropriate interventions with Hispanics.* Paper presented at the Cross Cultural Competence Conference, San Diego Mental Health Services, San Diego.

Report

> Schafft, G., Erlanger, W., Rudolph, L., Yin, R. K., & Scott, A. C. (1987). *Joint study of services and funding for handicapped infants and toddlers, ages 0 through 2 years* (Final Report for Contract No. 300-85-0143). Washington, DC: U.S. Department of Education, Division of Innovation and Development, Office of Special Education Programs.
> U.S. Bureau of the Census. (1984). Projections of the population of the United States, by age, sex, and race: 1983 to 2080. In R. J. Koski (Ed.), *Current population reports* (Series P-25, No. 952, Tables C and F, pp. 6, 8). Washington, DC: U.S. Government Printing Office.

Sections of journals (other than articles)

Use brackets for punctuation of departments such as Letters, Editorial, and Book Reviews in the reference list.

> Hartman, A. (1991). Words create worlds [Editorial]. *Social Work, 36,* 275–276.

Unpublished manuscript

> Farber, B. A. (1979). *The effects of psychotherapeutic practice upon psychotherapists: A phenomenological investigation.* Unpublished doctoral dissertation, Yale University, New Haven, CT.

Use of Cities and States in Reference Citations

In reference citations and in text, NASW follows Associated Press style for the omission of states and countries, except for Washington, DC. Use DC with Washington in text and in references.

Use standard two-letter postal abbreviations for all states when listed in reference list or the author blurb. In text, include a comma before and after a state (which is spelled out).

Example: Data for this study were gathered from a sample of 191 individuals in Allegheny County, Pennsylvania, who were at high risk for institutionalization.

Do not cite the state with the following cities:

Atlanta	Honolulu	Oklahoma City
Baltimore	Houston	Philadelphia
Boston	Indianapolis	Pittsburgh
Chicago	Los Angeles	St. Louis
Cincinnati	Miami	Salt Lake City
Cleveland	Milwaukee	San Diego
Dallas	Minneapolis	San Francisco
Denver	New Orleans	Seattle
Detroit	New York	

Do not cite the country with the following cities:

Berlin	Luxembourg	Quebec
Geneva	Macao	Rome
Gibraltar	Mexico City	Singapore
Guatemala City	Monaco	Stockholm
Havana	Montreal	Tokyo
Hong Kong	Moscow	Toronto
Jerusalem	Ottawa	Vatican City
Kuwait	Paris	
London	Peking	

If the name of a state or country is in the name of an institution in a references list, do not include the state or country name with the city.

Example: Tempe: Arizona State University, *not* Tempe, AZ: Arizona State University

statistics and math

All data reported must be subjected to statistical analysis, except for descriptive reports. Authors are responsible for the statistical method selected and for the accuracy of their data. Results of statistical tests can be presented in the text, in tables, and in figures. Describe all statistical methods in the text and reference those methods with appropriate literature citations. Descriptions should include information such as sample sizes and number of replications.

REPORTING REQUIREMENTS FOR SPECIFIC TESTS

When the results of a statistical test are reported, certain elements of the test are essential to provide readers with the importance of results. A list of common statistical tests follows. Listed with each test are the elements that should be reported. For some tests, examples illustrate the format in which these elements should be presented.

Analysis of Variance (ANOVA)
F (df values) = F value, p level.

Example: $F(1, 28) = 15.75, p = .05$

Regression
Report the correlation coefficient (r) and slope (usually 1) $\pm$ standard error of measurement (SEM).

Example: ($r = .86, 1 \pm SEM$)

Student–Newman–Keuls Test
Report the separation of means ($\bar{X}$) and associated analysis of variance.

t Tests
Report the t value, degrees of freedom, and the probability level or alpha level, as appropriate.

Example: $t(2) = 1.16, p = .05$

COMPUTER PROGRAMS

If a statistical test is performed with a published computer program or a commercially available statistics package, name the test and cite the reference or the user's manual as appropriate. Do not cite the original reference for the statistical test.

> *Example:* In text, with a procedure performed with SPSS software, name the procedure and cite the appropriate pages from the SPSS manual. Reference the manual in the reference list as follows: Nie, N. H., Hull, D. H., Jenkins, J. C., Steinbrunner, K., & Bent, D. H. [1985]. *Statistical package for the social sciences* (2nd ed.). New York: McGraw-Hill.

For more information on statistics or for statistics not mentioned in this section, please refer to the following books:

Jaeger, R. M. (1990). *Statistics: A spectator sport* (2nd ed.). Newbury Park, CA: Sage Publications.

Weinbach, R. W., & Grinnell, R. M., Jr. (1987). *Statistics for social workers*. New York: Longman.

Also see chapter 4, "The Quantitative Research Report," by Ann Abbott, in this book.

COMMON STATISTICAL ABBREVIATIONS

df	degrees of freedom
n	the number in a sample
N	all the elements in a universe
p	probability level
r	Pearson correlation coefficient
r^2	coefficient of determination
R	coefficient of multiple correlation
R^2	coefficient of multiple determination
SD	standard deviation
SE	standard error
$\bar{X}$ or *M*	mean
χ^2	chi-square (lowercase Greek chi)
α	alpha
β	beta
Σ	sigma (sum of)

MATH AND STATISTICS TEXT STYLE

ANOVA
Analysis of variance. Write out at first mention.

Decimal Fractions
Decimal fractions within a discussion need not be carried out to the same number of digits. In other words, if you have cited 34.32 and 36.4, do not add a zero to 36.4.

Decimal fractions that are being compared and are all of the same measure should be consistently carried out to the same number of digits. (This rule includes tables.) Please note that for chi-square values, decimals are carried out to two places only.

In scientific contexts decimal fractions of less than 1.00 are set with an initial zero if the quantity expressed can equal or exceed 1.00.

Examples: A mean of 0.73, the ratio 0.85

If the quantity never equals 1.00, as in probabilities, levels of significance, correlation coefficients, and factor loadings, no zero is used.

Examples: $p = .05$, $r = .10$

Greek Letters
Spell out Greek letters in text. Use the letters only in equations. Do not italicize Greek letters used in equations. Be sure to indicate whether these letters are uppercase or lowercase.

Italics in Equations
In equations, italicize all letters (except Greek letters) as appropriate.

NA, Dash
In tables, use NA to mean not applicable and a dash to mean data not available.

NS
Not significant (abbreviated NS [no italics]). Use only in tables. Define at first mention (usually by a footnote to the table).

Percent
Spell out percent when used in text. Use a percent sign (%) only in tables.

Percentages and Numerals (n values)
When providing only numerical data (*n* values), percentages of the total sample population are optional. When reporting only percentages, supply numerical sizes (*n* values).

Probability Levels
In tables, standard probability levels are denoted by asterisks. One asterisk (*) means $p \geq, \leq,$ or $= .05$; two asterisks (**) means $p \geq, \leq,$ or $= .01$; three asterisks (***) means $p \geq, \leq,$ or $= .001$.

Scales
The following scales are often used in generalizability studies involving Cronbach's alpha: a three-point scale where $1 =$ never, $2 =$ sometimes, and $3 =$ often; or a five-point scale ranging from $1 =$ "strongly agree" to $5 =$ "strongly disagree."

subheadings

Subheadings guide the reader through the article and provide a visual break in lengthy stretches of type. Subheadings should be succinct, meaningful, and similar in tone, as well as uniform and pertinent. They should accurately indicate the topic of the text that follows, and they should be as short as possible.

Follow outline style: If you are using a secondary subheading, then provide at least one other secondary subheading under the same principal subheading. However, in a few cases, use of outline style may seem contrived. In those cases, it may be necessary to make an exception to this rule.

Delete numbers from subheadings. Also, delete "The" or "A" as initial words of a subheading, if possible. Never include a reference citation in a subheading.

Capitalize the initial letter of the first and last words and all other words except articles (for example, "the," "a"), conjunctions (for example, "but," "and"), "to" in infinitives (for example, "to Practice"), and prepositions.

Refer also to "Titles and Headings" under the section entitled "Capitalization."

tables

A sample table is shown on page 251.

▶ Type each table double spaced on a separate sheet of paper and place after the reference list and any figures at the end of the manuscript. Number these pages sequentially, following the last text page number.

▶ Number all tables consecutively, beginning with Table 1. Be sure all tables are mentioned in the text.

▶ Table titles should be as short as possible while giving an accurate idea of the information included in the table.

▶ Capitalize main words in table column headings; capitalize only the first word in table stubs.

▶ Insert commas after thousands digits (for example, 2,025, *not* 2025).

▶ For footnotes, use the following order of elements:

NOTE. [Explanations referring to table *as a whole*.]
NA = not applicable; NS = not significant;
dash = data not available.

SOURCE. [or SOURCES.] Use complete reference citation so that table can stand on its own.

TABLE 3. Differences between Characteristics of People Who Were Never Poor, Occasionally Poor, and Persistently Poor

	Never Poor vs. Occasionally Poor		Persistently Poor vs. Occasionally Poor		Persistently Poor vs. Never Poor
	Beta Coefficient	Standard Error	Beta Coefficient	Standard Error	Chi-square
Constant (alpha)	6.3620*	.3424	-5.0250*	.7151	NA
Single throughout survey	-.9939*	.1049	1.2300*	.2290	173.53*
Gained a spouse	-.9616	.6038	-6.2500	27.5000	2.62
Lost a spouse	-.9894*	.1914	-.5837	.5606	27.80*
Residence in the South	-.3582*	.0933	.6228*	.1583	54.12*
Female	-.3953*	.1023	.3043	.1958	22.57*
Black	-.9991*	.1270	.1061	.1833	57.26*
No education	-2.2520*	.2934	1.3040*	.5618	65.07*
Primary school	-1.2900*	.1480	1.5510*	.4400	120.81*
Some high school	-.6198*	.1699	1.4270*	.4645	32.80*
High school graduate	-.3997*	.1671	.9380*	.4830	13.49*
Age 75 and older	-.2285*	.0195	-.1228	.1545	5.88
Rural residence	-.5691*	.0971	.2337	.1958	22.57*
Likelihood ratio for the null model[a]	5,774.8	(4,608)			
Likelihood ratio for the postulated model[a]	4,826.6	(4,584)			
Likelihood ratio difference between null and postulated model[a]	948.2*	(24)			

NOTE: N = 4,610; NA = not applicable.
[a]Degrees of freedom are in parentheses.
*$p < .05$.

Sample table

[a] [Explanations referring to *specific items* in a table.]
[b]
[c]

$*p = .05, **p = .01, ***p = .001$. [Asterisks are used only for levels of probability. There should be no = between the asterisk and the *p*.]

Refer also to the section entitled "Statistics and Math."

unbiased writing

NASW is committed to the fair and equal treatment of all individuals and groups. The material published by the NASW Press should not promote stereotypic or discriminatory attitudes and assumptions about people. Language that might imply sexual, ethnic, or other kinds of biases, discrimination, or stereotyping may not be used. Language can reinforce either inequality or balanced, accurate, and fair treatment of individuals.

Recast writing that uses male pronouns so that it means all people. Use plurals when possible to avoid gender reference.

Be sure that terms for groups of men and women are parallel. (In other words, don't use "male" doctors with "women" doctors.)

Change terms that give the impression that only people of one gender perform certain duties or work in certain professions (for example, use "stevedore" instead of "longshoreman," "police officer" instead of "policeman").

In case examples, use both masculine and feminine names for clients, social workers, doctors, patients, and others.

Styles and preferences for nouns referring to ethnic groups change over time. In some cases, even members of a group disagree about the preferred name at a specific time. Try to ascertain the most acceptable current terms and use them. Refer to *The Social Work Dictionary* for the appropriate name for a specific ethnic group. Also check *The Chicago Manual of Style*, sections 7.32 and 7.33. Change or expand terms for groups that could be read as negative or pejorative. Use terms that acknowledge difference, but that also allow for differences among members of the group (for example, black Americans, white Americans, Puerto Rican individuals, rather than blacks, whites, or Puerto Ricans).

Avoid language that implies a moral judgment on behavior or lifestyles. For example, say "people with AIDS," rather than "AIDS victims" or "innocent victims of AIDS." "High-risk groups" implies that some kind of demographic trait, rather than behavioral practice, is responsible for AIDS exposure. A more appropriate term is "high-risk behavior." In regard to "HIV" versus "AIDS," many people still confuse exposure to HIV with the disease. Well over 1 million people are believed to have been exposed to the virus; some 230,000 AIDS cases had been diagnosed as of June 1992. Always explain the difference.

BIASED AND UNBIASED TERMS

Biased	Unbiased
bag lady/bag man	street person, homeless person
businessman	executive, business executive
chairman	chair
congressman	member of Congress, representative, legislator, delegate
con man	con artist
Mary, an epileptic, had no trouble doing her job.	Mary, who has epilepsy, had no trouble doing her job.
fits, spells	seizures, epilepsy
housewife	homemaker
male nurse	nurse; specify gender only if important to the discussion
man a project	hire personnel, employ staff
mankind	humans, human beings, people
manpower	work force, personnel, human resources, workers
mothering	parenting, nurturing
peeping Tom	voyeur
An African American student, John James works as a part-time clerk.	John James works as a part-time clerk.
Not the type to stay at home and bake cookies, Betty Wong has chosen a career in politics.	Betty Wong has chosen a career in politics.

Some of the examples of biased and unbiased language come from *The Nonsexist Word Finder*, by R. Maggio (Oryx Press, 1987), and *Guidelines for Equal Treatment of the Sexes in McGraw-Hill Book Company Publications.*

usage

Refer to the following pages for terms to avoid and to use. Consult *Webster's Ninth New Collegiate Dictionary* or *The Social Work Dictionary* (2nd ed.), for terms not found in this list. If you choose to use a word listed in *Webster's*, please be sure that the word is the best possible choice for use in a social work context. Also, please use only the primary spelling listed in *Webster's*.

TERMS TO AVOID AND TO USE

The following is a list of commonly misused words and expressions to avoid and, in many cases, the appropriate preferred term for each one.

due to, when used for "because of," "owing to," and "on account of." "Due," an adjective, should be attached only to a noun or pronoun, not a verb.

> *Example:* "his failure was due to . . ." *but* "he failed because of . . ."

Can also use "was a result of."

e.g. Use "for example"

employ Use only in reference to working; otherwise, use "use."

> *Examples:* She is employed at a local agency.
>
> The authors used the following methods: . . .

etc. Use "and so on," "and so forth," "and the like."

execute Use "implement."

feel, for "think" or "believe"; instead, use "feel" only for emotions.

i.e. Use "that is."

in order to The word "to" is usually enough.

prior to Use "before."

service (verb) Use "serve" or "give service to."

since, unless referring to time. Otherwise, use "because."

the fact that The word "that" is usually enough.

utilize Use "use."

where, to mean anything other than location. Use "when."

while, unless referring to time. Use "and," "but," "although," or "whereas."

COMMONLY USED TERMS

adj = adjective   n = noun
adv = adverb   v = verb

A

acknowledgment
acquired immune deficiency
    syndrome (AIDS)
acting out (n)
acute care hospital
ad hoc (roman, *not* italics)
administration (Bush
    administration)
adviser
African American (adj, n)
aftercare (adj)
after-school (adj)
Aid to Families with Dependent
    Children (AFDC)
all-black-male school
alpha level
Asian American (adj, n)
azidothymidine (AZT)

B

Beck's Depression Index (BDI)
biopsychosocial
birthweight (n), low-
    birthweight baby
black person or black American
black power movement

C

caregiver
caregiving
caseload
Chicano/Chicana
child care (adj, n)
child rearing (n)
child-rearing (adj)
child welfare agency
chi-square test, chi-square
    value

civil rights movement
coauthor
co-coordinator
coleader
community at large
communitywide (adj)
control subjects (*not* controls)
countertransference
coworker
Cramer's *V*
Cronbach's alpha

D

database (adj, n)
day-by-day (adj)
day care (adj, n)
decision maker
decision making (n)
decision-making (adj)
diagnosis related groups (DRGs)
dideoxycytidine (DDC)
dideoxyinosine (DDI)
discharge planning (adj, n)
disk
DSM-III–R (*Diagnostic and
    Statistical Manual of Mental
    Disorders, Third Edition–
    Revised*; no italics when
    abbreviated)
DSM-IV (*Diagnostic and
    Statistical Manual of Mental
    Disorders, Fourth Edition*; no
    italics when abbreviated)

E

eldercare
elementary school–age children
ensure (to make sure; also see
    "insure")
ex-patient
ex-wife

F

family-centered (adj)
family functioning (n)
family life education program
family services agency
family welfare work
federal government
fee-charging (adj, n)
field service training
flextime
follow-up (adj, n)
follow up (v)
Food Stamp Program
food stamps
freelance
full-time
fundraiser
fundraising

G

gay liberation movement
GED (general equivalency
    diploma)
grassroots (adj, n)
group-serving agencies
group therapy program
group work

H

halfway house
Head Start
health maintenance
    organizations (HMOs)
high school–age
Hispanic people
home health care
homemaker
home health aide
human services

I

in-house
in-kind (adj, adv)
inner city (n)

inner-city (adj)
inpatient
in-service training
insure (use only in reference to
    financial guarantees)

L

lay off (v)
layoff (n)
laypeople, layperson
leisure-time (adj)
lifestyle (n)
long-term-care referral
low-cost housing
lower middle class (n)
lower-middle-class (adj)
low-income (adj)

M

macrolevel (adj, n)
macropractitioner
macrosystem (adj, n)
many-faceted (adj), but
    multifaceted
Medicaid
Medicare
member-at-large (hyphenate
    when used as a title)
metaanalysis
Mexican American (adj, n)
micropractitioner (adj, n)
microsystem (adj, n)
middle age (n)
middle-aged (adj)
middle class (n)
middle-class (adj)
middle-income (adj)
Model Cities Program

N

narcotic addiction
National Institute of Mental
    Health (NIMH)

National Institutes of Health
(NIH)
Native American
near-crisis situation
near-poor (adj)
near-poor people (n)
non–social worker
non-English-speaking

O

often-overlooked (adj)
old age (n)
old-age (adj), but old age
pension
one-to-one relationship
on-the-job training
outpatient
outreach (adj, n, v)

P

parent–child interaction
parent–child problems
parent–teacher association
part-time
past, *not* last (when referring to
time that has passed but there
is a future: over the past 10
years)
payer
Payment-in-Kind (for the
agricultural program only)
payment in-kind
peer group (n)
peer-group (adj)
peer review (adj, n)
people (for large groups):
people with AIDS (PWAs)
percent (following number or
figure), but "percentage"
without number or figure
person-in-environment
persons (for exact or small
numbers): persons with AIDS
(countable: 10 persons with
AIDS)

policy maker
policy-making (n)
post-hospitalization
posttest
preferred provider organizations
(PPOs)
pretest
problem solving (n)
problem-solving (adj)
program planning (adj, n)
psychoanalytic
psychosexual
psychosocial
public school districts
public welfare (adj, n)
public welfare administration

R

relief giving (n)
relief-giving (adj)
residential treatment (adj, n)
role perception
role play (n)
role playing (n)
role-playing (adj, v)
role-set

S

school-age (adj)
schoolchild
schoolteacher
schoolwork
sex-role stereotyping
single female–headed families
sit-ins
slum-dweller
social security amendments
social security laws
social services
social worker–client
relationship (*not* worker–
client relationship)
standard setting (n)
standard-setting (adj)
Supreme Court

T

teenage
teenagers (*not* teens)
third-party payments
Third World
time-series analysis
time span

U

under way (adj)
underway (n)
United States (n), U.S. as adj
upper middle class (n)
upper-middle-class (adj)
up-to-date

V

Veterans Administration (VA)
vice president
visiting teacher program

W

War on Drugs

War on Poverty
well-being (n)
white-collar housing
-wide (close up most words
    with this suffix)
women's liberation
women's liberation movement
women's movement
work force
workload
workplace
work setting
workyear
worldview

Y

youth (singular), youths
    (plural)

Z

zip code (n)

PART IV

appendixes

A *contract examples*

This appendix includes three types of contracts an author may encounter. The examples given are contracts used by the NASW Press, so the wording and provisions may vary from publisher to publisher. However, these contracts are sufficiently typical that they will give authors an idea of what they can expect from other publishers.

agreement form for contributors to collective works

This form (Figure A.1) is used for all contributions to NASW Press journals. Essentially, the author transfers the copyright to the NASW Press, authorizes NASW to prepare the article for publication, and certifies that he or she has the rights to the article and has accomplished all appropriate actions to make the article publishable. The agreement form spells out various other details to protect the author and the publisher.

book contract

A book contract (Figure A.2) specifies the agreement between the publisher and the author in great detail. In addition to transferring the copyright and certifying the right to do so, the author agrees to a specific delivery date, royalty rates, preparation for publication, and so forth. The NASW Press contract has recently been revised to include a mediation clause in case of any disputes.

261

National Association of Social Workers, Inc.
750 First Street, NE, Suite 700, Washington, DC 20002-4241
(202) 408-8600 • (800) 638-8799 • Fax: (202) 336-8310

Manuscript Number

AGREEMENT FORM FOR CONTRIBUTORS TO COLLECTIVE WORKS

Title of manuscript _____

_____

By _____

For publication in _____

1. I specifically transfer to the National Association of Social Workers, Inc. (NASW), full and complete ownership of any copyright I may have with respect to the work entitled above. (If there is more than one author, I also certify and represent to NASW that I am the duly authorized agent for any or all other authors of the work and I am authorized to make this agreement on their behalf.)

2. I agree to refer to NASW all requests to republish or reprint the whole or any part of my work, including my own requests.

3. I have obtained written permission to use any quotations or excerpts from another work not in the public domain or covered by fair use provisions of U.S. Copyright law. Proper acknowledgment has been given for such use of other materials in the new work.

4. I will supply original artwork for any illustration or figure in my manuscript. I understand that such art must be rendered in black ink, preferably by a professional illustrator, or on a laser printer. If I wish, NASW will arrange for an artist and forward the bill to me for payment.

5. I agree that the editor will do what is necessary to prepare the article for publication—including changes in title, style, and format to conform to editorial usage, format, and NASW style. Changes may include such last-minute deletions as are necessary to meet the requirements of space and format. I understand that I may be requested to update data and other material before publication.

6. I understand that I will receive a copy of the edited article for review before it is sent to the printer and that the printer's proofs are not provided, except for technical research articles.

7. I have disguised identifying information (names of persons, organizations, and so on) in the case examples used in this article and have substituted comparable material.

8. I am supplying herewith an informative abstract (up to 150 words) that distills the key concepts in the article. I understand that this abstract will be published at the beginning of the article. I also grant permission for the abstract to be published and indexed in *Social Work Research & Abstracts* and to be placed in the *Abstracts* online database.

9. I understand that I will receive complimentary copies of the issue in which my article appears. For regular articles, each author will receive five copies; for articles published in special columns, each author will receive two copies. Reprints are available for a fee in quantities of 50 or more. The cost of the reprints will depend on the number of printed pages. NASW will sent a rate sheet after publication.

10. I have read the policy in regard to overlapping submissions, which appears on the reverse side, and I affirm that my work is in compliance.

11. I understand that NASW approaches any case of plagiarism as an issue of professional conduct.

Date _____ Signed _____
Author (and/or duly authorized agent)

(over)

Please supply the following information, printed or typed, for use in connection with publication:

Dr. _____   Mr. _____   Miss _____   Ms. _____   Mrs. _____

Name _____

Highest academic degree earned _____ Certification earned (e.g., ACSW) _____

Job title _____

Agency/School _____

Address _____   Phone (   ) _____

_____   Zip _____

Home address _____   Phone (   ) _____

_____   Zip _____

Permission is hereby granted _____ not granted _____ to publish an address where I may be contacted by readers seeking additional information about my article.
Please use my business _____ home _____ address.

If this paper was delivered at a conference, institute, or workshop, please supply the following:

Name of meeting _____

Date (month/day/year) _____ Place (city, state) _____

NASW POLICY ON PLAGIARISM

The use of another author's ideas, words, or data without attribution is considered plagiarism, whether the use is deliberate or accidental. NASW views any incidence of plagiarism as an issue of professional misconduct and a violation of the Code of Ethics.

POLICY STATEMENT ON OVERLAPPING SUBMISSIONS

It is recognized that in the case of large-scale research studies, more than one article might be generated from the core material available. However, in such cases, it is the clear responsibility of the author to state in the work under consideration that the paper is part of a larger study and to annotate fully other articles from the same study that are already published, in press, or in process.

If such information has been withheld and substantive portions of the material under review or already accepted by NASW have been published or submitted for publication elsewhere, the editorial boards and committees that function as subunits of the Communications Committee can, at their discretion, reject or withdraw acceptance of such articles, if it is deemed that publication could lead to violation of publications policy or NASW adherence to the copyright law.

Rev. 9/92

Author Contract
[Book Title]

MEMORANDUM OF AGREEMENT made this *[date]* between the NASW Press (National Association of Social Workers, Inc.), 750 First Street, NE, Washington, DC 20002-4241 (hereafter referred to as the Publisher), and *[Author(s) or Editor(s)]*, whose address is *[address]*, hereafter referred to as the *[Author or Editor]*).

1. **Transfer of Copyright Ownership**

   The Author(s) *[or Editors], hereby irrevocably and exclusively transfers* to the Publisher any and all rights, titles, and interests, including copyright, all subsidiary rights, and all rights to all forms of publication in all languages throughout the world, in a work with the draft title of *[working book title]*.

2. **Preparation of Manuscript for Publication**

   The Author *[or Editor]* agrees to deliver to the Publisher on or before *[expected date]* ("Manuscript Delivery Date") two complete copies (an original and a clean copy) of the manuscript of the Work in the English language, satisfactory to the Publisher in form and content. The Author *[or Editor]* agrees to cooperate with the Publisher in making such changes as are deemed necessary to complete the final manuscript for publication. The author *[or Editor]* agrees to provide such additional work as the Publisher deems necessary and to furnish, in a form satisfactory to the Publisher, all drawings, photographs, or other graphic or supplementary materials that may be necessary to illustrate or supplement the text. The acceptability of any revisions and supplemental materials is of the essence to the obligations of the Publisher under this agreement and may not be waived except by the mutual written agreement of the Publisher and Author *[or Editor]*. In the event the Author *[or Editor]* fails to provide any graphic or supplementary materials or permissions as requested by the Publisher within the time set by the Publisher or fails to provide them in a form acceptable to the Publisher, the Publisher may have the materials prepared and may, at the Publisher's election, charge such costs directly to the Author *[or Editor]* under this Agreement. The Publisher agrees to notify the Author within sixty (60) days of receipt of the manuscript whether the manuscript is or is not acceptable to the Publisher for publication. If the Author *[or Editor]* fails to deliver a complete and finished manuscript and related materials outlined above within sixty (60) days of the Manuscript Delivery Date or any date established by the Publisher for completion of revisions, unless it has been postponed by mutual written agreement, the Publisher, at its sole election, may terminate this agreement. The Publisher may retain another Author *[or Editor]* to

   (continued)

264

complete the manuscript and shall deduct such expenses from amounts due to the Author *[or Editor]* under this agreement.

3. Publication

The Publisher agrees to publish the Work within a reasonable period after delivery of the complete and acceptable manuscript at its own expense and at such time and in such style and manner as the Publisher shall deem best suited to its sale.

4. Copyright

The Publisher shall have the sole and exclusive right to register and protect the copyright of the Work, in the name of the Publisher or otherwise in the United States and elsewhere. If the Publisher is unable to complete publication, all rights revert to the Author *[or Editor]*.

5. Default by the Publisher

In the event the Publisher has not published the Work within the time specified, unless publication has been delayed for any reason stated in the Agreement for circumstances beyond the control of the Publisher, and if the Publisher, after written demand by the Author, does not schedule the Work for publication within twelve (12) months following the receipt of such a demand, the Author shall have the right, as the Author's sole and exclusive remedy, to terminate this agreement by written notice to the Publisher. In no event shall the Publisher be obligated to publish the work if, in the Publisher's opinion, the work violates copyright; or the rights of privacy, publicity, or any other right of any person; or contains libelous or obscene matter.

6. Author's *[or Editor's]* Warranty

(a) The Author *[or Editor]* warrants that he or she is the sole proprietor of the Work and of all rights therein and has full power to make this agreement; that the Work has not been previously published, is original except for such excerpts from copyrighted works as may be included therein with the written permission of the copyright owners thereof; that it is unencumbered; that it is not libelous or obscene; and that it does not infringe any copyright or violate any statute or any personal or property right at common law. The Author *[or Editor]* will indemnify the Publisher against all costs, expenses (including attorneys' fees), and damages arising from any breach of these warranties. These warranties shall survive any termination of this agreement.

(b) The Author *[or Editor]* agrees that so long as the Publisher shall continue to publish the Work, he or she will not (without prior consent thereto in writing by the Publisher) write, publish, or print or cause to be written, published, or printed, or participate therein, any other form of said Work or any other work of such extent or character that might

(continued)

interfere with or reduce the sale of the Work that is the subject of this agreement.

(c) The Author *[or Editor]* shall be responsible for obtaining at his or her own expense all permissions for the use of copyrighted material. Such permissions shall be satisfactory to the Publisher in form and content and shall be delivered by the Author *[or Editor]* at the time of delivery of the manuscript.

7. **Author's *[or Editor's]* Royalty**
   The Publisher agrees to pay the Author *[or Editor]* royalties as follows:

   (a) A royalty based on the net amounts received by the Publisher from sales of all copies of the Work, to be calculated as follows:
   10% on the first 3,000 copies
   12½% on copies from 3,001 to 6,000
   15% on copies from 6,001 or more

   (b) In the case of copies of the Work sold at a discount of 50 percent or more from the retail price, the rate provided in 6(a) shall be reduced to 5 percent. No royalty shall be paid on any copies (1) sold below or at cost, including expenses incurred, or (2) furnished gratis to the Author *[or Editor]*.

   (c) A royalty based on any permissions fees received for reprinting any portion of the Work. The royalty percentage shall be 10 percent during the time the Work is in print and 15 percent if permissions fees are received after the Work no longer is in print. The Publisher shall grant permission to reprint no more than 10 percent of the Work at any time the Work is in print.

   (d) The Publisher shall render to the Author *[or Editor]* annual statements of account as of the 30th day of June and shall mail statements to the Author *[or Editor]* along with checks in the amounts due thereon within 90 days of the 30th day of June. In making accountings, the Publisher shall have the right to allow for a reasonable reserve sufficient in light of industry standards and, whenever possible, the actual return percentage in the sale of the Work and to be adjusted accordingly in each accounting period.

   After two years following the publication date, regular royalty statements and payments need not be issued by the Publisher until accumulated earnings from all sources, due and payable, exceed $10.00 unless requested in writing by the Author.

   (e) Should the Author receive an overpayment, the Author agrees that the Publisher may deduct such amount from any further earnings of the Work.

(continued)

8. Author's *[or Editor's]* Copies

The Publisher shall give to the Author *[or Editor]* 10 complimentary copies upon publication of the Work, and the Author *[or Editor]* may purchase additional copies at the Author/Editor's discount of 40 percent from the retail price for free distribution, but not resale as long as the work is in stock.

9. Revised Editions

As may be requested by the Publisher, the Author *[or Editor]* agrees to revise the work or to cooperate in arranging for others to prepare a new edition. If the Author *[or Editor]* is unable or unwilling to prepare the revision for any reason, the Publisher, at its sole discretion, may engage another person or persons to prepare the revision. The Publisher may arrange for the preparation of the revision by such other persons at its own expense, and any fees paid by the Publisher may be deducted from amounts otherwise payable to the Author *[or Editor]* under Paragraph 5 hereof.

10. Proofreading and Changes in Proof

The Author *[or Editor]* agrees to read, correct, and return promptly all proof sheets and to pay all charges in excess of 10 percent of the cost of typesetting for alterations that the Author *[or Editor]* shall make in proof after type has been set in conformity with the edited manuscript, which the Author *[or Editor]* has cleared.

11. Use of the Author's *[or Editor's]* Name and Likeness

The Publisher and any licensees or assigns of the Publisher's rights shall have the right, in connection with the exercise of any of such rights, and in advertising and publicity, to use the name, image, likeness, and biography of the Author *[or Editor]*.

12. Termination

Should the Publisher fail to keep the work in print, and after written demand from the Author *[or Editor]* decline or neglect to bring it back into print within six (6) months, the Publisher's rights under this Agreement shall terminate, provided that all obligations of the Author *[or Editor]* to the Publisher have been met. It is understood that the Work shall be considered to be in print if any rights granted are being exercised or are under contract to be exercised anywhere in the world. If, at any time after first publication the Publisher wishes to discontinue publication for any reason, the Publisher may do so upon written notice to the Author *[or Editor]*, in which event this Agreement shall terminate and all rights granted shall revert to the Author *[or Editor]* upon the termination date set forth in such notice from the Publisher. For thirty (30) days after the date of any such termination, the Author

(continued)

[or Editor] shall have the right, but not the obligation, to acquire from the Publisher (a) any printer's materials under the control of the Publisher, if any continue to exist, at fair market value; and/or (b) any inventory of the Work under the control of the Publisher, at the manufacturing cost of the last printing. If the Author *[or Editor]* does not exercise such right within such thirty (30) days, the Publisher may dispose of any such materials or inventory without any further obligation to the Author *[or Editor]*. The Publisher shall execute a written assignment of the Publisher's copyright to the Author *[or Editor]* upon termination.

13. Mediation Clause

The parties agree to submit any dispute or claim arising out of this Agreement to mediation before a mutually acceptable third party to be selected at the time.

14. Arbitration Clause

Any dispute or claim arising out of this Agreement shall be submitted by the parties to arbitration by a mutually acceptable arbitrator, or if there is none, to the American Arbitration Association, in accordance with the Association's rules. Judgment on any award rendered by an arbitrator may be entered in any court of competent jurisdiction.

15. Right of First Refusal

If, pursuant to the United States Copyright Act, the Author *[or Editor]* (or, if deceased, the successor of the Author *[or Editor]*) has the right to terminate the rights granted hereunder and elects to exercise such rights as provided pursuant to such Act, after such termination, the Author *[or Editor]* shall not exercise or dispose of such rights except in accordance with the following procedure: Commencing with the date of such termination, the Author *[or Editor]* and the Publisher shall negotiate in good faith for a period of not less than sixty (60) days with respect to mutually agreeable terms and conditions. If the parties are unable in good faith to arrive at a mutually satisfactory agreement for such publication, the Author *[or Editor]* shall be free to offer the rights terminated elsewhere, provided, however, that prior to entering into any agreement with any such third party, the Author *[or Editor]* shall first give the Publisher the opportunity to agree, within ten (10) business days, to match the terms offered by the third party which the Author *[or Editor]* is willing to accept.

16. Binding Agreement

This Agreement shall be binding upon and inure to the benefit of the heirs, executors, administrators, successors, or assigns of the Author *[or Editor]* and the successors, assigns, and licensees for the Publisher, but

(continued)

no assignment by either party, other than an assignment by operation of law or by the Publisher to a person, group, or corporation currently or hereinafter associated with the Publisher shall be made without the prior written consent of the other party.

17. Laws
This Agreement shall be subject to the laws of the District of Columbia.

18. Entire Agreement
This Agreement constitutes the entire understanding of the parties and may be modified or terminated only by a written statement executed by both parties.

For the AUTHOR *[or Editor]*:   For NASW PRESS:

_____   _____
Date   Date

_____   _____
Author *[or Editor]*   Executive Editor

_____
Social Security Number

work for hire

Section 101 of the 1976 Copyright Law of the United States of America (revised July 1, 1985) defines a work made for hire as

1. a work prepared by an employee within the scope of his or her employment; or
2. a work specially ordered or commissioned for use as a contribution to a collective work. (p. 5)

Authors who are commissioned to write articles for major works, such as the NASW Press's *Encyclopedia of Social Work,* sign work-for-hire agreements (Figure A.3).

FIGURE A.3 NASW Press Work-for-Hire Agreement

Encyclopedia of Social Work

NATIONAL ASSOCIATION OF SOCIAL WORKERS
750 First Street, NE, Suite 700, Washington, DC 20002-4241 • (202) 408-8600 • (800) 638-8799

Work-for-Hire Agreement

We, the undersigned, agree that all research for and writing of _____

_____

[working title] prepared for the *Encyclopedia of Social Work*, 19th edition,
shall be considered works made for hire prepared for the NASW Press,
a division of the National Association of Social Workers, in accordance
with sections 101 and 201(b) of the United States Copyright Law.

_____
Author Name

_____
Date

_____
For the NASW Press

_____
Date

B *copyright and permissions*

Publishers copyright material so they can control and protect all future uses of the work. In addition to defending their own copyright rigorously, publishers also take great care to avoid violating anyone else's copyright.

obtaining permissions

When authors must ask permission to reprint depends, in part, on the total length of the original work and on the type of work it is. For example, permission is required to use all cartoons, artwork, photographs, tables, figures, newspaper articles, and even a single line of music or poetry. For text, a standard rule of thumb for shorter pieces is that if the quotation is 10 percent or more of the original work, the author should seek permission. For longer pieces, the NASW Press requires that permission be obtained for any quotation of 300 words or more, although some publishers permit quotation of fewer than 500 words without requesting permission.

Obtaining permissions can be a time-consuming task; therefore, the author should request permission well in advance of an anticipated publishing date. Providing all the information the publisher needs to respond will enhance the likelihood that an author will receive a positive response in a timely manner. The Permission to Reprint form shown here as Figure B.l is the form that the NASW Press provides to authors for their use. Authors always are responsible for obtaining permissions, and no publisher will go to press until all written permissions are in hand.

271

FIGURE B.1 NASW Press Permission to Reprint Form

Permission to Reprint

I am requesting permission to reprint the following:

Title _____

Author _____

Originally Published in _____

_____

Publisher _____

Date of Publication _____ Pages _____

Opening Line _____

Closing Line _____

The material will be used in _____

to be published by the NASW Press in _____

☐ Your material will be used in its original form.
☐ A copy of the proposed changes is attached.

A standard credit line will be used unless you request specific wording. Granting the NASW Press rights to reprint in no way restricts republication of your material in any other form by you or by others you authorize. If you do not control these rights in their entirety, please inform the NASW Press where else to write.

_____

I hereby give my approval of the use of the work as specified above. The NASW Press is authorized to include this material in the current text and in future revisions and editions for distribution throughout the world and in all languages. This authorization includes the right to approve, without charge, the publication in Braille, records, tapes, or large type editions for the visually impaired.

_____

Signature   Title   Date

Please return to the NASW Press, 750 First Street, NE, Suite 700, Washington, DC 20002.

NASW PRESS

NATIONAL ASSOCIATION OF SOCIAL WORKERS • 750 First Street, NE, Suite 700, Washington, DC 20002-4241 • (202) 408-8600 • (800) 638-8799

Publishers often require payment of a fee for permission to reprint. Although fees can be as low as $20 for a figure, the use of a popular cartoon or a piece of music may result in a fee of several hundred dollars. Publishers occasionally waive permission fees, particularly for items that will not be sold. Authors of books that require substantial permissions should be certain of their arrangement with their publisher. The general practice is for the author to pay for the permissions or for the publisher to pay the initial costs and to deduct them from future royalties.

giving credit

Even if permissions are not required, authors still must give full credit for the source of the material they are quoting. Citations must include the following:

- ▶ name of the author of the material being quoted or paraphrased
- ▶ title of the chapter or article in which the material originally appeared
- ▶ title of the book or journal in which the material originally appeared
- ▶ year of publication
- ▶ place and name of the publisher of the book in which the chapter appeared
- ▶ volume number if relevant
- ▶ page number.

As with permissions, authors are fully and solely responsible for preparing complete and accurate citations.

C ethics in publishing

Professional publishing involves three primary actors: the author, the publisher, and the reader. Each has an ethical responsibility. Although some of the following apply only to publishing in professional journals, others apply to all forms of publishing.

author's responsibilities

- ▶ Submit a manuscript to only one journal at a time.
- ▶ Submit only original materials to a journal—not manuscripts that have been published elsewhere in any form.
- ▶ Identify clearly previously published materials that are included in a book proposal.
- ▶ Submit only the author's own material; plagiarism is an infringement of property rights.
- ▶ Provide full documentation in references.
- ▶ Obtain all necessary permissions for the use of cartoons, photographs, artwork, tables, figures, newspaper articles, a single line of poetry or music, or text references of 10 percent of the original work or 300 words or more.
- ▶ Avoid the "Least Publishable Unit" syndrome; do not try to milk six articles out of a study that merits only one or two.

publisher's responsibilities

- ▶ Provide a fair, objective review within a reasonable time frame.
- ▶ Ensure that reviewers are scrupulous in their handling of the manuscript.

- ▶ Offer the author an opportunity to update the material if there is a time lag between the acceptance of the completed manuscript and the publication date.
- ▶ Protect the author's work by preventing copying without permission and proper attribution.
- ▶ Ensure that potential readers have access to the published work.
- ▶ Present the material in the best possible way.

reader's responsibilities

- ▶ Quote accurately and keep material in the proper context.
- ▶ Provide appropriate documentation.
- ▶ Do not violate copyrights.

D *journal publishers*

Following are the human services journals that the NASW Press has designated as "core," to be fully abstracted.

ADMINISTRATION IN SOCIAL WORK
    Editor: Rino Patti
  Address: School of Social Work
             University Park
             Los Angeles, CA 90007

AFFILIA
    Editor: Carol Meyer
  Address: School of Social Work
             Columbia University
             McVickar Hall
             622 West 113th Street
             New York, NY 10025

AMERICAN JOURNAL OF ORTHOPSYCHIATRY
    Editor: Milton F. Shore
  Address: American Association of Orthopsychiatry
             19 West 44th Street, Suite 1616
             New York, NY 10036

ARETE
  Managing
    Editor: Miriam L. Freeman
  Address: University of South Carolina
             College of Social Work
             Columbia, SC 29208

AUSTRALIAN SOCIAL WORK
  Editor: Elizabeth Rabbitts
  Address: 28 Ethie Road
          Beacon Hill, N.S.W. 2100
          Australia

THE BRITISH JOURNAL OF SOCIAL WORK
  Editors: David B. Smith
          Richard Hugman
  Address: Lancaster University
          Department of Social Science
          Cartmel College
          Bailrigg, Lancaster
          LA1 4YL, England

CHILD AND ADOLESCENT SOCIAL WORK JOURNAL
  Editor: Florence Lieberman
  Address: 315 Wyndcliff Road
          Scarsdale, NY 10583

CHILD WELFARE
  Editor: Carl Schoenberg
  Address: *Child Welfare*
          Child Welfare League of America
          440 First Street, NW, Suite 310
          Washington, DC 20001-2085

CLINICAL SOCIAL WORK JOURNAL
  Editor: Jean L. Sanville
  Address: 1300 Tigertail Road
          Los Angeles, CA 90049

FAMILIES IN SOCIETY: THE JOURNAL OF
CONTEMPORARY HUMAN SERVICES
  Editor: Ralph Burant
  Address: *Families in Society*
          Family Service America
          11700 West Lake Park Drive
          Milwaukee, WI 53224

THE GERONTOLOGIST
  Editor: Rosalie A. Kane
  Address: *The Gerontologist*
          Division of Health Services Research and Policy
          University of Minnesota
          420 Delaware Street, SE, Box 197
          Minneapolis, MN 55455

HEALTH & SOCIAL WORK
Editor: Judith Ross
Address: *Health & Social Work*
NASW Press
750 First Street, NE, Suite 700
Washington, DC 20002-4241

INTERNATIONAL SOCIAL WORK
Editor: Francis J. Turner
Address: York University
School of Social Work
4700 Keele Street
Downsview, Ontario
Canada M3J 1P3

THE JEWISH SOCIAL WORK FORUM
Editor: Edwin Simon
Address: 433 Links Drive East
Oceanside, NY 11572

THE JOURNAL OF ANALYTIC SOCIAL WORK
Editor: Jerrold R. Brandell
Address: School of Social Work
Boston University
264 Bay State Road
Boston, MA 02215

JOURNAL OF CONTINUING SOCIAL WORK EDUCATION
Editor: Thomas J. Kinney
Address: *Journal of Continuing Social Work Education*
School of Social Welfare/Rockefeller College
University of Albany, Richardson Hall
135 Western Avenue
Albany, NY 12222

JOURNAL OF GERONTOLOGICAL SOCIAL WORK
Editor: Rose Dobrof
Address: Brookdale Center on Aging
Hunter College
425 East 25th Street
New York, NY 10010-2590

JOURNAL OF MARITAL AND FAMILY THERAPY
    Editor: Douglas H. Sprenkle
    Address: *Journal of Marital and Family Therapy*
               Purdue University
               Marriage and Family Therapy Program
               1268 Marriage and Family Therapy Center
               West Lafayette, IN 47907-1268

JOURNAL OF SOCIAL SERVICE RESEARCH
    Editor: Shanti K. Khinduka
    Address: George Warren Brown School of Social Work
               Washington University
               St. Louis, MO 63130

JOURNAL OF SOCIAL WORK AND HUMAN SEXUALITY
    Editor: David A. Shore
    Address: 3215 Illinois Road
               Wilmette, IL 60091

JOURNAL OF SOCIAL WORK EDUCATION
    Editor: Frederic C. Reamer
    Address: Council on Social Work Education
               Assistant to the Editor
               Journal of Social Work Education
               1600 Duke Street
               Alexandria, VA 22314

JOURNAL OF SOCIOLOGY AND SOCIAL WELFARE
    Editor: Robert D. Leighninger, Jr.
    Address: Associate Editor
               Journal of Sociology and Social Welfare
               School of Social Work
               Louisiana State University
               Baton Rouge, LA 70803

JOURNAL OF TEACHING IN SOCIAL WORK
    Editors: Florence W. Vigilante
               Harold Lewis
    Address: Hunter College School of Social Work
               129 East 79th Street
               New York, NY 10021

PUBLIC WELFARE
Editor: Bill Detweiler
Address: *Public Welfare*
American Public Welfare Association
810 First Street, NE, Suite 500
Washington, DC 20002-4267

RESEARCH ON SOCIAL WORK PRACTICE
Editor: Bruce A. Thyer
Address: *Research on Social Work Practice*
School of Social Work
University of Georgia
Athens, GA 30602

SCHOOL SOCIAL WORK JOURNAL
Editor: Joan Fedota
Address: SSWJ
P.O. Box 2072
Northlake, IL 60164

SMITH COLLEGE STUDIES IN SOCIAL WORK
Editor: Joan Laird
Address: Smith College School for Social Work
Lilly Hall
Northampton, MA 01063

SOCIAL SERVICE REVIEW
Editor: John R. Schuerman
Address: Social Service Review
969 East 60th Street
Chicago, IL 60637

SOCIAL WORK
Editor: Ann Hartman
Address: *Social Work*
NASW Press
750 First Street, NE, Suite 700
Washington, DC 20002-4241

THE SOCIAL WORKER/LE TRAVAILLEUR SOCIAL
Editor: Marie Emond
Address: Myropen Publications
55 Parkdale Avenue
Ottawa, Ontario
Canada K1Y 1E5

SOCIAL WORK IN EDUCATION
    Editor: Paula Allen-Meares
    Address: *Social Work in Education*
                NASW Press
                750 First Street, NE
                Washington, DC 20002-4241

SOCIAL WORK IN HEALTH CARE
    Editor: Gary Rosenberg
    Address: Mount Sinai Medical Center
                1 Gustave Levy Place
                Box 1246
                New York, NY 10029

SOCIAL WORK RESEARCH & ABSTRACTS
    Editor: Stuart Kirk
    Address: *Social Work Research & Abstracts*
                NASW Press
                750 First Street, NE, Suite 700
                Washington, DC 20002-4241

SOCIAL WORK WITH GROUPS
    Editors: Roselle Kurland
                Andrew Malekoff
    Address: Hunter College School of Social Work
                129 East 79th Street
                New York, NY 10021

E   *NASW Press books*

The NASW Press publishes high-quality professional books of relevance to social workers and other professionals in social welfare and the human services. It welcomes proposals for books on a variety of topics and seeks submissions for several different publications programs. In general, the NASW Press focuses on scholarly books and monographs that contribute to the advancement of knowledge and practice in social work.

major programs

The press has five major book programs:

▶ scholarly texts
▶ reference works
▶ practice series
▶ continuing education series
▶ study guides for credentialing and other exams.

Authors are invited to submit proposals for any of these programs.

SCHOLARLY TEXTS

In 1992, the NASW Press has over 75 scholarly titles in print, and it continues to focus primarily on this program while it builds other programs. NASW Press books are widely used as required and recommended reading in schools of social work. To be accepted, a proposal should demonstrate rigorous scholarship, good writing, and the potential to fill an existing need in the field.

REFERENCE WORKS

As a publisher of reference works, the NASW Press is probably most well known for its *Encyclopedia of Social Work* and *The Social Work Dictionary.* The press seeks proposals for other high-quality reference works, particularly those that will be of use to students and practitioners of social work.

PRACTICE SERIES

Designed for the busy practitioner, books in this new series are expected to be concise, fact based, and accessible. The finished product will be short and visually appealing. Criteria for the series include the following:

▶ utility for social work practitioners
▶ based on facts, well documented
▶ clear, strong writing
▶ 150 manuscript pages or fewer.

Strong preference will be given to manuscripts that are distinguished by innovation and creativity. "How-to" manuscripts are particularly well suited for this series.

CONTINUING EDUCATION SERIES

The NASW Press has designed this series to provide training modules for use in social services agencies. Proposals should demonstrate a strong usefulness for practice and should detail how the materials have been tested in practice settings. Written clearly for staff development, training modules in this series are expected to provide sufficient guidelines for presentation that an agency could use them without requiring trainers from outside the agency.

STUDY GUIDES

One of the most well-used books published by the NASW Press is *A Study Guide for ACSW Certification, 2nd edition,* by Ruth Middleman. The press seeks proposals for other study guides related to credentialing, licensing, and other standardized exams. Like the continuing education series, proposals for study guides must demonstrate a clear, strong potential for training.

review process

All proposals for an NASW Press book are reviewed by members of the NASW Press Book Committee. The Book Committee, which is a subcommittee of the NASW Communications Committee, articulates policy and reviews proposals. The chair of the Book Committee sits on the Communications Committee; the chair and all members of the Book Committee must be published authors who are members in good standing of NASW.

Book committee members read and rate manuscripts, advise the NASW Press staff on content, and make recommendations for publication. The chair may ask expert readers to read and rate specialized manuscripts. At least two reviewers, in addition to the chair of the Book Committee, read and rate each proposal.

For all programs, reviewers will consider the following:

▶ Does the proposal demonstrate a contribution to social work knowledge?
▶ Does it meet the press's standards for presentation? Is the methodology consistent, the concept clear, the documentation precise? Is the proposal readable?
▶ Does the proposal appear to have a sufficient potential audience?
▶ Is the method and style appropriate for the intended audience?
▶ Is the material timely?
▶ Is the subject innovative? Of professional significance? Of broad interest?
▶ Are other comparable materials available?
▶ Does the subject matter relate to NASW priorities?

Reviewers may ask to see revisions based on their comments. If the decision to publish is favorable, authors will receive a contract that may include requests to adapt or change the manuscript as necessary, according to the reviewers' comments. An off-press date will be determined when the final manuscript is delivered.

Reviews may take three to four months to complete. All submissions are acknowledged upon receipt.

guidelines for book proposals

The quality of a book proposal is a key factor in selling the project to a publisher. The information should be succinct, yet comprehensive enough to enable members of the Book Committee to undertake a thorough review. Even if the author submits a full manuscript, he or she also should submit a book proposal that describes the book's purpose, the potential audience for the book, and the author's qualifications to write the book.

PROSPECTUS

Although the prospectus should be no longer than six pages, it should contain vital information about the book. The author should establish a clear rationale or purpose for the book and describe how he or she will accomplish the purpose. The author must demonstrate that he or she has enough comprehensive, valid material to justify a book rather than a journal article. Features that make the book unique should be described.

The book prospectus should include an accurate assessment of the market for the book, as well as a critique of existing books now competing in the market. If the book is intended for classroom use, the prospectus should include an estimate of how many students are enrolled in courses for which the book would be used and note whether it would be used as a central textbook or a supplemental text. If the book is directed toward practitioners, the authors should estimate how many practitioners practice in the particular area and explain how they would use the book in their work.

Identification and assessment of competing books will be weighed carefully during the review. In addition to determining whether a market exists, members of the Book Committee use the assessment to gauge the author's knowledge of the literature in the area. In describing other books, the author should include the authors, titles, publishers, and years of publication. The author also should describe the strengths and weaknesses of each book and indicate how the proposed book will be superior or different.

The prospectus should include an estimated timetable for the completion of the manuscript, which should be considered carefully because it will be written into the book contract if the proposal is accepted. Estimated completion dates should be realistic, but not so far in the future that timeliness would be affected. In addition, the author should estimate the number of typed, double-spaced manuscript pages, including artwork or tables, the final manuscript will contain.

AUTHOR'S BACKGROUND

A full vita, which includes the author's educational background, work experience, and a list of publications, should be attached to the book prospectus. In addition, the prospectus should note any special qualifications that bear on the author's ability to produce the book. If there is to be more than one author, the prospectus should include information for each.

BOOK OUTLINE

A detailed outline and draft table of contents should accompany the prospectus. Authors should include sufficient information on the outline so the reviewers can easily see the flow of the book and the major points covered in it. If the book is intended to be a collection of articles by several authors, the editor should provide the names of the prospective authors, as well as the articles they are expected to write. Further, the editor should indicate how he or she will achieve an even balance of high-quality articles.

The NASW Press requests an introduction and one or two representative chapters for the initial review. Members of the Book Committee review these chapters for the author's writing style and indications of the author's skill in developing the subject. It is wise, also, to indicate how many chapters are completed so the press can request additional chapters if they are available.

inappropriate submissions

The NASW Press regrets that it is unable to review the following:

▶ fiction or other materials intended for a general audience
▶ dissertations or master's theses
▶ curriculum guides for schools of social work
▶ "readers" or other collections of previously published materials
▶ general conference proceedings.

Currently, the NASW Press publishes materials directed to the professional social worker or related professional, not to the consumer of services. Doctoral or master's theses must be reworked to meet the criteria of a book before they will be considered for publication.

payment for authors

The NASW Press is a competitive book publisher in terms of royalties paid to authors and the average number of copies sold per title. The standard royalty schedule is as follows:

- first 3,000 copies—10 percent of net sales
- 3,001 to 6,000 copies—12.5 percent of net sales
- over 6,000 copies—15 percent of net sales.

If there is more than one author or editor, royalties are divided. Royalties, based on net sales during the fiscal year that ends June 30, are paid annually within 90 days of June 30. The press does not pay royalties to authors of articles in a collected work of original articles.

submissions

Authors should send five copies of a prospectus, typed double spaced, for review. Forward all submissions to

Executive Editor
The NASW Press
750 First Street, NE, Suite 700
Washington, DC 20002-4241

F *NASW Press journals*

The four NASW Press journals—*Social Work, Social Work Research, Health & Social Work,* and *Social Work in Education*—publish unsolicited manuscripts. All submissions are subject to peer review. The editorial boards of all four journals use the following policies and procedures in reviewing, rating, and selecting manuscripts for publication.

initial processing

When a manuscript arrives at the NASW Press, the staff enter it into the records of the appropriate journal and mail an acknowledgment of receipt to the author. The acknowledgment states NASW's expectation that the manuscript has not been published elsewhere and is not under review by any other journal. An author can expect to receive an acknowledgment within approximately four weeks after he or she mails a manuscript.

The staff remove the cover sheet that identifies the author and do a preliminary screening to be sure that the manuscript meets the basic criteria for submissions. The manuscript then is assigned to members of the editorial boards or consulting editors who act as reviewers, according to procedures set by each journal. The staff assign manuscripts to reviewers based on the reviewer's self-reported areas of expertise and the number of manuscripts already assigned to them. All manuscripts, except letters and some columns, are reviewed anonymously. (See the section in this appendix on Individual Journals for column procedures.)

reviewers

The names of editorial board members and consulting editors appear on the masthead of each journal. Although the author can assume that the reviewers of his or her work are among those persons listed on the masthead, specific reviewers remain anonymous.

The president of NASW appoints members of the editorial board, who review manuscripts and set policy for the journal. Editorial board members, who must be NASW members in good standing, must also have a strong publishing background. The president considers skills and knowledge, geographic location, gender, and ethnic origin when appointing members of the editorial board. To maintain a pool of reviewers large enough to review manuscripts in a timely manner and to cover the areas of expertise required, editors-in-chief appoint consulting editors to act as reviewers. Consulting editors must meet the same criteria as do members of the editorial board. From time to time, editors-in-chief also may consult other reviewers for their expertise in specific subjects.

selection process

Generally, at least three reviewers, including the editor-in-chief, read every manuscript. In rating manuscripts, the reviewers consider factors such as the following:

▶ contribution to social work knowledge
▶ currency
▶ clarity of presentation
▶ utility and relevance to social work practice
▶ appropriateness to the journal
▶ originality
▶ adequate documentation
▶ organization
▶ style and readability.

In addition to recommending acceptance or rejection, the reviewers are asked to write comments that will help an author improve the manuscript. These comments are mailed to the author with the decision letter unless a manuscript is accepted outright. All information related to the review of manuscripts is confidential and is not revealed to others except for the comments provided to the author.

Manuscripts will not be rejected for publication because they are controversial or present unpopular stances or positions other than the prevailing view. Editorial boards seek original manuscripts that will stimulate professional dialogue.

decisions

The editor-in-chief of each journal makes the final decision on publication on the basis of the reviewers' ratings, the balance of subject matter, articles on similar topics already accepted or in the literature, and other similar editorial considerations. Decisions on manuscripts are released only to the authors and reviewers.

Although every effort is made to arrive at an early decision, the process generally takes a minimum of three to four months. Authors should be aware that reviewers volunteer their time and that the process may be slower during certain times of the year, such as the summer. Authors should feel free to inquire about the status of their manuscripts if they think the process is taking longer than it should. The NASW Press staff will be happy to provide a status report on the progress of the review; however, they cannot release decisions over the telephone.

As soon as the editor-in-chief has made a decision, the staff notifies the author in writing. The possible decisions are "accept for publication," "accept on condition of minor changes," "reject but encourage resubmission," and "reject."

ACCEPT FOR PUBLICATION

If a manuscript is accepted for publication, the author will receive a letter of acceptance with an agreement form. The author should return the agreement form with the necessary signatures and information as soon as possible.

The press edits all manuscripts according to house style; in addition, the editorial boards reserve the right to make other changes, subject to the author's approval. Authors receive a copy of the edited manuscript for review and approval. They also may be asked to update or clarify references. In the final stages of production, the NASW Press may make changes in a manuscript to conform to the format and space requirements of the journal in which it is to appear. Although the press does not generally provide galley proofs, courtesy galleys are mailed to authors if time permits when such changes are made.

On publication, the author receives five complimentary copies of the issue in which the article appears. The author also receives a form that he or she may use to order reprints.

ACCEPT ON CONDITION OF MINOR CHANGES

At times, the editorial board will be prepared to accept a manuscript provided that certain changes are made. These changes
generally are relatively minor. When this decision is made, the
press returns one copy of the manuscript to the author with the
reviewers' comments specifying the changes that should be made.
A decision to accept on condition of minor changes does not
guarantee final acceptance.

Authors who resubmit their manuscripts should specify, on a
separate, unsigned cover sheet, the changes they have made and
should mark the first page of the revised manuscript with the word
"revision" and the date the revision is submitted. (Five copies of
the cover sheet should be submitted with five copies of the revised
manuscript.) The author may also use the cover sheet to discuss
any recommended changes he or she believes should not or cannot
be made.

If the editor-in-chief accepts the revised manuscript, the author
will receive an acceptance letter and an agreement form. The
standard editing procedures will then be followed.

REJECT BUT ENCOURAGE RESUBMISSION

This decision is made when a manuscript holds promise but needs
considerable work. When an author receives this decision, the
editor-in-chief has determined that the journal would be interested
in reviewing a revised manuscript. The press returns one copy of
the manuscript to the author with the reviewers' comments specifying the changes that should be made.

Authors who resubmit their manuscripts should follow the same
procedure for the cover sheet and number of copies to be submitted
as for revised manuscripts in the category Accept on Condition of
Minor Changes.

When revisions arrive at the NASW Press, they are sent to the
original reviewers with a copy of all the reviewer's comments the
author received.

If the editor-in-chief accepts the revised manuscript, the author
will receive an acceptance letter and agreement form. The standard
editing procedures will then be followed.

REJECT

Editorial boards retain the prerogative to reject or accept any
contributions to their journals. The press will forward copies of the
reviewers' comments to the author with a decision letter. Authors
who receive rejection letters should be aware that the acceptance

rates for NASW Press journals are low. Editors hope that authors will find the reviewers' comments useful in their own evaluation of how they should proceed with their work. Authors may want to consider submitting their manuscript to another journal or a less formal newsletter.

REFERRALS

The editorial board of each journal evaluates manuscripts independently. Although an editorial board will not take an initiative to move manuscripts from one journal to another, individual reviewers may suggest in their comments to the author that the manuscript may be more appropriate for another journal. A manuscript rejected by one journal may be submitted to another NASW Press journal; however, the press recommends that authors use the reviewers' comments to revise a rejected manuscript before they submit it to any other journal.

individual journals

SOCIAL WORK

Social Work, established in 1956, is a professional journal published by the NASW Press, a division of NASW, and provided to all NASW members as a membership benefit. The journal is dedicated to improving practice and advancing knowledge in social work and social welfare. The editorial board welcomes manuscripts that yield new insights into established practices, evaluate new techniques and research, examine current social problems, or bring serious critical analysis to bear on problems in the profession. Literary articles that deal with issues of significance to social work will also be reviewed.

Manuscripts on specific topics often are selected from the pool of accepted articles to form theme issues. From time to time, the editorial board puts forth calls for papers on issues of major importance to the field.

Articles

Manuscripts for full-length articles should not exceed 18 to 20 pages, including all references and tables, typed double spaced with one-inch margins on all sides. The entire review process is anonymous. At least two reviewers critique each manuscript; then the editor-in-chief makes a decision taking those reviews into account.

Columns

Notes from the Field includes descriptions of programs, research projects, types of innovative practice, or other discussions that may be of interest to the profession. Initial reports of works in progress may be submitted to this column. Manuscripts may be more descriptive than analytical and do not require the depth of documentation necessary for full-length articles. Manuscripts submitted to Notes from the Field are reviewed by the editor-in-chief anonymously. Although the maximum length for these manuscripts is four to six pages, typed double spaced with one-inch margins, the journal invites shorter accounts.

Op-Ed features readers' comments and opinions on current issues in the profession. It offers writers an opportunity to present their opinion on issues that have an impact on social work or social work clients. The maximum length of manuscripts for this column is five to seven pages, typed double spaced with one-inch margins. Op-Ed submissions are reviewed anonymously by the editor-in-chief.

Points & Viewpoints provides readers an opportunity to respond substantively to an article previously published in the journal and to challenge the premises, studies, and intellectual positions in that article. It was created to stimulate dialogue that helps the profession evolve and respond to changing conditions. Manuscripts are reviewed anonymously by the editor-in-chief. If a manuscript is accepted, the author of the original article will be asked to respond to it. Manuscripts may be shortened and included as a Letter to the Editor if the original author declines to respond. The maximum length for this column is seven pages, typed double spaced with one-inch margins.

Book Reviews are considered an essential component of the professional literature, and the editorial board subscribes to the philosophy that a book review can be as enlightening as an article. Thoughtful critiques are essential in guiding the practitioner, educator, and student to important resources in the field. The book review editor selects books and other materials for review, solicits reviews, and determines whether reviews will be published. Although the journal attempts to publish all solicited reviews, publication is not guaranteed. Unsolicited reviews are not accepted.

The journal welcomes *Letters to the Editor.* Readers are encouraged to send brief comments on issues covered in the journal or other points of interest to the profession that will extend dialogue. Although all letters are acknowledged and read, not all can be published. Selected letters may be shortened to fit the space available. The optimum length for letters is one or two pages, typed double spaced with one-inch margins.

SOCIAL WORK RESEARCH

Social Work Research is a professional journal committed to advancing the development of knowledge and informing social work practice. The journal is one of the chief outlets for primary research articles in social work and social welfare. As a repository for an evolving body of knowledge, it makes an important contribution to the quality of educational materials and social work practice.

The editorial board seeks manuscripts that include analytic reviews of research, theoretical articles pertaining to social work research, practice-based research, evaluation studies, and diverse research studies that contribute to knowledge about social work issues and problems. Criteria for acceptance include readability, sound methodology, and utility for practice.

Articles

Manuscripts for full-length articles should not exceed 18 to 20 pages, including all references and tables, typed double spaced with one-inch margins on all sides. The entire review process is anonymous. At least three reviewers critique each manuscript; then the editor-in-chief makes a decision taking those reviews into account.

Columns

Research Notes presents brief reports on research findings that do not lend themselves to full-length articles. Reports may examine the results of a study, methodological issues, or works in progress and should include information on the research questions and the general methodology. The column also provides a forum to present research findings and ideas from studies that are in their early stages. Submissions are selected through the standard review process. Manuscripts should be no longer than seven pages, typed double spaced with one-inch margins on all sides.

Letters from readers are strongly encouraged. Readers may react to articles published in the journal or comment on contemporary issues in social work research that have not been covered in the journal. Although space precludes publishing every letter received, all will be considered. Letters should not exceed three manuscript pages.

Selected Government Reports presents the latest in government publications. Although the column usually contains lists of reports, from time to time reports are reviewed. Unsolicited reviews are not published.

HEALTH & SOCIAL WORK

Health & Social Work, established in 1976, is a professional journal committed to improving social work practice and expanding knowledge in the field of health care. Health is defined broadly to include both physical and mental health. The editorial board welcomes manuscripts on all aspects of health that are of professional concern to social workers. The journal carries articles on practice, social policy and planning, legislative issues, innovations in health care, and research.

Health & Social Work strives to balance issues with articles that appeal to its broad constituency. Most issues contain some articles that address direct services and some that address policy issues. The editor-in-chief often groups related articles in an issue, and the editorial board invites articles on special themes from time to time.

The articles must do the following to be generally acceptable to the reviewers:

- ► be important to social work and relevant to health
- ► contain a clear statement of purpose and a consistent focus
- ► expand current knowledge
- ► build on the work of others
- ► contain a current and appropriate literature review
- ► include relevant medical information, such as etiology, prognosis, and hereditary factors, if disease specific
- ► clearly present the complete methodology if a research article
- ► be well organized with a logical, orderly presentation
- ► soundly support the conclusions with data or a logical argument
- ► contain a clear explication of the implications for social work.

Articles

Manuscripts for full-length articles should be no longer than 18 pages, typed double spaced with one-inch margins on all four sides. The entire review process is anonymous. At least three reviewers critique each manuscript; then the editor-in-chief makes a decision taking those reviews into consideration.

Columns

Designed specifically to stimulate publication of more material written by and of particular interest to practitioners, *Practice Forum* provides an outlet for descriptions of practice innovations and action research. The editor of Practice Forum invites practitioners to submit brief articles that describe new and effective programs, techniques, or policies and often assists authors in developing articles for the column. Manuscripts should not exceed eight pages, typed double spaced with one-inch margins.

National Health Line reports current legislative and political issues that have implications for social work practice in health settings. It provides a link between social work practice and health care policy. The editor of the column seeks to present contemporary issues that have the greatest potential impact on social work clients. Although the editor writes the column, readers are invited to submit suggestions for topics to be covered.

Viewpoints features readers' comments and opinions on current issues in the profession. It offers writers an opportunity to express their opinion on issues that may have an impact on social work or social work clients in health or mental health settings. The maximum length of manuscripts is seven pages, typed double spaced with one-inch margins.

Book Reviews includes critiques of books and other materials of professional interest to social workers in health and mental health. Reviewers are asked to provide substantive, balanced reviews that address the strengths and limitations of the publication. The book review editor selects books and other material to be reviewed, solicits reviews, and determines whether reviews will be published. Although the journal attempts to publish all solicited reviews, publication is not guaranteed. Unsolicited reviews are not accepted.

The editorial board invites *Letters to the Editor* that comment on issues covered in the journal or other points of interest to social workers in health or mental health settings. Letters enhance the professional dialogue in the journal. Although all letters are acknowledged and read, not all can be published. Letters selected by the editor-in-chief may be shortened to fit the available space. Letters should be no more than two pages, typed double spaced with one-inch margins.

SOCIAL WORK IN EDUCATION

Social Work in Education, established in 1978, is a professional journal that publishes materials relevant to social work services in education through the life span. Education is broadly defined to include early intervention programs and preschool, elementary, and secondary education. The journal addresses audiences that include school social workers and other pupil personnel professionals and professionals in educational institutions, family agencies, child and family health and mental health agencies, and the juvenile justice system.

The editorial board encourages practitioners to share their practice knowledge. The board welcomes articles on innovations in practice, interdisciplinary efforts, research, program evaluation, legislation, policy, and planning. As a practice-oriented journal, *Social Work in Education* seeks to represent the broad spectrum of educational activities; controversial manuscripts that will encourage dialogue are welcomed. The editorial board particularly invites manuscripts that emphasize practice and cultural diversity.

Because the journal represents the breadth of social work practice in education, the preference is to vary the content within a single issue. From time to time, however, the journal publishes special issues on themes of importance to the field.

Articles

Manuscripts for full-length articles should not exceed 18 to 20 pages, including all references and tables, typed double spaced with one-inch margins on all sides. The entire review process is anonymous. At least three reviewers critique each manuscript; then the editor-in-chief makes a decision taking those reviews into account.

Columns

Trends & Issues provides program and policy updates on local, regional, or national developments. Authors are encouraged to address programmatic responses to social trends, changes in policy, innovative programs, reforms in the field, and other events that have generalizable implications for practice. Manuscripts should be short—no more than eight pages, typed double spaced with one-inch margins. The editor of this column may assist authors in developing potential articles for this column.

Practice Highlights describes exemplary social work services in educational settings. Authors are encouraged to submit descriptive case studies of their direct work with individuals and families. The editorial board encourages a strong emphasis on interdisciplinary collaboration. Intended as a practitioner-to-practitioner resource, the column is more relaxed in style than are the regular articles. Manuscripts should be short—up to six pages, typed double spaced with one-inch margins. The editor of this column may assist authors in developing potential articles for this column.

Resources for Practice provides reviews of books, films, videotapes, software, and other professional resources of interest to school social workers and their colleagues. The editor of this column selects materials for review, solicits reviews, and accepts or rejects the review. Although every effort is made to publish solicited reviews, reviews are not guaranteed publication. Unsolicited reviews are not accepted.

As Readers See It provides a forum for letters and comments from readers. The editorial board welcomes opinions of interest to the field, as well as comments on articles published in the journal.

guidelines for submitting manuscripts

Authors should submit five complete copies of manuscripts assembled in the following order:

- ▶ a cover sheet with all author identifications and addresses
- ▶ a title page with no author identification
- ▶ an abstract of about 150 words
- ▶ text
- ▶ references
- ▶ tables and artwork.

All copy, including references, tables, and figure captions, should be typed double spaced on one side of opaque paper with a one-inch margin on all four sides. Illegible copies, single-spaced material, and material typed on both sides of the paper will not be reviewed. Avoid script fonts or dot matrix printers. Although the NASW Press requests computer disks when manuscripts are accepted, it is not necessary to submit a disk initially.

The cover sheet should contain the full title of the manuscript; the names, degrees, titles, addresses, and telephone numbers of the authors; and the date of submission. If there is more than one author, the authors should be listed in the order in which the authors wish to see their names appear if the article is published. One author should be designated the corresponding author to whom the authors wish all correspondence related to the manuscript to be addressed. For theoretical or discussion articles, only those authors who participated in the actual writing should be listed as authors. For research-based articles, authors should be listed only if they played a major part in the design and analysis of the study. The cover sheet, which is removed and held in the NASW Press office, is the only component of the manuscript that should identify the author or authors.

The NASW Press uses the author–date citation style outlined in this volume. Authors should incorporate footnotes into the text. The total package should not exceed 20 pages. Editorial boards have requested that the staff of the NASW Press return any manuscripts of 25 pages or more.

Authors should designate the journal of choice when submitting a manuscript. Manuscripts for all NASW Press journals should be mailed to

[Insert journal title here]
The NASW Press
750 First Street, NE
Suite 700
Washington, DC 20002-4241

Submitting a manuscript directly to an editor-in-chief at another address will delay the review process.

The NASW Press is not responsible for the loss of a manuscript in the mail. Authors should retain at least one copy of any manuscript. Unless the press requests revisions, manuscripts will not be returned. All manuscripts are acknowledged on receipt. The review process generally takes four months.

G *NASW Press policies*

The following NASW Press policies may be of particular interest to the readers of this volume.

disclaimers

The NASW Press publishes scholarly journals that are dedicated to expanding social work knowledge and informing social work practice. Opinions in the journals are those of the authors and do not necessarily reflect the official position of NASW. The mention of trade names in the journals does not constitute an endorsement by the National Association of Social Workers.

overlapping submissions

The NASW Press recognizes that a large-scale research study may generate more than one article. However, in these cases, it is the clear responsibility of the authors to state in the work under consideration that it is part of a larger study and to annotate fully other articles from the same study that are already published, in press, or in process.

If such information has been withheld and substantive portions of the material under review or already accepted by an NASW Press journal have been published or submitted for publication elsewhere, an NASW Press editorial board can reject or withdraw acceptance of the articles at its discretion. Such actions will be taken if it is determined that publication could lead to violation of the press's publications policy or NASW's adherence to the copyright law.

A manuscript will be deemed an overlapping submission if it shares the following with another article or articles:

▶ identical language
▶ substantive portions of similar or paraphrased language
▶ identical conclusions
▶ identical implications.

Although a large-scale study may yield more than one article, it is essential that each article add new information to the profession's knowledge base. Succeeding articles should build on each other, rather than rework the same information. The addition of methodology and data to a literature review does not constitute a new article if the conclusions and implications are identical.

prior consent

The NASW Press must assume that content in conference presentations, journal articles, books, or other materials presented to NASW by an author is available for general dissemination. It is the responsibility of the author, not the NASW Press, to determine whether the disclosure of this material requires the prior consent of other parties and, if so, to obtain that consent.

prior publication

NASW Press journals publish original articles that have not been published previously and are not under consideration by other publishers. Prior publication includes

▶ articles previously published in other scholarly journals
▶ articles previously published in the popular press
▶ articles previously published in agency or company newsletters or magazines
▶ articles previously distributed through one of the online document delivery services.

Articles that have been published previously will not be reviewed. If a manuscript has been accepted before the existence of prior publication is known, acceptance will be withdrawn as soon as the NASW Press learns of the prior publication.

publication of the professional work of NASW leaders

All NASW Press publications seek to attain the highest quality of material. No one is denied access to publication. All submissions are processed in the same manner and reviewed by referees, with no prejudice for or against members of the Communications Committee and editorial boards, consulting editors, or other NASW staff and volunteer leaders. All submissions to NASW Press journals are reviewed anonymously.

unbiased communication

In the interest of accurate and unbiased communication, authors should not use language that may imply sexual, ethnic, or other kinds of discrimination, stereotyping, or bias. NASW is committed to the fair and equal treatment of individuals and groups, and material submitted to the NASW Press should not promote stereotypical or discriminatory attitudes and assumptions about people.

use of professional titles

NASW Press journals are dedicated to improving social work practice and to increasing knowledge in the field. Authors do not need to be either professional social workers or NASW members to submit manuscripts. The criterion for submission is clear relevance to social work.

All manuscripts for NASW Press journals are reviewed anonymously (that is, reviewers do not learn authors' names or titles during the review). However, if the author of an accepted manuscript is a professional social worker, the title used in the author's blurb at the end of the article will reflect the profession. Titles such as "psychotherapist" or "family counselor" will not be used to substitute for social work titles. Certification and licensing designations, such as ACSW and LCSW, will be published.

H reference library for authors

The books listed here are the editor's choices of the references that are most useful for authors and editors alike in the human services. For readers interested in reading about writing, see the Suggested Reading list in chapter 2, "Basic Writing Techniques."

citations and references

A uniform system of citation (14th ed.). (1981). Cambridge, MA: Harvard Law Review Association.

American Psychological Association. (1983). *Publication manual of the American Psychological Association* (3rd ed.). Washington, DC: Author.

Beebe, L. (1992). *Professional writing for the human services.* Washington, DC: NASW Press.

Garner, D. L., & Smith, D. H. (1984). *The complete guide to citing governmental documents: A manual for writers and librarians.* Bethesda, MD: Congressional Information Service.

grammar

Hodges, J. C., & Whitten, M. E. (1984). *Harbrace college handbook* (9th ed.). New York: Harcourt Brace Jovanovich.

information

Barker, R. (1991). *The social work dictionary* (2nd ed.). Silver Spring, MD: NASW Press.

Ginsberg, L. (1992). *Social work almanac.* Washington, DC: NASW Press.

Illustrating science: Standards for publication. (1988). Bethesda, MD: Council of Biology Editors.

Minahan, A. (Ed.-in-Chief). (1987). *The encyclopedia of social work* (18th ed.). Silver Spring, MD: National Association of Social Workers.

Tufte, E. (1983). *The visual display of quantitative information.* Cheshire, CT: Graphics Press.

Tufte, E. (1990). *Envisioning information.* Cheshire, CT: Graphics Press.

publishing outlets

Mendelsohn, H. N. (1992). *An author's guide to social work journals* (3rd ed.). Washington, DC: NASW Press.

spelling

Random House dictionary of the English language—Unabridged (2nd ed.). (1987). New York: Random House.

Webster's ninth new collegiate dictionary. (1985). Springfield, MA: Merriam-Webster.

style

University of Chicago Press. (1982). *The Chicago manual of style* (13th ed.). Chicago: Author.

Strunk, W., Jr., & White, E. B. (1979). *The elements of style* (3rd ed.). New York: Macmillan.

Words into type (3rd ed.). (1974). Englewood Cliffs, NJ: Prentice Hall.

Also see American Psychological Association (1983) and Beebe (1992) under "Citations and References" in this appendix.

usage

Bernstein, T. M. (1965). *The careful writer: A modern guide to English usage.* New York: Atheneum.

Copperud, R. H. (1980). *American usage and style: The consensus.* New York: Van Nostrand Reinhold.

Fowler, H. W. *Modern English usage* (2nd ed., rev. by E. Gowers). Oxford, England: Oxford University Press.

index

the editor

Linda Beebe is associate executive director for communications at the National Association of Social Workers. Before assuming responsibility for the association's marketing, media relations, and publishing programs, she was director of publications. She has worked as managing editor for national advocacy groups and has directed numerous publishing and continuing education programs at the state and local levels.

the contributors

Ann A. Abbott, PhD, ACSW, is associate professor at the School of Social Work at Rugters, The State University of New Jersey. Currently she is a National Institute for Drug Abuse, National Institute on Alcohol Abuse and Alcohol, Office of Substance Abuse Prevention faculty fellow developing substance abuse content for social work curricula. She has a bachelor's degree in psychology from St. Norbert College and an MSS and a PhD in social work and social research from Bryn Mawr College. Dr. Abbott is president-elect of the National Association of Social Workers. From 1989 to 1992 she served on the NASW Book Committee and from 1991 to 1992 on the editorial board of *Social Work Research & Abstracts*.

Lisa Ann Braxton is staff editor for the NASW Press. She has a bachelor's degree in journalism from Hampton University and a Publications Specialist certificate from The George Washington University. She is a former reporter for the *Richmond News Leader* and for radio station WNAB-AM in Bridgeport, Connecticut. She is also editor of the Washington Association of Black Journalists' bimonthly newsletter.

William H. Butterfield, PhD, is associate professor of social work at the George Warren Brown School of Social Work, Washington University. His most recent publications have appeared in the *Journal of Social Service Research, Journal of Sociology and Social Welfare,* and *European Journal of Applied Physiology and Occupational Physiology.* From 1986 to 1989 he was a member of the editorial board of *Social Work Research & Abstracts* and since 1989 has served as consulting editor.

Christina Davis is staff editor for the NASW Press. Before joining NASW in 1991, she edited publications for the Entomological Society of America, the International City Management Association, the American Chemical Society, and University Press of America. She volunteers as editor-in-chief of *The Riverdale* (Maryland) *Town Crier* and is a member of the Women's National Book Association and Bookbuilders of Washington.

Howard Goldstein, DSW, is professor emeritus, the Mandel School of Applied Social Sciences, Case Western Reserve University. He has 20 years of direct practice in family agencies and private practice and has taught at San Diego State College, the University of South Carolina, Dalhousie University (Nova Scotia), and Case Western Reserve University. In 1991 he received the Richard Lodge Prize from the Adelphi University School of Social Work for outstanding contributions to social work theory. His books include *Social Work Practice: A Unitary Approach; Social Learning and Change: A Cognitive Approach to Human Services;* and *Creative Change: A Cognitive–Humanistic Approach to Social Work Practice.* He is now at work on a book based on a study of older adults who grew up in orphanages and a book on practice with hard-to-reach clients.

Ann Hartman, DSW, is dean and Elizabeth Marting Treuhaft Professor at the Smith College School for Social Work. She is a graduate of Wellesley College and received her MSW from Smith College and her DSW from Columbia University. Before assuming the deanship at Smith College, she was on the faculty of the School of Social Work at the University of Michigan. She is an eminent lecturer, author, teacher, and clinician. Her publications include *Family-Centered Social Work Practice; A Handbook of Child Welfare; Helping Families Beyond Placement;* and *Finding Families: An Ecological Approach to Family Assessment in Adoption.* She is currently editor of *Social Work,* the journal of the National Association of Social Workers.

Trudi E. Jacobson, MA, MLS, is bibliographic instruction coordinator at the University Library, University at Albany, State University of New York, where she develops and teaches library instruction classes, including numerous CD-ROM sessions, for undergraduate and graduate students in a variety of disciplines. Previously she was reference services coordinator at Siena College Library, Loudonville, New York. She has an MLS and an MA from the University at Albany and is coauthor of the forthcoming book *State-of-the-Art Fact Finding* and the author of numerous articles. She has presented papers at Critical Thinking and CD-ROM conferences to both librarian and faculty audiences.

Kathryn Hyde Loomis is senior editor at the NASW Press, where she works on the association's books, journals, and reports. Previously she was assistant editor with Aspen Publishers, where she worked on five scholarly journals, and book editor with Three Continents Press. She has a master's degree in English from Georgetown University and a bachelor's degree in Spanish from Mount Holyoke College.

Henry N. Mendelsohn, MA, MLS, is associate librarian and bibliographer and reference librarian for social welfare and criminal justice at the Governor Thomas E. Dewey Graduate Library for Public Affairs and Policy, University at Albany, State University of New York. He is author of *An Author's Guide to Social Work Journals,* now in its third edition, and *A Guide to Information Sources for Social Work and the Human Services* and a contributor to the 18th edition of NASW's *Encyclopedia of Social Work.* He has also contributed to other reference books as well as to social work and library science journals.

Stephen D. Pazdan is staff editor for the NASW Press. Before joining NASW he was production editor with the Entomological Society of America, where he produced the *Bulletin of the Entomological Society of America* and additionally worked on four scholarly journals. He has a bachelor's degree in journalism from the University of Maryland.

Nancy A. Winchester is director of editorial services at the National Association of Social Workers, where she manages the production of the association's books, journals, and reports. Before coming to NASW she was a book editor with the National Academy of Sciences, Information Resources Press, and the American Physiological Society. She has a master's degree in business administration from Boston University and a bachelor's degree in zoology from the University of Maryland.

ORDER FORM

☐ *Send me the NASW Press publications checked below.*

Qty.	Title	Item #	Price	Total
____	Professional Writing for the Human Services	1999	$ 26.95	
____	An Author's Guide to Social Work Journals	2197	$ 24.95	
____	Social Work Almanac	1964	$ 29.95	
____	**NASW Writer's Special**	A15	$ 73.65	
____	**NASW Super Reference Work Special**	A12	$169.00	
			+ 10% postage & handling	
			TOTAL	

☐ I've enclosed my check or money order for $ _____ .

☐ Please charge my credit card: ☐ NASW Visa   ☐ Other Visa   ☐ MasterCard

CREDIT CARD NUMBER   EXPIRATION DATE

SIGNATURE

NAME

ADDRESS

CITY   STATE   ZIP

(Payment must accompany this order. Make checks payable to **NASW Press**.*)*

Send to
NASW Distribution Center
P.O. Box 431
Annapolis JCT, MD 20701

Or call toll free—
1-800-227-3590

NASW PRESS

To Help You Publish

FROM NASW PRESS . . .

Professional Writing for the Human Services, *edited by Linda Beebe.* Learn basic writing techniques, how to conduct a literature search, how to write qualitative and quantitative research reports, and how to present statistical data graphically. Delve into the mysteries of the peer review process and discover how to package your journal article or book proposal to best advantage. NASW's own style and reference guides plus information on the production process, ethical issues, copyright concerns, and more make this the most comprehensive writing guide available for the human services. An excellent resource for all forms of professional writing. **$26.95**

An Author's Guide to Social Work Journals, Third Edition, *by Henry N. Mendelsohn.* Helps authors find the right journal for their manuscript. Provides detailed publishing requirements and guidelines for over 130 human services journals plus a selected bibliography on style and writing guides. **$24.95**

Social Work Almanac, *by Leon Ginsberg.* The most comprehensive compilation of statistical social welfare data available in one source. Provides clear, succinct information on virtually every human services category. Entries include basic demography, income, children, crime and delinquency, education, health, mental health, older adults, social welfare issues, and the social work profession. **$29.95**

Save 10% with the NASW *Writer's Special.* **. . a collection of new publications designed to help you research, write, and find the appropriate publisher for your work.**

Human services writers from the neophyte to the experienced author can prepare their writing and research for publication with the valued reference books featured in NASW's **Writer's Special.** For years, writers have depended on NASW for the information they need to publish in the human services. Now, for the low price of $73.65, you will receive three of NASW's top reference books for writers—**Professional Writing for the Human Services;** the widely used and useful **Author's Guide to Social Work Journals,** third edition; and the long-awaited **Social Work Almanac.**

Save Even More with the NASW Super Reference Work Special!

The NASW **Super Reference Work Special** includes six of the top reference works for the human services—all in one convenient package—and at a 15% savings! The **Super Reference Work Special** includes all the books included in the **Writer's Special**—*plus* NASW's classic reference collection—the two-volume **Encyclopedia of Social Work** (18th Edition), the **1990 Encyclopedia of Social Work Supplement,** and the 2nd edition of **The Social Work Dictionary**—all the human services reference works you need, at the special price of $169.00.

To take advantage of the NASW **Writer's Special** or **Super Reference Work Special,** or to order any of the above NASW Press publications, see the order form on the reverse of this card.